This Book must be returned to
the Library on, or before, the
last date shown below

5. JUL. 1964

25. FEB. 1974

EUROPEAN UNITY
AND THE
TRADE UNION MOVEMENTS

The Council of Europe annually awards a number of research fellowships, which are intended primarily for persons prepared to undertake research work of European interest, in the various member countries of the Council of Europe. The object is to encourage research into the following questions, considered in the light of their present-day importance: (a) political, economic, social, educational and scientific problems connected with European integration; (b) European civilisation (philosophy, history, literature and the arts). Fellowship holders are required to write a thesis in any one of the languages of member countries of the Council of Europe or the States acceding to the European Cultural Convention.

A selection of the most valuable studies is being published in the present series called "European Aspects".

EUROPEAN ASPECTS

A COLLECTION OF STUDIES RELATING TO EUROPEAN INTEGRATION

PUBLISHED UNDER THE AUSPICES OF THE COUNCIL OF EUROPE

SERIES D: SOCIAL SCIENCE

NO. 2

R. COLIN BEEVER

EUROPEAN UNITY

AND THE

TRADE UNION MOVEMENTS

A. W. SYTHOFF-LEYDEN

1960

A Thesis submitted to the Council of Europe, Strasbourg, in fulfilment
of the terms of a Research Fellowship, awarded in 1957

C

213452

Soe Sei

CONTENTS

ACKNOWLEDGEMENTS

Grateful thanks are due to the Council of Europe whose award of a Research Fellowship made this study possible.

Gratitude is owed, also, to the United Kingdom Council of the European Movement and to the Charles Henry Foyle Trust for their interest, and generous supplementary financial assistance.

The author's natural disposition towards trade union causes, as well as his occupation as a trade union research worker, should be declared. Viewpoints taken, conclusions reached and policies suggested in Part Five, or elsewhere, are entirely on the author's responsibility, and should not be taken as committing the Council of Europe or other sponsors in any way.

Those people all over Western Europe who so readily made their experience and knowledge available are too numerous to mention individually, but the generosity of them all in Community Secretariats, national and international trade union organisations, intergovernmental organisations and national embassies was much appreciated. But special mention must be made of Donald Bowers and Lionel Murray of the TUC Secretariat, Harm Buiter of the Trade Union Secretariat of the six Community countries, Walter Schevenels of the European Regional Organisation of the ICFTU, and Messrs. W. H. Marsh, F. Kenny, D. Taylor and J. R. Lloyd Davies, Labour Counsellors in the British Embassies in Brussels, Bonn, Rome and Paris respectively; all of whom gave very freely of their time and experience.

Special thanks are due to Raymond Oliver for his translations, patient reading of the draft text and his valuable suggestions for its greater clarity; to Peter Rosenfeld and to Alie and George Watkins for their great assistance with translations; also to Kenneth Wardle, Marion Gabb, Pauline Thomas and Vilma Thomas for their encouragement and volunteered secretarial help.

PREFACE

The signing of the Treaties establishing the European Economic Community and the European Atomic Energy Community, or Euratom, by the foreign ministers of Western Germany, France, Italy, Belgium, the Netherlands and Luxembourg, in Rome on 25 March 1957, opened out a new chapter in European history, which had begun with the setting up of the European Coal and Steel Community (ECSC) in 1952. The task of drafting treaties of this sort, to make them acceptable to countries of differing economic interests, historical backgrounds, cultures and political outlooks, is, in itself, a feat requiring great skill and tenacity of purpose. But if the signing of such treaties by the plenipotentiaries of the six powers is remarkable, the second stage of persuading the national legislatures of these countries to ratify the Treaties is, perhaps, an even greater achievement. Each national parliament is composed of elected members representing different political parties, different localities, differing trade and industrial interests; and each of them is subject to the pressure of particular interests.

The fact that the Economic Community and the Atomic Energy Community can become realities, in these circumstances is evidence that the six countries have each experienced a sufficiently strong common desire for unity in Europe to override the objections which could arise from the natural conservatism of those affected.

Of all the organised interest groups at work in the social and economic life of a modern nation, few, if any, have greater influence than the organised employees, speaking through their trade unions. Quite apart from the numerical strength of the trade unions, few other organisations are so closely geared to the everyday changes in society as to be able to bring immediate and heavy pressure to bear on those responsible for actions adversely affecting their interests. European integration is bound to bring in its wake a host of new problems for the trade unions. It might have been supposed, therefore, that they would generally oppose the Rome Treaties. The opposite has been true. National and international trade union organisations in Western Europe have been in the vanguard of those desiring a closer-knit Europe, with the important exceptions of the World Federation of Trade Unions and its affiliates.

The reasons for this support, and the impact which European integration has had, and will have, on the trade union movements, and *vice-*

versa, are the basis of the present study. It was inevitable that measures as far-reaching as the ECSC and the Rome treaties would confront the trade union movements with new factors, and cause them to take stock of their position. The national movements have had to consider, among other things, what alterations to their international machinery were appropriate to a more unified Europe.

Although this study was originally completed during the early months of 1959, the advent of the European Free Trade Association plan, directly after that, made it necessary to revise the text and to add a new chapter to Part Three. The seven countries forming this Association: Britain, Norway, Sweden, Denmark, Austria, Switzerland and Portugal; were among the chief of those which had been trying, through negotiations in the OEEC, to set up a wider Free Trade Area for Western Europe which would have included the Common Market countries. Although the original negotiations failed in that object, the declared aim of the new Association, set up as a second best, is still to negotiate a wider agreement with the Common Market countries.

Details of the original Free Trade Area plan, which are included, therefore, are of more than historical interest, and are very relevant to the fundamental problems over which the "Six" and the "Seven" must resolve their differences. The resolution of these differences is still causing a great deal of discussion and diplomatic activity at the time of writing.

The European Free Trade Association can hardly be described as an integration project because it does not have the supranational features of the Communities of the "Six". It is better described as intergovernmental. Consequently, trade union functions in it are unlikely to be as great as those in the Common Market. The study therefore deals with the viewpoints of the trade union national centres of the Association countries more briefly than with the "Six". The exception is Britain, which has, in its TUC, the strongest trade union movement in Western Europe. British trade unionism would play a major role in any wider link-up, and full account of its views is taken in the study.

Trade unionists are far from being novices in international dealings, as international trade union movements existed even before the beginning of the century. In recent years, international trade union organisations have played an important role in planning common action on issues of importance in many countries. True international viewpoints have emerged, which have taken precedence over national interests in a number of fields. International trade union organisations have been taken into consultation with the United Nations organs and their special agencies, as well as with a number of other intergovernmental organisations. In some cases their representatives have the right to speak or vote in plenary sessions of such organisations, and to submit items for the agenda, and memoranda for consideration by delegates.

The experience gained by the trade union movements in these international activities is valuable to them in facing their problems in the new, integrated, Europe, which is emerging. But the picture is a complex one, because in most of the countries affected there are several trade union movements rather than one, divided along political or religious lines. And there are three separate trade union internationals, reflecting these divisions at international level. There is little immediate prospect of this framework changing radically, but there is a shortage of collated information on how the picture is drawn, now, for Western Europe which this study attempts, in a necessarily limited way, to remedy.

Because, in certain instances, national trade union viewpoints carry at least as much weight as those put forward by the international organisations, their views are set out separately, in Part Four. It has not been possible, in a work of this scope, to give any detailed consideration to specific industrial sectors of the Common Market, except by way of illustration, and for this reason individual trade unions have not been studied; only the national federations of unions, or national centres, as they are generally known.

This, by and large, gives a balanced picture, as the individual unions, with one or two exceptions, have been content to agree the general lines of policy towards integration questions through the medium of their national centres. It is these general lines which form the basis of the study.

The dynamic nature of the integration process creates difficulties in writing a study that is not to be out of date almost as soon as it is completed. Events have moved with great rapidity, and it was to be expected, therefore, that attitudes to integration projects would be in a continuous state of flux concerning detailed matters, as has proved to be the case. Much of the data used was collected in the first half of 1958; a good deal of it by interview or correspondence with the people most directly concerned, owing to the scarcity of published statements. Developments of major importance, during 1959, concerning the trade union position, have been incorporated in the study, but the possibility remains of some modifications in matters of detail since 1958 having gone unrecorded, especially if unpublished, as is sometimes the case.

The non-availability of published material on a number of trade union aspects of integration made it necessary to obtain a good deal of the information from unpublished documents, or by direct interview.

The supply of this information would have been further restricted in some cases, if sources were to have been divulged. Partly for these reasons the annotation of this work, and the bibliography attached, are limited in scope. Footnotes are mostly reserved for occasions where direct quotes are made from published documents. This system has the advantage of leaving a text, already complicated by the need to use a wide range of initials, as unobstructed as possible, so that the reader is not unnecessarily distracted. As a further small concession to readability, certain formal or correct names such as European Economic Community, United Kingdom, Federal Republic, etc., have been rendered less formally as Common Market, Britain, Germany, etc., where the precise meaning is not in doubt.

The study is not intended to be a history of trade union participation in Western European integration. It is an attempt to set out a good deal of factual matter that has not previously been brought together, concerning the role of trade union organisations in the integration process; together with an evaluation of that role. The Conclusion attempts to indicate the lines along which international trade union policy and structure might develop in its own best interests, and consistently with the responsible and essential role which it is recognised trade unionism plays in modern industrial nations.

LIST OF ABBREVIATIONS

Full names or descriptions given here are in English only. Titles in other languages which are represented by abbreviations listed, are given in full, in those languages, on the first occasion they occur in the text, if they are of major importance, or are used frequently.

AF of L	American Federation of Labor.
AFL-CIO	American Federation of Labor-Congress of Industrial Organisations.
CFTC	French Confederation of Christian Workers.
CGC	French White-Collar Workers' Federation.
CGD	German Christian Trade Union Federation.
CGIL	Italian General Confederation of Labour.
CGT	French General Confederation of Labour.
CGT-FO	French Trade Union Centre which was postwar breakaway from CGT.
CGT (Lux)	Luxembourg General Confederation of Labour.
CIO	Congress of Industrial Organisations in the United States.
CISC	International Federation of Christian Trade Unions.
CISL	Italian Confederation of Workers Unions (Christian).
CNV	Dutch Protestant Trade Union Federation.
CSC	Belgian Christian Trade Union Federation.
DAG	German White-Collar Workers' Federation.
DBB	German Civil Service Federation.
DGB	German Trade Union Federation.
DSF	Danish Trade Union Federation.
ECE	United Nations Economic Commission for Europe.
ECSC	European Coal and Steel Community.
EDC	European Defence Community.
EEC	European Economic Community.
EFTA	European Free Trade Association.
EPU	European Payments Union.

ERO	European Regional Organisation of the ICFTU.
Euratom	European Atomic Energy Community.
EVC	WFTU-affiliated Dutch Trade Union Centre.
FGTB	General Federation of Labour of Belgium.
FIL	Italian Labour Federation.
FTA	Free Trade Area.
GATT	General Agreement on Tariffs and Trade.
ICFTU	International Confederation of Free Trade Unions.
IFBWW	International Federation of Building and Woodworkers.
IFCCTE	International Federation of Commercial Clerical and Technical Employees.
IFTU	International Federation of Trade Unions.
ILO	International Labour Organisation, or International Labour Office.
IMF	International Metalworkers Federation.
ITF	International Transport Workers' Federation.
ITS	International Trade Secretariat.
JTUAC	Joint Trade Union Advisory Committee to the OEEC.
KAB	Dutch Catholic Trade Union Federation.
LCGB	Luxembourg Christian Trade Union Federation.
LCGIL	Free Italian General Confederation of Workers.
LO	Swedish Trade Union Federation.
MIF	Miner's International Federation.
MRP	French Catholic Political Party.
NATO	North Atlantic Treaty Organisation.
NVV	Netherlands Federation of Trade Unions.
OEEC	Organisation for European Economic Co-operation.
ÖGB	Austrian Trade Union Federation.
TUC	Trades Union Congress.
TUI	Trade Union International (Trade Departments of the WFTU).
UIL	Italian Labour Union.
UNESCO	United Nations Educational, Scientific and Cultural Organisation.
USS	Swiss Trade Union Federation.
WFTU	World Federation of Trade Unions.

PART ONE

THE INTERNATIONAL TRADE UNION MOVEMENTS

CHAPTER I

CHANGE AND DIVERSITY

There is no single statement of policy in existence which can be said to represent the views of the international trade union movement on the subject of Western European integration. The reason is that there is no one organisation which can truly claim to speak on behalf of the whole trade union movement; for there is not one trade union movement at the international level, but several. They include two which are very large and influential though in rather different spheres, and one which is very much smaller. These three between them have all but a small minority of trade unionists in Western Europe affiliated to them through their respective trade union national centres, so that they figure predominantly in all aspects of this study.

The International Confederation of Free Trade Unions (ICFTU) has by far the largest affiliated trade union membership in Western Europe; over 80% of the total. The ICFTU's report on the activities of the Confederation, presented to its fifth World Congress in Tunis, in July 1957, claims a European total of 24,509,000. As it claims no affiliates in Eastern Europe, this can be taken to be a wholly Western European membership. It gives the ICFTU's world membership as 53,814,822 on 1 January 1957, comprising 124 affiliated organisations in 88 countries and territories.

The second of the international trade union organisations, the World Federation of Trade Unions (WFTU), claims a larger affiliated world membership than the ICFTU. The organisation's General Secretary, Louis Saillant, put the figure at ninety millions in his report to the WFTU World Trade Union Congress in Leipzig, in October 1957. No separate estimate of its Western European affiliates is available, but all save a minute part of its strength in this area is contained in the membership of the *Confédération Générale du Travail* (CGT) in France, and the *Confederazione Generale Italiana del Lavoro* (CGIL) in Italy.

Exact membership figures for these two organisations are unobtainable, but estimates of CGT membership vary from one to one-and-a-half millions, and that of the CGIL is generally believed to be about three millions.

This gives the WFTU a nominal Western European strength of four to four-and-a-half millions. However, no trade union membership figures given in France or Italy are very reliable, as they can include, usually anybody, from a fully paid up member to a worker who has been hopefully presented with a union card, but has paid no subscriptions. The head offices find it almost impossible to obtain exact figures, or to make clearcut definitions of who is entitled to call himself a member, as is done in most other European countries. The organisations are therefore prone to be optimistic in their membership estimates–sometimes excessively so.

This tendency to exaggerate memberships also applies to the international trade union organisations, and probably more particularly to the WFTU and to the International Federation of Christian Trade Unions (CISC),[1] which is the third of the main trade union internationals. These two organisations are less forthcoming than the ICFTU in giving detailed analyses of the totals that they claim.

The CISC has a membership of between three and three-and-a-quarter millions in Western Europe, according to the figures supplied to the Yearbook of International Associations. The bulk of this is in France, Belgium and the Netherlands. The worldwide membership was about four millions, in 47 countries, at the beginning of 1956.

It is apparent from all these figures that the ICFTU has by far the largest membership and influence in Western Europe of all the trade union internationals, and the organisation will therefore be dealt with at greater length, further on. At the same time, it should be borne in mind that both the WFTU and the CISC wield very strong influence in some Western European countries, and little, or none at all, in others. This could have important consequences.

Progress in integration trends in Western Europe necessarily depends on a high measure of agreement between all the countries concerned. Therefore any large organisation with considerable public influence in one country may tilt the balance of national opinion on matters concerning integration. If it should tilt the balance in a direction which does not coincide with the views of other countries, then it could be said that this organisation was indirectly altering the course of international negotiations.

A large national trade union centre could find itself in such a position. Although it is not necessarily suggested here that any of them have

1. Will be referred to throughout this study by its French initials, CISC; that is, *Confédération Internationale des Syndicats Chrétiens*. The English initials, IFCTU, which are in fairly common usage, elsewhere, are easily confused, on sight with ICFTU, the abbreviation for the International Confederation of Free Trade Unions.

altered the course of events concerning integration in this way, that possibility does exist.

The Post-War International Trade Union Scene

The history of the international trade union movement from the early days of World War II is an unhappy one. The old International Federation of Trade Unions (IFTU), which up till that time had brought together most of the main trade union national centres of the western world, almost collapsed before the political and military campaigns of the Hitler government, which smashed many of its strongest affiliates. In June 1940 the IFTU had hastily to move its headquarters from Paris to London, where the Trades Union Congress (TUC) provided it with offices for the duration. It still had the support of the American Federation of Labor (AF of L) and the TUC, and of the trade union federations in Sweden and Switzerland. But there was little it could do except maintain its existence until the war was over and trade union and other reconstruction could begin.

However, the resuscitation of the IFTU after the war would have proved a difficult task, owing to changed circumstances, and, in fact, it never came about. Instead, the TUC took a decision in October 1943 to call a world trade union conference which would consider both the furtherance of the war effort and problems of reconstruction for peace. They felt that the IFTU was not a suitable body to convene such a conference because its rules would prevent the attendance of Soviet trade unionists with whom the TUC were co-operating successfully in wartime alliance. The IFTU rules would also prevent certain other large trade union centres being represented because they only made provision for one representative organisation per country. This would have excluded from the conference, among others, the Congress of Industrial Organisations (CIO), in the United States, which was a well-established breakaway from the AF of L, whose hostility it still incurred.

The TUC believed that international trade union solidarity was essential for a lasting peace and was prepared to make the attempt to have something approaching universal representation at an international gathering. It therefore envisaged a conference which would be exploratory only, in order that the trade union organisations which had hitherto been in opposition to each other could get together without feeling compromised. This solution, the TUC thought, would leave open the question of whether the IFTU could be brought back to full life, and it was hoped that the AF of L, who wished for such a revival, would agree to attend the special conference along with the rival CIO and the Russians.

In spite of the TUC's early initiative the conference, in fact, did not meet until 6 February 1945, and then without the AF of L, which adhered to its view that any such conference should have been called by the IFTU, and so declined to attend. The conference set up an interim, or preparatory committee to act as an executive, and a sub-committee of this interim committee then proceeded to draft a constitution for a proposed new international trade union organisation. The result was submitted to a second conference convened in Paris in September and October 1945, and was approved.

The conference represented 56 countries or territories and 83 national and international trade union organisations. The AF of L was the only important absentee.

After the constitution was adopted, the conference continued to sit as the first Congress of the World Federation of Trade Unions (WFTU). One of the rules adopted stated that affiliation should be confined, where possible, to a single national trade union centre from each country. However, the Christian trade union observers who had attended the conference wished to keep their separate national centres and international federation, if they joined the new organisation. The conference pointed to the new rule and disallowed the Christian proposal, as there were already non-denominational centres in the countries concerned seeking affiliation. The Christians therefore decided not to associate themselves with the WFTU, and have maintained their separate organisations since.

Members of the IFTU General Council had been present at the conference, and had now become parties to the establishment of the WFTU.

They accordingly decided to wind up the IFTU when they next met in December 1945. Although the AF of L still opposed the IFTU dissolution, all the other organisations affiliated to it had now joined the WFTU. The General Council of the IFTU therefore dissolved the organisation as from 31 December 1945, without even calling a special congress.

Walter Citrine was at this time still the General Secretary of the British TUC, and also President of the IFTU. As such, he was one of the most respected figures in the trade union world. He had warned the delegates at the first international trade union conference in London, the previous February, that, to avoid future difficulties they should not, in any new trade union international, seek to reach fundamental decisions on majority votes; but by common consent. He continued:

"Nor must we forget that we are trade unions and not political bodies. We combine to raise the standard of the worker, to reduce his hours of work and give him an increasing measure of control over his work. Here we have common ground as I am sure we shall find out when we come to consider the subject of the immediate trade union demands. The moment, however, that we approach politics, we find divergencies amongst us. Let us pursue as actively as we wish within our respective countries our national political policies, but I warn you that a trade union international which imports into its operations political principles or philosophies is endangering its stability and effectiveness."[1]

It appeared at the outset as if Citrine's advice had been taken to heart, because the preamble to the new WFTU constitution, contrary to many trade union constitutions, contained no expressions of ultimate political aims, or their method of achievement; save for the non-controversial post-war determination which was restated, to struggle for the "extermination of all fascist forms of government and every manifestation of fascism". It looked as if a formula may have been found whereby the trade union representatives of capitalist, communist, socialist and catholic countries could work together for industrial purposes in a common organisation.

But it was not to be. The honeymoon period for the trade unions lasted no longer than it did for the governments of the great powers after the war.

And to a substantial degree the rifts in the new WFTU, which became increasingly severe from 1947, were a direct reflection of the international political events.

Louis Saillant, of the French CGT, had been elected General Secretary of the WFTU. He had a number of assistant secretaries who represented, approximately, the international balance of power in the organisation. Saillant had been acceptable to most because of his reputation in France as a worker in the wartime underground movement, and later as head of the the National Resistance Council. At the time of his election he was not thought to be associated with the communist movement, but, as time went on, it appeared to West European and American trade unionists that he was becoming a mouthpiece for Soviet policies, and a strong critic of the non-communist countries. In fact it was thought that the whole organisation of the WFTU was being used whenever possible to advance Soviet policies. Arthur Deakin of the TUC protested

---

1. *Forty-Five Years*, by W. SCHEVENELS, pp. 334-336.

along with others, but the protests had no lasting effect, and events moved from bad to worse.

After several attempts to patch matters up, the final split came at the WFTU Executive Bureau meeting in Paris on 17 to 21 January 1949. The representatives of the British TUC, the American CIO and the Dutch Unions walked out in protest. Before the second WFTU Congress opened in Milan in June that year, nearly all the other West European trade union organisations had quit. The immediate cause of the Anglo-American-Dutch walkout was a procedural dispute, but the fundamental differences which had made the final act inevitable are worth-while recalling.

There had been, and still was, a deep division in the WFTU concerning their attitude to the Marshall Plan, which proposed to dispense American financial aid to European countries, to help them in their postwar recovery. Most of the West European trade unionists, and naturally the Americans, had been all in favour of the plan, but the Soviet unions, plus the largest French and Italian federations, had sharply attacked it. The WFTU had followed the same line in its publications, and in the speeches of some of its senior officials. This was possible because of the large number of communist sympathisers who had found their way into the WFTU hierarchy and now exercised, together, a controlling power. The separate elements of the WFTU were splitting along the clear and distinct lines of the cold war which was dividing the world outside, and for very similar reasons.

Another major factor leading to the split was the failure to find a formula which would bring the International Trade Secretariats (ITS) into close association with the WFTU. These international trade union organisations, which co-ordinated the activities in different countries of workers in the same industries, had long been an accepted feature of the international trade union scene. Pre-war, they had enjoyed a very high degree of autonomy in their association with the IFTU, but now the WFTU wanted to make them into trade departments of its own organisation, and curb their independence.

The ITSs would not tolerate this, and were becoming suspicious, anyway, of the Communist leanings of the WFTU. They, themselves, were in favour of the Marshall plan, and they also wanted to keep on good terms with the AF of L (which was still opposed to the WFTU) with a view to their expansion on the North American continent. For all these reasons antipathy between the ITSs and the WFTU grew, and the International Federation of Transport Workers, at its Congress in July 1948, led the way by declaring its independence of any trade union international until such time as there was one more congenial to it. Two months later the other ITSs, in joint conference, likewise declined to accept WFTU suzerainty. Their attitude was a major factor in the eventual WFTU split, as they had strong support from the American, and most of the West European trade union delegates to the WFTU.

Another factor contributing to the final rift was the split in the French trade union movement, the CGT. This took place in December 1947, and was along similar lines and for similar reasons of pro and anti-communist feeling within the same organisation. For these, and other lesser reasons, the WFTU officially ceased to represent world trade union opinion in January 1949, and became the organisation of the eastern bloc of the trade union world only.

Broadly, then, the confused events of the post-war scene began with the TUC decision to call an international trade union conference. The pre-war International Federation of Trade Unions was still officially in existence, but its rules would have prevented universal representation at the conference; hence the British initiative for an *ad hoc* conference. The powerful American Federation of Labor did not attend because it was diffident about joining forces with Soviet unions, and thought the IFTU should have called such a conference. The AF of L's rival organisation, the Congress of Industrial Organisations, was not squeamish about sitting down with the Russians, however, and they, together with French, Soviet and other representatives at the conference, pressed for, and obtained the setting up of a new international, which came into existence at a second international conference. The new international was named the World Federation of Trade Unions. It was not very long before internal dissensions along East-West political lines, became serious. They came to a head in January 1949 over a fairly technical issue when the British, American and Dutch executive Bureau representatives walked out.

But the major differences were over the Marshall Plan and the independence of the International Trade Secretariats.

It did not take the breakaway elements very long to decide on the formation of a rival trade union International that would represent the trade union viewpoint of the western world. They named it the International Confederation of Free Trade Unions.

CHAPTER II

THE INTERNATIONAL CONFEDERATION OF FREE TRADE UNIONS

The ICFTU Constitution was adopted at a conference in London in November and December 1949, which had been convened by a preparatory committee set up during a similar conference called by the TUC, and held in Geneva five months previously. The London Conference sat first as the World Free Labour Conference, and then itself became the first ICFTU Congress, when the constitution had been approved.

The new International contained all the trade union national centres which had broken away from the WFTU plus a number of others. The most important of the others was the AF of L. For the first time it was working together with the CIO, which was also affiliated. At its inauguration the ICFTU represented 87 national and international trade union organisations, with an estimated 48 million workers in 53 different countries.

The ICFTU is sometimes loosely termed the "socialist" trade union international, presumably to make an easy distinction between it and the communist and christian internationals.

The term is misleading. It need only be borne in mind that both the AF of L and the CIO in the United States were, and still, in amalgamation, are powerful members of the new organisation. Any suggestion that it was socialist would certainly have alienated the Americans.

The fact that all the affiliates of the new International were united in their opposition to Communist systems, and their trade unions, did not indicate that they held similar views on more positive political issues. Far from it. While Western European trade unionism generally had, and still has, a tradition of socialism, most trade union organisations in Western Europe are not directly allied with socialist parties. Britain has the closest link between trade unions and party. But a number of national centres affiliated to the ICFTU are at pains to deny any direct or official link with any party, socialist or otherwise, while admitting, usually, that they have general socialist sympathies. Others are more in harmony with Social Democratic Parties often considered to be a little to the right of socialists, politically.

In view of this position, great care was taken to draft a constitution for the ICFTU which would be acceptable to socialist and non-socialist viewpoints alike. The constitution's preamble and declared aims therefore avoid all mention of socialism and political means or objectives. The wording focuses, instead, on the freedom of the individual and of trade unions, and on the importance of democratic systems. The keynote is set by the first of the declared aims:

> "to establish a powerful and effective international organisation, composed of free and democratic trade unions, independent of any external domination and pledged to the task of promoting the interests of working people throughout the world and of enhancing the dignity of labour."

The WFTU, of course, had set out with a deftly worded constitution which also avoided political controversy. But whereas the WFTU fell down on the task of maintaining political independence, the ICFTU has managed, with one or two minor exceptions, to keep peace with, and among, its affiliates. It has done this by following the advice of Walter Citrine, quoted earlier, of avoiding political action or statements which were likely to be controversial between its own members. The Confederation has broadly confined itself to industrial activities, or political pressure on matters closely allied to industry, and the well-being of trade unionists working in it.

Another of the aims of the Confederation, set out in the constitution, indicates the general approach of the organisation to problems of economic integration. It reads in full:

> "to advocate, with a view to raising the general level of prosperity, increased and properly planned economic co-operation among the nations in such a way as will encourage the development of wider economic units and freer exchange of commodities and to seek full participation of workers' representatives in official bodies dealing with these questions."

The ICFTU would seem bound to support any movement to bring about European co-operation in view of this clause, if for no other reason. And, in fact, it has done so with enthusiasm.

The other main aims of the Confederation set out in its constitution, are to gain a greater recognition of trade unions and their rights and provide assistance to them where necessary; to promote mutual assistance among them; to resist totalitarian influences; to help people in countries suffering from the after-effects of the war; to establish full employment, improved working conditions and higher living standards; to further conomic, social and cultural progress of all peoples, particularly in under-developed countries; to eliminate forced labour; to establish working relationships with international organisations of all kinds in order to further ICFTU aims; to support the establishment of a world system of collective security; to foster educational and publicity work which will increase the workers' knowledge and understanding, and particularly to supply affiliated organisations with trade union data concerning other countries.

When the ICFTU was set up, representatives from the christian national trade union centres in France and Belgium attended the inaugural conference. The delegates from the other national centres in those countries, and from the non-denominational trade union centre in the Netherlands, objected to their presence. These christian national centres were already affiliated to their own International, the CISC, and the non-christian trade unionists from these three countries were of the opinion that their rivals were not trade unions in the true sense, but were susceptible to government or employer pressure because of their denominational character. The christian representatives denied this, and they were allowed to remain in the conference.

The ICFTU later decided that the christian trade union national centres should be welcomed into affiliation provided that they accepted the principle of attaching themselves to one international only. This was tantamount to saying that the Christian International, which had been re-started soon after the war, should disband itself. This it refused to do, with the result that no christian national centre has affiliated to the ICFTU. The only case that may be regarded as something of an exception to this is that of the Italian Confederation of Labour Unions (CISL), which has arisen from a postwar split of the Italian trade union movement. The organisation is very predominantly Christian Democrat (Roman Catholic), with a small number of Social Democrats, and others, included. In spite of this it has never been affiliated to the CISC, but has chosen to associate itself with the ICFTU instead.

After the big breakaway from the WFTU in 1949, and the inauguration of the ICFTU by the dissenting elements, it did not take the former organisation long to start a big campaign for international co-operation between them, in order, they claimed, to further working class interests and trade union solidarity on an international front.

The WFTU pressure on the ICFTU to co-operate with them on items of common policy has been maintained ever since, but the ICFTU has fought off all thoughts of joint action and has flatly and consistently refused to co-operate with the WFTU, at an official level, on any issue whatever. Each organisation has kept up a running propaganda campaign against the other, and the ICFTU even produces a publication called "Spotlight", which it describes as a "monthly bulletin of news from the dictatorship countries".

Other ICFTU publications include a fortnightly "Information Bulletin", a monthly "Free Labour World" and a two-monthly "Economic and Social Bulletin", besides a number of special monographs, reports, pamphlets and study guides. All publications are normally produced in English, French, German and Spanish; a range wide enough to satisfy most affiliates. The Italian affiliates suffer from special difficulties, because there are no ICFTU publications in their language.

The ICFTU has an extensive educational programme, apart from its publications. It organises, or co-sponsors a large number of courses and schools, and each year an international school is held in a different country. The Confederation maintains its own Training College for Asian trade unionists in Calcutta and has recently started to give three-month training courses at its Brussels headquarters for trade unionists from economically underdeveloped countries. The Regional Organisations of the ICFTU also organise a number of schools and other educational activities in their own areas. In September 1954 the European Regional Organisation held a trade union school in the Netherlands on "The Problems of European Unification".

In Western Europe the ICFTU has nineteen separate trade union centres affiliated to it, listed in its 1957-8 Yearbook. Only Italy and Spain have two organisations affiliated–the other countries one each. The Spanish trade union organisations are both small ones, in exile. The Saar originally had a separate union affiliation, but this is now part of the German trade union federation. The full list of Western European countries with affiliated trade union centres is: Austria, Belgium, Britain, Denmark, France, West Germany, Greece, Iceland, Italy, Luxembourg, Malta, the Netherlands, Norway, Spain, Sweden, Switzerland and Trieste.

The ICFTU maintains relations with a large number of international organisations, most of them United Nations Special Agencies or intergovernmental organisations of a regional character. It has official consultative status with the U.N. Economic and Social Council, the U.N. Food and Agriculture Organisation, the U.N. Children's Emergency Fund, the International Labour Organisation, the Intergovernmental Committee for European Migration, the Organisation for European Economic Co-operation, and the Council of Europe. The ICFTU maintains contact with a number of other international organisations. It has also declared its support for NATO–the North Atlantic Treaty Organisation.

At the Brussels headquarters of the ICFTU a staff of approximately seventy is employed. Branch offices, each with a very small staff, are situated in Paris, Geneva and New York, and are mainly for the purposes of liaison with the various international organisations mentioned. The ICFTU Regional Organisations have separate offices. These are in Mexico, New Delhi and Brussels, and serve the Inter-American Regional Organisation of Workers (ORIT), the Asian Regional Organisation (ARO), and the European Regional Organisation (ERO), respectively. In addition, small ICFTU sub-offices are maintained in Brazil, Trinidad, Tokyo, Singapore, Indonesia, Ghana, Kenya and Chile.

The ICFTU finances are raised from affiliation fees on the basis of £3.15s. sterling per annum per thousand members up to five million, and £2.10s. per annum per thousand for additional members over five million. The total affiliation is abour 54 million, and only Britain, Germany and the United States have affiliates in excess of five million. The annual income of the ICFTU over the last few years has been in the region of £164,000, and little or none of this has remained unspent.

The supreme authority of the ICFTU is its Biennial Congress. Among the Congress's functions are the election of a General Secretary and an Executive Board. The General Secretary is the central figure in the organisation and has wide powers and responsibilities in connection with general administration, the maintenance of contact with affiliated organisations, and the dissemination of information by general publications, and concerning Congress and Executive Board meetings. The holder of the office since the organisation's inception has been J. H. Oldenbroek, originally the General Secretary of the International Federation of Transport Workers, the second largest of the ITSs affiliated to the ICFTU.

The Executive Board is composed of 25 members elected by Congress on a regional basis, weighted to reflect membership totals in each region. Europe has six members. The Board elects its own President. The present holder of the office is Arne Geijer, President of the Swedish Federation of Trade Unions, and a Social Democratic member of Parliament. It is interesting to note that the first holder of this highest ICFTU office, Paul Finet, a veteran Belgian trade union leader, was, in 1958, made President of the High Authority of the European Coal and Steel Community, the first full European integration project, and held this position until September 1959.

The Executive Board is responsible for the running of the ICFTU between Congresses, and it has to prepare and submit a report on activities to each Congress. It must meet at least twice a year. Questions of urgency or importance are dealt with by a sub-committee of seven, again chosen on a weighted, regional basis.

The Congress, itself, has a number of other important tasks to perform at its biennial meetings, apart from the election of a General Secretary and Executive Board. It must elect, also, a Credentials Committee and a Standing Orders Committee and decide which agenda items should be discussed by separate Commissions.

It considers reports on the activities of the Confederation in the preceding two years and proposals for activities for the next two years. Congress vets the financial reports and decides on any proposed amendments to the constitution.

In connection with Congress it is interesting to note another indication, to be found in the constitution, of the influence of Walter Citrine's philosophy. It reads: "The endeavour of Congress shall be to secure the widest possible measure of agreement rather than the carrying of simple majorities". This is clearly to dissuade ICFTU affiliates from pushing resolutions of a highly contentious nature to a vote, thus risking a split in the Confederation.

All national centres affiliated to the ICFTU may send delegates to Congress, with full power to speak and vote. The number of delegates may be as many as twenty per organisation, according to size. However, the sliding scale gives the smaller national centres a higher proportionate basis of representation than the larger ones. There is also special provision for ITS representation, described elsewhere.

Membership of the ICFTU is open to "all *bona fide* national trade union centres accepting the aims and constitution of the Confederation". It is not necessarily confined to one trade union centre per country, as in the old IFTU. Indeed, it is not even confined to national centres (i.e. national federations having a number of affiliates), but is open also to individual trade union organisations. Any trade union which affiliates becomes entitled to normal membership rights and is eligible to send delegates to Congress.

The constitution makes provision for Regional Organisations to be established for certain areas, as and where necessary. In practice, there are three Regional Organisations operating; those for the Inter-American Region, for Asia and for Europe. At the end of 1959 plans were well advanced to set up an African Regional Organisation (AFRO), in addition. Organisations affiliated to the Confederation are eligible for regional membership. The terms of reference of these Regional Organisations are very wide, i.e.: "to deal with problems affecting the workers and the trade unions in their respective areas and to further the aims and objects of the Confederation as set out in this constitution".

The Regional Organisations have their separate rules, and finances raised on an affiliation basis. But the rules, budget and accounts have to be approved by the ICFTU Executive Board, and, in addition, six-monthly reports on activities must be submitted. But a large measure of independence is left in the hands of the Regional Organisations, as will be seen.

CHAPTER III

THE I.C.F.T.U. EUROPEAN REGIONAL ORGANISATION

While each of the three Regional Organisations works within the same generous limits laid down in the ICFTU Constitution, their tasks, in practice, differ fairly widely owing to different circumstances and requirements in those parts of the world in which they operate. The ERO has been actively concerned with the problems of Western European integration for a number of years, and its work therefore requires to be examined in some detail. The work of the other two Regional Organisations, though important, does not directly concern the present study, however.

All organisations affiliated to the ICFTU in the European Region are entitled to become members of the ERO if they accept its statutes. In fact all of them are members, and the ERO statutes guarantee them the same autonomy as they enjoy with the ICFTU. The ERO's competence extends to all countries in Europe and also to any country adjacent to the borders of Europe where a trade union organisation has exercised its right to apply for ERO membership, and has been accepted. In practice, there is no such organisation in the ERO.

The ERO's membership is thus neatly comprised of the Western European affiliates of the ICFTU, no more, no less. These, it will be recalled, are in Austria, Belgium, Britain, Denmark, France, West Germany, Greece, Iceland, Italy, Luxembourg, Malta, the Netherlands, Norway, Spain (in exile), Sweden, Switzerland and Trieste–totalling about 24.5 million members.

The whole of the aims of the ICFTU Constitution are reproduced as Article One of the ERO Statutes. These are not the organisation's only guide to action, however, as it also has a list of eight tasks set out in Article Two. They are, in brief, to endeavour to secure new ICFTU affiliations in the Region; to help existing free trade union organisations in the Region, and to try and establish new ones; to promote conferences and discussions on a Regional basis with a view to obtaining agreement among the trade union organisations about Regional problems; to co-ordinate the free trade union activities in the Region, and where necessary to represent the ICFTU on international organisations; to collect and distribute information concerning trade unions and all social matters appertaining to them in the Region; to advise the ICFTU Executive Board on applications for affiliation from organisations within the Region; to advise the Executive Board about measures to promote the interests of affiliated organisations within the Region and, lastly, to carry on constant propaganda for the achievement of ICFTU aims.

The general picture of the ERO which emerges from this definition of its tasks is that of an international trade union forum for the European Region. This is also what the organisation has become, in fact. The ERO is not an international federation of trade unions with central powers over its affiliates, although the large measure of agreement that has often been achieved in its meetings has sometimes given the mistaken impression that this must have been accomplished by the overriding of minority views. The impression has been present at times when there have been forceful statements concerning Western European integration problems.

The surprising fact is that, huge and complex though the subject is, there has been agreement on fundamental attitudes by nearly all ICFTU affiliated national centres in Europe, independently of the ERO's centralising influence. The ERO could not have done its co-ordinating work so well, or formed the positive policies it has done on integration questions, had it not been for the similar outlook of its affiliates in the first instance.

As in the ICFTU itself, the supreme authority of the ERO is a biennial delegate congress. It is known as the European Regional Conference. Its basis of representation is similar too–the number of delegates increasing with the increasing membership of the affiliates, but, measure for measure, weighted in favour of the smaller trade union organisations. The Conference may meet more frequently than every two years if an extraordinary meeting is deemed necessary.

The official languages at the meetings of the Regional Conference are English, German, French and a Scandinavian language.

The functions of the Conference are in most ways parallel with those of the ICFTU Congress. It has to consider reports on the last two years' activities and deliberate on the proposals for the next two years, consider the financial reports and budgetary proposals and elect officers and committees. The latter include the Credentials Committee, the Standing Orders Committee and the Executive Committee. Officers to be elected are the President, four Vice-Presidents and the General Secretary, each for a period of two years, which is also the mandate for the Executive. The General Secretary's appointment is subject to ICFTU confirmation.

The Executive Committee is composed of the President, the General Secretary, and six other full members. The President and the six members each represent one of the following geographical groups:

Britain–Malta
Germany
Scandinavia (Denmark, Norway, Sweden)
France – Spain
Austria–Switzerland
Benelux (Belgium, the Netherlands, Luxembourg)
Italy–Trieste–Greece

There is an unusual provision for substitute members of the Executive to be elected by Conference, also. These substitutes may attend the meetings of the Executive and are entitled to receive all minutes, agendas and other documents appertaining to the meetings. This provision is to enable countries not represented by a full Executive member to participate in the meetings, and be fully informed, nevertheless. There are either one or two substitute members for each group according to the number of countries in it. Substitutes are proposed by the groups, but elected by Conference. Substitute members may speak at Executive meetings, but may not vote, unless they are replacing full members.

The Presidency of the ERO seems to be a British privilege. Up to his retirement in 1957, the position was held by Sir Charles Geddes (now Lord Geddes), who has been Chairman of the TUC, and since then, Sir Alfred Roberts, also a member and past chairman of the TUC's General Council, has occupied the seat. The election of a British President is not just an act of deference to ERO's largest affililate. It is a genuine tribute by other European trade unionists to the individuals, themselves, and to what they regard as a British capacity for good chairmanship. Not only in the ERO, but also in the meetings of the ILO Workers' Group, European trade unionists have paid spontaneous tribute to the capacity of both these men to be fair to all sides and to expedite the business on the agenda, even by strict rulings against irrelevant speeches.

If it were not for these widely shared feelings about British chairmen, the ERO might not work as effectively. The reason is that continental European trade unionists are rather suspicious of Britain's traditional insularity from continental problems. For an organisation as deeply committed to the European unification movement as the ERO, it might have been considered injudicious to have a President representing the one country that was considered likely to drag its feet on the question. But, in fact, Geddes, himself, became a convinced "European", and there is no reason to suppose that his successor damps down, in any way, the activities of the ERO on integration questions.

The Executive Committee is constitutionally the next highest authority of the ERO, after the Conference.

Its terms of reference are:

"to advise the General Secretary, to supervise his activities and to submit recommendations to the Regional Conference on all matters concerning the activities of the Regional Organisation."

It also has to approve the ERO budget, fix the place and date of the Regional Conference and prepare its agenda. The meetings of the Executive are not on set dates, but are convened according to need and convenience, several times a year.

The ERO has found it necessary to have a number of committees to look into specialised questions - particularly on the various aspects of Western European integration. This question has been largely the prerogative of the Economic Committee, which had five reports prepared on the liberalisation of trade, the balance of payments, investment policy, full employment and the problems of European integration. These were eventually approved by the Committee and by Regional Conference. Committee meetings are normally held in Brussels at the ERO headquarters.

Members of the Executive Committee find that their positions carry a heavy responsibility, and are very time-consuming, particularly when attendance at other ERO committee meetings is also required. It is usually the case that all Executive members have full time executive or administrative posts in their own individual unions or national trade union centres, or both. They are therefore extremely busy men. The ERO responsibilities are a great additional burden, not only in the sense of time spent at meetings, and travelling to and from meetings abroad, but also in the amount of reading, study and consultation that is an essential part of the job.

In order to be able to carry out this job effectively, an Executive member must have a good working knowledge, not only of the briefs prepared for him, but of the broader implications of the economic and political topics which will be debated at the meetings. He may then see trade union policy in the perspective of the general international scene. He must be sufficiently versed in economics and social subjects to have an understanding of the technical questions on his agenda, and must be shrewd and industrious enough to read news of those events abroad which will determine the attitude of his colleagues on the Executive.

All this, in addition to full time duties at home, is a considerable task for anybody. But most of the Executive members are not men who have been fortunate enough to receive university education, or professional training as economists. They are more usually self-educated men whose knowledge and experience have been gained during a gradual rise to the top of the trade union movements of their own countries. The successful performance of their international trade union duties, in these circumstances, is no small accomplishment.

The members of the ERO Executive Committee elected in 1958 were—G. Canini of the Italian CISL (1st substitute from Italian UIL, 2nd substitute from Greece); C. Mourges of France; K. Nordahl of Norway[1]; C. van Wingerden of the Netherlands (1st substitute from Belgium, 2nd substitute from Luxembourg); F. Klenner of Austria (substitute from Switzerland); and L. Rosenberg of Germany. The President, Sir A. Roberts, represents Britain. He and the General Secretary make up the eight members of the Committee.

The ERO has a small secretariat of its own, headed by the General Secretary, which may be given assistance by ICFTU specialist staff, in Brussels, when urgently needed. All committees therefore have drafts prepared in advance on any major subject on the agenda, and expert advice on technical or other problems for which they seek a solution. Normally, such draft reports are considered by representative specialist committees before being submitted to the full Executive. This was done in the case of the five reports on various aspects of European integration.

The Executive Committee representatives usually have sufficient time to submit draft statements of policy thus arrived at to the experts employed in their own national trade union centres, if desired, before any final decisions are taken at a subsequent ERO Executive meeting. After the national expert has analysed a document for the benefit of a delegate, it is quite possible that it will be submitted to the executive body of the national centre for full discussion, if it concerns a major issue, or is likely to be controversial.

The delegate will thus have every opportunity to be fully briefed when he has to attend the next ERO Executive meeting.

The salaries of the Regional Secretariat (apart from that of the General Secretary, who is paid by the ICFTU) are borne by the ERO. The ERO, itself, is financed by dues from its affiliated trade union organisations. The level of dues is decided by the Regional Conference,

---

1. The Scandinavian trade union movements regularly meet together to discuss policy and co-operation, and, arising from this, they have, for some years, operated a system to share out international delegations. Norway has the ERO delegate, Sweden the ILO delegate, and Denmark the ICFTU delegate.

and they are payable quarterly. The whole cost of the running of the ERO has to be met from these resources. However, subject to the approval of the ICFTU Executive Board, the Regional Conference may levy supplementary contributions to meet extraordinary expenditure.

The General Secretary

Article Nine of the ERO Statutes states:

"The management of the affairs of the Regional Organisation shall be in the hands of the Regional Conference, the Executive Committee and the General Secretary of the ERO whose respective authorities shall rank in the order indicated."

This is a normal state of affairs in many organisations, and it is a well-recognised fact that the General Secretaries of them are subject to the control of the Executive, and in the last instance, of Conference. It is also well recognised that General Secretaries, in practice, have a wider measure of independence than may be suggested in constitutions. The reason is that day-to-day decisions, often of an important nature, require to be made without delay. It is seldom practical to call an Executive meeting for these purposes, and so the responsibility falls on the General Secretaries, whose actions are later confirmed, almost without exception.

Because of their continuous participation in events, and contacts with people, General Secretaries are usually far better informed than any of their Executive members have a chance of being. They are therefore in a position not only to advise the Executive on general events and technical points, but to use their expertise to initiate policy, although this is, theoretically, not one of their functions. If a particular General Secretary is a man of long experience, then it is almost certain that his personal authority will be the dominating factor in his organisation's work, and sense of direction.

Conferences may be the supreme authorities of organisations, but they meet infrequently, and their cumbrous nature makes them unsuitable bodies for determining the finer points of policy. It is normally for them to approve, or (unusually) disapprove, the general lines of policy in the last period under review, and to indicate the general lines of policy they wish to see in the forthcoming period. Conferences usually accept their General Secretaries' advice on what is practical and possible concerning the topic under discussion. Delegates to conferences also know that their General Secretary will be the man who has to carry out the directives, and that he will have to decide later, normally after consultation with his Executive, whether he is able to carry out the policy of Conference, or whether the emphasis or direction of that policy will have to be altered in the light of changing circumstances.

The conclusion is that while it is usual for organisations to stipulate that Conference is the policy-making body, that the Executive is there to implement the policy and work out details, and that the General Secretary's job is to administer the whole; it is recognised, in practice, that the General Secretary, as the constant factor in all this process, must achieve a status and authority greater than that of a paid administrator and servant of the organisation, which the constitution sometimes suggests is his only role.

If the above is true of organisations in general, it is certainly to be expected that it will hold good for an international body of the character of the ERO. And so it does. The fact that Conference meets only every two years tends to lessen its direct influence on policy issues, and a meeting as heterogeneous as an international trade union conference is rather more unwieldy than the average delegate conference. This is accentuated by the language problem. Four languages are used at the ERO Conference, but even so, a considerable number of delegates have to manage with an understanding of a tongue other than their native one.

The ERO Executive Committee is more in a position to exert a direct and consistent influence on the organisation's activities than is the Conference. But even the Executive has a number of limitations on its functioning which throw heavy responsibilities back on to the General Secretary. Because the meetings are not statutory, members of the Executive may not always know of them sufficiently far in advance to ensure attendance. In any case, it is difficult to arrange a date convenient to all members when each of them has so many important national commitments. And some delegates have to allow up to two days travelling time for attendance at Executive meetings, in addition to the duration of the meeting itself.

All these factors tend to make attendances patchy, and substitutes often have to take the place of delegates. The element of continuity in the Executive is thereby reduced, making it less easy for it to exercise its policy-making functions. This is not to say that the Executive voluntarily relinquish any of their policy-making rights. It is hardly conceivable that a body containing such a high proportion of trade union General Secretaries and Presidents should voluntarily delegate any policy-making powers at all, were it not for the number of physical obstacles to be overcome in getting to grips with their problems.

In consequence of these factors, the General Secretary of the ERO is a man who must shoulder big responsibilities in all aspects of the ERO's work. Whether or not he should choose to become leader of the organisation, he will almost certainly find himself, willynilly, in a position to exercise the option.

Walter Schevenels, the man who has occupied the position since the ERO's inception in 1950, has not fought shy of work or responsibility. He is a man of adequate resourcefulness and industriousness for the job. Schevenels is a trade unionist of long experience, and an inveterate and indefatigable fighter on behalf of all organised workers. He is a Belgian, and was originally a metalworker and a trade union organiser in his own country. From the beginning of 1931, right up to its dissolution at the end of 1945, he was the General Secretary of the old International Federation of Trade Unions. The stormy political and trade union weather of the 1930s and early 1940s could hardly have provided a more gruelling task for any trade unionist. In spite of this long and hard schooling, Schevenels was passed over in favour of Saillant when it came to choosing the General Secretary of the newly formed WFTU in 1945. This was largely because of his unpopularity with the French and Russian trade unionists, who considered him too right-wing. However, he was given a post as Assistant General Secretary and put in charge of relations with the ITSs, a position he later resigned when his differences with the WFTU official policy on the subject reached breaking point.

An ex-President of the ERO, Charles Geddes, has described Schevenels as "a Belgian by birth but a European by conviction of many years standing"[1]. As such he is well fitted to speak for the ERO in its determination to carry out that part of its constitution which requires it to advocate:

> "increased and properly planned economic co-operation among the nations to attain wider economic units, freer exchange of commodities, and the full participation of workers' representatives in the resulting structure".

Schevenels' personal convictions take him beyond the advocacy of economic integration in Western Europe. He believes that a supranational government for Western Europe will be necessary to control the economic integration, and to act as a bulwark against the encroachment of communism, although the ERO, itself, has not yet gone as far as this.

The ERO then, under Schevenels' leadership (for such it is), since its inception, has been in the vanguard of the movement to propagate the European Idea. It was not necessary for him to use his persuasive powers

1. Broadcast talk on the BBC Third Programme, entitled "Wages and the Common Market", reproduced in *The Listener* of 4 April 1957.

to convince most of the ERO's affiliates of the advantages of integration in Western Europe. Nearly all of them were convinced that a move in this direction was not only desirable, but essential. Opinions varied on the form integration should take, and the speed with which it should proceed. But on the basic principle of the inevitability of integration there was general agreement. Some were active in the acceptance of the principle while others gave it passive recognition.

The broad distinction between the active and the passive assentors to integration is that the former belong to the six countries which are members of the European Coal and Steel Community (ECSC), the European Economic Community (EEC)and the Euratom treaty, i.e. the Benelux countries, France, Germany, and Italy. The passive assentors are the remainder of the ERO affiliates, but particularly Britain, Denmark, Norway, Sweden, Austria and Switzerland.

Once it was found that Britain did not intend to become a full member of the ECSC, the interest of the active supporters of integration in the ERO naturally became centred on the problems of integration in the "Six" countries. Consequently, a great deal of the ERO's time has been devoted to the problems of these countries, and even more time has been used for this purpose since the European Common Market and Euratom proposals became subjects for serious negotiations.

Although vitally interested and concerned in the process of integration in the "Six", Schevenels never let himself or the ERO become devoted to it, to the exclusion of the wider Europe. The ICFTU has consultative status with a number of international organisations, operating in Western Europe, and Schevenels personally plays a large part in the liaison work involved, necessitating him keeping well abreast of the problems and opinions of all the ERO's affiliates. He is, for instance, the General Secretary of the Joint Trade Union Advisory Committee (JTUAC) to OEEC, the Organisation for European Economic Co-operation. Although much of the day-to-day work of this Committee is done by an Assistant Secretary and his staff at the ICFTU-ERO Paris Office, Schevenels is largely responsible for the broader policy decisions, and goes to Paris himself, from time to time, when official consultations with the OEEC take place. He also represents the ICFTU at certain committee meetings and at plenary sessions of the Council of Europe in Strasbourg.

The Approach to Integration

The wider prospects of Western European co-operation and integration are kept very much in mind by the ERO, and one example was the problems concerning the original Free Trade Area (FTA) proposals, and the countries concerned with them. The ERO's initiative in this last question, however, came not from Schevenels, or the active support- ers of integration form the "Six" countries, but from the British TUC.

The TUC had previously been the most passive of all the ERO assentors to integration. It was on the insistence of the TUC, however, that a special meeting of the ERO was called in Brussels, in May 1957, to determine the organisation's attitude to the FTA.

The reason for the sudden heightening of British interest in European affairs was because the FTA proposals had come from the British Government, and the TUC had felt it necessary to determine its own attitude, as Britain was to be the senior partner. The statement of policy passed by the ERO at this specially convened meeting was similar in many ways to the TUC's own statement, published six months previous- ly, except on the problem of the possible inclusion of agriculture in the scheme, and one or two other points. On agriculture, the TUC had accepted the British Government's view that it should not be included, while the ERO thought that inclusion in some form was essential.

It is useful at this stage to consider the broad outline of the ERO's views, and why they are held.

In 1952, at the inception of the first Western European economic integration project, the Coal and Steel Community; trade unionists supported the principle of integration, but were somewhat apprehensive about the outcome. Since that time it has been found that the wages and conditions of miners and metalworkers in the Community countries have improved generally, and not worsened, and support for integration has consequently grown stronger among trade unionists.

Thus, in August 1955, under the auspices of the ICFTU-ERO, a trade union conference for the revival of the European Idea was held in Brussels. A statement issued by the conference sets out concisely the dominating themes of the ERO's thinking over a period of years on the whole subject of Western European integration. It says:

> "The necessity of raising living standards and for securing full employment in all countries is the determining reason for the free trade unions to seek European-wide solutions of the economic problems. The free trade unions demand that every step towards economic co-operation and integration should be accomplished within the framework of a policy of full employment and social progress in general, including an upward adjustment of social conditions."

This Brussels conference was a special one, devoted exclusively to the purposes of supporting Western European integration. Its main intentions were to associate, publicly, the European trade unions and the international campaign for the European Idea, and secondly to urge the ICFTU-affiliated national centres, and all other trade union organisations, to do all they could to influence the climate of opinion in their own countries. It was stressed that integration could only succeed if it had the full support of the workers, and if those workers were represented, through their organisations, on the steering committees and administrative and consultative bodies which may be engaged in bringing the European projects into being.

It may be observed from this that the international trade union movement does not believe that its own efforts and pressures at international level are sufficient, in themselves. The ICFTU and the ERO have always recognised the reality that, at least during the formative periods of integration projects, the main burden of responsibility for keeping a watching brief must remain with the movements at national level. The view is held that it is the national movements which must keep up consistent pressure to influence public opinion. They must also influence the governments responsible for negotiating new treaties, to ensure that they move in the right direction and provide the necessary safeguards and guarantees for the workers.

While the limitations of the ERO have been realised, this has by no means meant that it has taken a back seat in the various events concerning integration. It has attempted to exert pressure from the international level whenever and wherever possible, through Schevenels and other ICFTU representatives who are in frequent contact and consultation with various intergovernmental organisations. The ERO has also achieved wide publicity for its views by the passing and circulation of resolutions on integration questions, particularly by the Biennial Conferences. These resolutions are also intended to stimulate the ERO's affiliates into national action which will be consistent with the ERO's outlook.

The ICFTU has subjected the various integration proposals and draft treaties to analysis by its research staff, as they have been made known. It has subsequently been able to indicate, in fair detail, the lines of policy it wishes to see followed, and why, and to announce the various safeguards it considers necessary for the security of the workers. The comments made by the ERO in this way have nearly all been of an international, or European character, concerning general questions, and have not been concerned to a great extent with individual national problems. The tendency was to encourage the national affiliates to keep an international outlook on integration questions during their own campaigns, by following the ERO's lead. There is some evidence that this has, in fact, occurred.

Since 1950, the ERO has made a number of points repeatedly and consistently, concerning integration. Perhaps the most important of these is its insistence that integration processes must be used to maintain or attain full employment in all European countries. The ERO has said that the European Common Market could not be a success unless it was based on an expansionist policy which would keep the number of available jobs at a suitable level. The Common Market is seen as an excellent opportunity to make the most of wider markets by bringing full modern mass production and automation processes into play. This would not only keep the European economy constantly expanding through greater specialisation, in the ERO's view, but would also bring in its train an era of high employment and increasing living standards all round, provided the fruits of increased production were equitably distributed.

Great emphasis has been placed on this latter point. European integration, the ERO has argued, cannot function successfully unless supported by the workers. The workers will not support it unless it offers them a share of the material benefits accruing. Therefore the Common Market must be based upon, and dedicated to, the principle of expansion, and an equitable distribution of the economic benefits of expansion.

The ERO has not been content with stating its support merely for the broad principle of full employment. It has frequently and forcefully made the point that the responsible international bodies must work out schemes to ease the disruptions of the transitional period of the Common Market, or any similar treaty, as far as employment is concerned. Although trade unionists have not envisaged major upheavals of national economies–mainly because the transitional periods proposed have been long enough to ensure gradual change–they have realised that the European economy cannot be rationalised without changes in the industrial structure.

This must bring with it changes of jobs, removals to new areas and some transitional unemployment, in certain parts. The ERO has therefore insisted that the international bodies and the governments concerned must make provision to tide workers over the transitional period. They should also undertake schemes of vocational training where it is necessary to retrain workers for different jobs and industries, as a result of the Common Market.

Another aspect of integration on which the ERO has laid particular emphasis is the necessity that the trade union organisations should be represented and consulted at all levels in the structure of new European organisations set up to administer the Common market or other integration projects. The trade union leaders feel that they are not only in a position to speak on behalf of organised labour, but also on behalf of millions of consumers, as the organised workers form a high proportion of all consumers. They therefore insist that, if they are not allowed to tender their advice on all aspects and problems of the formation and working of integration projects, then these projects will become gravely out of touch with large sections of public feeling, and may thereby fail in their objects.

A resolution of the 1958 ERO Conference registered dissatisfaction at the inadequate degree and level of consultation that had been extended to the trade unions, by the governments which were attempting to negotiate a Free Trade Area. The ERO believes that it is essential to have a balanced controlling authority for any integration project, and that trade unionists should be nominated for a fair share of the seats on such authorities. Trade unions, it contends, have reached a status in present-day society where prominent figures from them should be nominated for executive positions on public bodies, as well as being taken into consultation on social and economic issues.

One of the major problems that the ERO sees arising from a more closely integrated Europe is wide anomalies in social benefits between different countries. The 1958 ERO Conference demanded, for Europe, the immediate ratification and implementation of all relevant ILO Conventions and Recommendations which would promote harmonisation; and encouraged other, separate, agreements, also. It has insisted, throughout its statements on integration, that an essential prerequisite of the Common Market was the harmonisation of social legislation in an upward direction. The ERO argued that if this was not done, a number of serious problems would arise. The legislation on social benefits differed so widely in the "Six", and in other countries of Europe, that it would not be possible to have the anticipated free movement of labour unless the position were rationalised.

Workers would certainly not move from countries where high social benefits were paid to those where low benefits were paid if they could possibly help it; especially if they had qualified for high benefits in their original country by a high personal contribution. Even more important, competition and trade would be unfair, it was said, once the tariff barriers were down, if the same product were to have different social charges included in its cost when produced in different countries.

For example, in countries where the employer paid a high contribution towards the workers' social benefits for sickness, unemployment, pensions, family allowances, or any other form of benefit, his total contribution bill was bound to be reflected in the price of the products to be turned out. His prices would therefore be higher, other things being equal, than similar products manufactured in countries where the employers' social welfare contributions were low.

The employers in the high-contribution countries would therefore regard themselves as being at a disadvantage under free trade. The trade unions are also strongly opposed to the anomalous situation, because they maintain it will bring pressure to bear to reduce the level of employer contributions in those countries where it is high. This would mean, if carried through, a cut in social benefits for their members, and a backward step in social standards. The unions have therefore demanded that social legislation be harmonised in an upward direction, and that social minimum standards be introduced, in order to bring about the dual advantages of high social benefits for workers in all the countries concerned, and fair competition in products between those countries.

The social minimum standards proposed for an integrated Europe were set out in a resolution on social harmonisation, passed by the ERO Conference, in 1958. The intention was that the standards should affirm certain principles; including the right of organisation and collective bargaining for trade unions, allied to the right to strike and to reject compulsory arbitration. Participation of workers in all levels of management should be ensured, and the necessity of full employment and a comprehensive scheme of unemployment insurance should be recognised. Equal pay for work of equal value must be put into practice, and hours of work must be shortened in a manner which includes wage consolidation. Overtime and Sunday work should be minimised, and adequately compensated; night work for women and young people should be abolished, and everyone should have adequate annual holidays. Special inspection measures for the safety and health of workers should be ensured, and finally, the standard of living should be cushioned against setbacks, by adequate social security systems.

The ERO, as a trade union organisation, is naturally primarily concerned with the material welfare of working people. But economic and social considerations are not by any means the only causes of ERO interest in integration questions. In fact, it is probably true to say that the fundamental inspiration of its integration campaign springs as much from political ideology as from economic involvement. The continental trade unionist has an objective and logical approach to political problems, and the division of Western Europe into a score or so of separate economic and political units seems to him outdated and irrational. The ERO reflects this view, and its statements have shown that it is no blind respecter of national sovereignties, but, rather, a firm advocate of strong supra-national institutions in an integrated Western Europe, at least as far as the six Community countries are concerned.

At the ERO Biennial Conference held in Frankfurt in May 1956, a resolution was passed which said, in part, that unless the international institutions which were to supervise an integrated Western Europe were strong, then the objectives of integration would not be achieved. The reason was that there were many obstacles to be overcome during the course of integration, and some of the greatest of these were entrenched national interests–both economic and political. The new international institutions must have sufficient authority to overcome obstacles arising from national interests. Therefore the determination of measures to be taken in the Common Market and Euratom must not be left solely to the whims of national governments or private monopolies.

The progress on negotiations for Euratom, or the European Atomic Energy Community, to give it its full name, was at all stages parallel with progress on the Economic Community Treaty. Now that both have entered their transitional periods, they have a common timetable and several common institutions. It was therefore logical that the international trade union movements, including the ERO, dealt with the two Treaties together in their statements.

There were, however, one or two aspects of the Euratom proposals which required separate comment. This the ERO gave, firstly at the Frankfurt Conference, and secondly after a meeting of its European Trade Union Committee on Atomic Energy, in Brussels, in November 1956. The Conference declared that the Euratom institutions must have full control of the production of atomic energy and fissionable materials in Europe in order to ensure that they would be used only for peaceful purposes. Six months later the special committee said that it considered public ownership of fissionable materials and their by-products was essential to ensure effective international control.

Another point made by the committee was that the increasing disproportion between the demand and supply of energy in Europe threatened the pace of economic and social progress. To eliminate this danger the closest co-operation of Western European countries was advocated, with a view to bringing about the quickest possible development of production and utilisation of atomic energy. This would reduce dependence on non-European sources of energy supply. It also stated that careful planning of investments was indispensable and that there should be a joint fund for the purposes of research, education, vocational training and production. The committee stressed the dangers of radioactivity and called for adequate precautions, and protection from this danger, for workers and the general public, alike. Particular mention was made of the risks of air, water and soil contamination by radio-activity.

Mention has already been made of the fact that the ERO has interests wider than the six Community countries in its advocacy of integration. The special conference in Brussels for the revival of the European Idea, convened by the ERO in August 1955, declared its support for the progressive liberalisation of trade between as many European countries as possible. It advocated a steady and systematic removal of tariff barriers.

The fact that the word "liberalisation" was used in this connection indicates that the ERO was prepared to lend support to schemes of economic co-operation in Europe that fell short of full integration within a customs union. This was well before the British Government had put forward its original plan for an Industrial Free Trade Area, and also before the OEEC Council set up a Working Party, in July 1956, to study the possibility of some such scheme.

Thus when the ERO Brussels Conference of May 1957 met, at the request of the TUC, the leading figures in it were already convinced that some form of association between the Community of the "Six" and other OEEC countries would have to come about. Some of them would have preferred that these other countries, especially Britain, should themselves have accepted the full membership and conditions of the Common Market Treaty. But realities had been recognised, and they had known for some time that these other countries could not be, or did not wish to be, members of a full customs union. The mood of the conference was that it was prepared to agree to proposals which would further the cause of European unity in its broadest conception, but was unwilling to sanction anything which might tend to weaken the fuller integration schemes, or jeopardise their chances of success. This approach was reflected in the final resolution adopted by the conference, and the resolution itself was reaffirmed, in its main points, by a further one, on the Free Trade Area, adopted by the ERO Conference of May, 1958.

The 1957 resolution was by no means as forthright in the views expressed as had been previous resolutions concerning the Common Market and Euratom. In places it had the tone of an academic discourse rather than a pointed policy statement.

This formula served to by-pass the points of disagreement, mainly between the TUC and the representatives of the Community countries.

Apart from the question of the possible inclusion of agriculture in a FTA, which was a well-recognised point of difference, and frankly admitted; the resolution successfully analysed the problems of the free movement of labour, the harmonisation of social legislation and the nature of FTA institutions, without committing anybody to anything.

To take one example, on the subject of the free movement of labour between countries. The British trade union movement is particularly sensitive about suggestions that foreign workers, other than from Commonwealth countries, should be allowed to earn a living in Britain. The British Government did not envisage the free movement of labour between the countries of a FTA, and gave an assurance that it would control its own policy in this respect. The TUC welcomed this assurance, and set out its own view on the subject in a memorandum it submitted to the British Chancellor of the Exchequer on 14 March 1957. It said:

"The introduction of the Common Market and the Free Trade Area may well generate further pressure towards the movement of labour both within and between the participating countries. It is doubtful whether there is much value in attempting any European policy on movements of labour, and the existing consultative machinery within OEEC and the ILO will require no modification."[1]

In contrast to this, the ERO's view, as set out in their August 1955 statement, was:

"Efforts must be made by agreements to ensure a freer movement of labour. In these agreements must be embodied social guarantees for the migrant workers as well as for the workers of the immigrant countries".[2]

This statement should be taken as referring mainly to the Common Market, but it nevertheless indicates the ERO's general approach to the subject. In the subsequent ERO statement on the FTA proposals the following compromise paragraph between the above distinct viewpoints emerges:

"Since the war there have been limited movements of labour between all the countries of Western Europe, and the introduction of the Common Market and the Free Trade Area will probably generate further pressure towards such movement both within and between the participating countries. While the Common Market Treaty provides for the free movement of labour between the participating countries, and for Government action to remove obstacles to such movement, the existing machinery within OEEC and the ILO should be able to play a useful part in assisting the movement of labour where necessary between the countries of the Free Trade Area."[3]

1. Trades Union Congress Report and Proceedings, 1957, p. 272, para. 316, sub-para. 16.
2. ICFTU publication *Free Labour World*, September 1955, p. 46, Part III, para. 8 of documented statement.
3. *Free Labour World*, June 1957, p. 42, para. 20.

By thus stating facts and avoiding comments, the ERO was able to recognise differences between its affiliates without resolving them. Divergencies of view on social harmonisation were similarly passed over by tactful wording in the ERO's FTA resolution. The Community Country members of the ERO believe in the upward harmonisation of social conditions by legislation, but the TUC did not want this in a FTA. It believes in the longer-established process of levelling up social standards, but not by legislative means. The resolution wording was acceptable to both viewpoints.

The Community-Country trade unionists' liking for strong international institutions and supranational powers is unacceptable to British trade unionists who prefer to maintain a high degree of national sovereignty. The ERO's resolution surmounted this difficulty with similar facility, by the following formula:

> "For the proper functioning of the Free Trade Area, a number of institutions will be necessary, even though their exact nature cannot be determined until the form and substance of the Area have been defined . . . It might be that in a Free Trade Area some departure from the unanimity rule (in the OEEC Council) would be necessary, but, as in the Common Market Treaty, the nature of the decision required (i.e. unanimous or majority) would vary according to the nature of the point at issue".[1]

The differences in viewpoint between the British and the continental trade unionists are fundamental and important because they indicate the obstacles that are to be overcome if a more comprehensive European Community than the "Six" is ever to emerge. British insularity from the continent is deep-rooted, and the British trade unionist's desire for independence in some of the respects outlined is a fairly true reflection of British attitudes as a whole to general questions of association with the European continent.

Care must be taken not to magnify these differences out of proportion. The British and continental trade union views on most of the problems arising in the course of European integration are rather closer. As for the rest of the ERO's resolution on its attitude to the FTA; its guiding principles are similar to those in previous statements on the Common Market and Euratom schemes. It is unlikely that the ERO will ever waver in its support of a FTA, or of any similar scheme that is put forward as a substitute. Even if the full-scale integration that a number of its affiliates would like to see does not come about, it is almost certain that the ERO will consider half a loaf to be better than no bread.

1. *Free Labour World*, June 1957, p. 44, para. 29.

Any new scheme which was to link the Common Market countries with other OEEC countries would have to find some sort of compromise between the British and French Governments' points of view. The trade union centres affiliated to the ICFTU in those countries broadly reflect their respective governments' views on the wider integration questions. It is therefore likely that a compromise between the governments would bring agreement between the TUC and the *Force Ouvrière*, the two national centres concerned. That would ease matters for the ERO which contains them both.

The ERO is in a somewhat difficult position. On the one hand it has Britain as its largest affiliate and financial contributor. It also has a British chairman. It is a well-known fact that the *Force Ouvrière* is not one of its strongest affiliates, and that it may even be weaker if it were not for the continuous support it receives from the ICFTU. In these circumstances, any undue partiality for the French viewpoint, shown by the ERO, would definitely not be pleasing to the TUC. On the other hand, if it appeared that the ERO were taking a British standpoint, the organisation would come under suspicion immediately from the national centres representing the six Community Countries.

The reasons for this are rather complex, but are concerned to some degree with personal relationships. They depend also on the fact that while the trade unionists of Germany, Italy and the Benelux countries have fewer substantial objections to the FTA proposals, in the way that France has, they do not wish to see the ERO playing too great a part in events concerning the Common Market, now that the Treaty is actually in operation. The governments of the Community Countries are a little jealous of their new status, and tend to approach European negotiations as a single unit, where the subject touches on agreements between Common Market countries and the others.

The trade unions of the Six Countries have a rather similar common approach, and are not happy if they believe that the ERO is being unduly deferential to an "outside" country, such as Britain, in any discussion on a wider association. Of course, the Executive members, themselves, can determine what is the ERO's viewpoint, in the last instance; but for reasons outlined earlier, the General Secretary's viewpoint is often taken as a valid, if provisional, statement of the Executive's policy. In these circumstances, the General Secretary has to take great care not to overstep the mark in attributing viewpoints to his organisaation, for fear of incurring the active displeasure of one or more of its affiliates.

However, difficulties of this nature have not been entirely avoided. It was certainly the wish of the ERO's General Secretary that his organisation should be very closely associated with the new international trade union structure that has been set up by ICFTU-affiliated national centres in the Community Countries. In view of the large part that the ERO has played in the promotion of the Rome Treaties, in the trade union world, it may have been thought that this anticipation would be fulfilled.

But, in fact, the trade union centres of the six Community Countries, meeting in Dusseldorf on 16 and 17 January 1958, decided that the ERO should have only a minor role in the new trade union co-ordinating machinery. This was possibly due to an unspoken feeling that the ERO, or its chief representative, may tend to speak with the voice of Britain and the Scandinavian countries which were, after all, outsiders, and had declined to join the Common Market and Euratom as full members when they had the opportunity.

Now that the ERO has been given a role in the "Little European" trade union structure of less status than had been thought likely, it is probable that the attentions of that organisation will come to be increasingly concerned with schemes to form a wider association. It is likely for two reasons. Firstly, that now the Rome Treaties are written, signed and under way, the ERO should have more time to devote to integration projects in less developed stages. Secondly, that it is generally believed by the ERO's central figures that the organisation would be able to play a leading part in any trade union structure designed specifically to co-ordinate trade union activities in the wider Europe. Indeed, the view is held by a number of prominent trade unionists that the ERO could become the actual co-ordinating body for trade unions in a wider scheme which linked, say, the "Six" with other OEEC countries. It is not likely that the ERO will undertake co-ordinating functions for the trade unions of the "Outer Seven" alone.

But if the former were to occur, there would be some change of emphasis in the nature of the ERO's functions. Instead of being mainly a forum for the interchange of national viewpoints, and a vehicle through which non-controversial resolutions (from the trade union viewpoint) could be passed, the organisation would be used more for the actual making of day-to-day policy on an international plane, as far as negotiations with a wider authority were concerned.

It is not likely that its status would be enhanced to the point where it had federal powers over its affiliates, or that it would become a party to international collective bargaining, concerning wages and major conditions of employment. The unions of the ICFTU have a healthy scepticism about the merits of trade union internationals with strong central powers.

Whatever the final pattern of economic and other forms of integration in Western Europe, it seems natural that the trade union organisations

of the area should adapt their structure to meet the changing circumstances. Where more and more decisions of an international nature are
taken in economic, political and social fields, then the trade unions will
in some way have to perform an increasing share of their own tasks at
a similar level.

At the present time the international free trade union movement (the
usual collective name for the ICFTU and its associates, which is self-
endowed) is little more than an expression of the various hopes and
aspirations of the national trade union centres which comprise it. These
national centres usually make use of the ERO only when it is convenient
for them to do so, and the organisation is therefore only really effective
as a discussion centre. But it is quite within the bounds of possibility that
it will become, in due course, a body for carrying out more far-reaching
trade union action on an international scale.

To sum up, the ERO is one of three Regional Organisations of the
ICFTU which are financially self-sufficient, and have a large measure of
autonomy. It is controlled by a Biennial Conference, an Executive
Committee and the General Secretary; and since it was founded has
devoted a large part of its time to promoting integration projects in
Western Europe. Its membership is composed of the ICFTU's Western
European affiliates, and its Executive has a balanced geographical re-
presentation. The General Secretary carries much of the burden of the
organisation's work, and is himself a forceful advocate of Western
European unification.

The ERO's policy on integration is accepted, more or less, by all its
affiliates, but as far as the particular case of the original FTA was concerned, the national centres in Britain and France were opposed to
each other's views, and neither of them were completely in line with
ERO policy. The ERO's main points of concern, throughout all the
integration events and proposals, have been to obtain full employment,
higher living standards, adequate representation, harmonised social
benefits and a number of other safeguards and guarantees for the trade
unionists of Western Europe. Although the ERO has not been invited
to play a large part, as yet, in the actual functioning of international
trade union machinery in the new Community, it is quite possible that
it may have a specific co-ordinating role to perform in a more widely
integrated Western Europe, should that come about.

CHAPTER IV

THE INTERNATIONAL TRADE SECRETARIATS

The International Trade Secretariats (ITS) are trade union organisations which co-ordinate on an international scale the activities of individual unions having a common industrial or craft background, or widely shared interests. They have affiliates in most countries of the Western Bloc of nations, but none from the Eastern Bloc. They work in close association with the International Confederation of Free Trade Unions (ICFTU) and most of the national trade union centres affiliated to it, although, constitutionally, they are quite independent bodies.

The ITSs have a history dating from 1889, when the typographical workers from thirteen countries banded together at a meeting in Paris to form the first Secretariat. Since that time the number of ITSs has fluctuated considerably. In 1958 there were nineteen. Their functions have varied hardly at all during this period, and their aims and objects today are very similar to those which were stated at the end of the last century. ITSs act as centres of information for all their affiliates, regarding conditions and progress in various countries.

They attempt to promote the interests of the workers in the industries in which they specialise. This is done by organisational help, general advice, and by financial aid, used sometimes for strike action or to resist lockouts. They also have two other major functions in helping to build trade unions in the poorly organised countries, and concerning themselves with the protection of migrating members. And they play a leading part in promoting the common trade union action of their affiliates in various countries.

The ITSs suffered heavy reverses and membership losses from 1932 because of the policies of Hitler. Many of them had their largest memberships, or their headquarters in Germany. Activities were brought almost to a standstill during the war, although the headquarters had been dispersed to other countries of Europe.

Most ITSs were reconstituted between 1946 and 1948, and they looked forward to the same sort of fruitful co-operation with the new trade union international, the World Federation of Trade Unions (WFTU), as they had previously had with the International Federation of Trade

Unions (IFTU). However the negotiations with the WFTU, which were intended to define the status of the ITSs, as trade departments of the new International, broke down. The Secretariats wanted more autonomy than the WFTU were prepared to allow. Therefore they did not affiliate to any International until the ICFTU was formed. The ITSs set up a co-ordinating committee in 1949 to speak jointly for them. This committee met the Executive Board of the ICFTU later in the year, and a satisfactory agreement was reached providing for successful co-operation with the ICFTU.

The formula for the new relationship stated that the ITSs should be independent in all problems concerning their particular industries, and in their own affairs. However, they would recognise the general lines of international trade union policy, as laid down from time to time by the ICFTU.

The bulk of the membership of the ITSs had always been, and still is, in Europe, which is also the favoured region for the situation of head-quarters. A high proportion of the Secretariat staffs are European, many of them from the smaller countries. A good number of American unions have affiliated to appropriate ITSs since the war.

However, anti-communist credentials among ITSs are not always as fully established as American unions would like to see, in spite of their joint refusal to become part of the WFTU in 1948. One ITS, for example, insists on having discussions with its WFTU counterparts in Geneva, in order to formulate joint policy, prior to meetings in the International Labour Organisation, on which they are both represented. Another Secretariat, the International Federation of Building and Woodworkers (IFBWW), accepted Yugoslav trade unions into affiliation, and two American unions representing woodworkers and upholsterers subse-quently withdrew in protest. The Yugoslav unions were later expelled.

The ICFTU has frowned on this assertion of ITS independence, which is out of line with general policy. This indicates that the ITSs are truly independent of the ICFTU. It also indicates that American affiliations are not likely to reach a peak unless the ITSs show a little less independ-ence, and behave in a manner more amenable to the chief figures in the AFL-CIO, who are passionate advocates of anti-communist conform-ism among trade unions.

The nineteen ITSs affiliated to the ICFTU have membership totals varying from over 7.5 millions to under nine thousand. The full list of ITSs, with membership totals, is as follows:

International Federation of Building and Woodworkers	1,992,363
International Federation of Commercial, Clerical and Tech-nical Employees	1,994,098*

Universal Alliance of Diamond Workers	8,980*
International Union of Food and Drink Workers' Associations	1,009,548
International Garment Workers' Federation	1,041,663
International Graphical Federation	630,027
International Union of Hotel, Restaurant and Bar Workers	533,239*
International Federation of Industrial Organisations and General Workers' Unions	1,245,482*
International Landworkers Federation	1,264,082
International Metalworkers Federation	7,711,387
Miners' International Federation	2,658,365
International Federation of Petroleum Workers	350,000°
Postal, Telegraph and Telephone International	1,649,382
International Federation of Unions of Employees in Public and Civil Services	1,505,976
International Shoe and Leather Workers' Federation	307,628
International Federation of Free Teachers' Unions	670,635
International Federation of Textile Workers' Associations	1,388,854
International Federation of Tobacco Workers	66,300
International Transport Workers' Federation	5,660,250

(*: as at 31 December 1955. °: estimated membership. All other figures as at 31 December 1956. Source: ICFTU Report to the Fifth World Congress, July, 1957).

The ITSs are financially self-supporting, and raise their money from affiliation fees. Each organisation has its own rules and constitution and decides the level of affiliation fees quite independently of the others. These levels vary a great deal, but as ITSs perform more functions with the growing importance of international machinery, their budgets naturally increase. This increase in activity and budgets, some of it attributable to European integration, applies particularly to the larger of the ITSs. At its Congress in 1954, the Miners' International Federation (MIF) found it necessary to increase its subscription rate from £3 to £8 sterling per thousand affiliated members.

The structure of the ITSs varies a good deal, as does the method of appointment, or election, of their executive bodies. It is usual among the larger of them to have a Congress as the ultimate controlling body, meeting, perhaps, every three years. Both the MIF and the International Metalworkers Federation (IMF) have an executive body to act in between congresses, and to meet once or twice a year. Both, also, have sub-committees of their executive which meet more frequently and lend the necessary continuity to the organisations' policies and activities.

Although both the MIF and the IMF have had a large stake in Western European integration since 1952, they have not formed any special European section of their own movements to deal with Coal and Steel Community problems. This is partly because of the heavy European membership in these ITSs, which leads to a good proportion of the time being devoted to European affairs, anyway.

The MIF and IMF each had representation on the trade union "Committee of 21" (now replaced by a similar committee in a larger framework covering the European Economic Community) which co-ordinated activities on an international scale at the ECSC headquarters in Luxembourg. They had an equal voice on the Committee with the national trade union centres and the mining and metalworkers unions from each of the six Community countries, in forging a truly international trade union policy for the coal and steel industries.

The International Metalworkers Federation, the largest of the ITSs, had some noteworthy things to say about European integration in its Report to the Eighteenth International Metalworkers Congress in Lugano, in September 1957. With its five years experience of the ECSC, it was particularly well fitted to assess the achievements and further prospects of integration, as far as trade unionists are concerned.

The IMF, of course, supports the principle of integration, along with all the other ITSs, which are morally obliged to follow the ICFTU's lead. But it makes an interesting criticism of unions in the ECSC which regard the Community simply as a stepping-stone to a more broadly integrated Europe. The IMF claims that by neglecting the social and economic aspects of trade union work in the Community, in favour of general political propaganda to promote further integration, these unions and national centres have got their sense of priorities wrong. It is maintained that there is much to be achieved in the social and economic fields of ECSC endeavour before the project can be called an unqualified success. It is in these fields that the trade unions should be concentrating their efforts.

Not that the IMF is against a more widely integrated Europe; on the contrary, it believes that further integration could lessen the effects of any recessions on the metal industry, which is normally most sensitive to them. It declares that under integration international measures could be taken to counteract recessions, and that :

"it is easier to pursue such a policy of combating trade cycles on the international, or at any rate the regional scale, than it is to do so at the national level, because in that way there is more likelihood of preventing the measures taken in each country from counteracting one another".[1]

The IMF also stated the view that the co-existence of a Common Market and the original Free Trade Area would have been good for Europe. The six Community countries would have been able to press ahead at their own speed without being held back by the other OEEC countries forming a Free Trade Area. Because the two projects would necessarily have been closely co-ordinated, it saw the Common Market having an indirect speeding-up effect on the rather lethargic approach of the potential Free Trade Area countries to integration. The Economic Community, itself, would have benefited from association with the Free Trade Area because it would have encouraged it to cultivate its outside trading relations, and prevented it becoming economically introspective.

Other ITSs, not as closely connected with integration, have also put forward their views and proposals during the course of statements supporting integration. The International Transport Workers' Federation (ITF), the second largest of the ITSs, made known its ideas at length during a statement at a public hearing in Munich, where the European Transport Ministers Conference had invited representatives of workers and employers to put their views. The ITF reproduced the statement in their "International Transport Workers' Journal" of December 1956.

Much of the statement is technical, but, broadly, it welcomed the proposed creation of a Common Market in Western Europe and stated that its primary objective should be to attain the highest level of production and productivity. This could not be done unless a common European transport market was created simultaneously with the integration of industry. Furthermore, it insisted that each means of transport should pay its way within that common market, and substantiated this view at length.

The ITF also wanted to see the creation of a European Transport Authority within the proposed European Commission of the Economic Community. This Authority should be empowered to create and control a common European transport market, sponsor improvements of social conditions in the industry and generally co-ordinate European transport. It should secure the co-operation of the transport workers' unions of the ITF in the carrying out of these policies.

The ITF believed that certain co-ordinating measures would have to

1. Report to the Eighteenth International Metalworkers Congress, September 1957, p. 105.

be taken in the various countries with the aim of achieving a harmonious co-operation between the different means of transport. Safety measures should be brought into line, internationally, and it was suggested that an independent committee of experts should be empowered to investigate the problem. It was thought that their findings would lead to uniform procedures, particularly for the fixing of maximum weights and dimensions of motor vehicles.

In September, 1957, the eighth Congress of the International Federation of Building and Woodworkers (IFBWW), in Munich, passed a resolution stressing the necessity of adequate trade union representation on European international organisations connected with integration. It was suggested that trade union influence could be brought to bear if affiliated organisations were to supply their IFBWW secretariat with more information, and if the activities of IFBWW representatives on various international organisations be co-ordinated. The IFBWW bulletin could be used as a rallying point, and affiliated organisations ought to use their influence, nationally, to ensure trade union representation on international delegations.

Another conference in Munich, in May, 1957, was that of the International Bank, Insurance and Social Insurance Employees. This is a trade section of the International Federation of Commercial, Clerical and Technical Employees (IFCCTE). A resolution was passed welcoming the establishment of the Common Market and hoping for its extended scope to other countries. Conference considered that it was necessary to bring about conventions and international agreements, on the social plane, on behalf of their own professions, in the various countries concerned. This should be done by increasingly close contacts between affiliated organisations, within the IFCCTE.

It is apparent from the ITSs' comments on integration questions that they concern themselves mainly with problems which will affect their own industries and memberships, and leave general policy largely to the ICFTU and its European Regional Organisation. This, of course, was intended in the original agreement between the ICFTU and the ITSs, concerning the division of functions.

Generally speaking, the relationships between the nineteen ITSs and the ICFTU and ERO seem remarkably smooth. Some friction inevitably occurs over such questions as the demarcation of responsibility, but there are few real disputes, all things considered. This is in large part due to the machinery that has been set up to co-ordinate the activities of the ICFTU and ITSs.

In 1952, it was decided that a Liaison Committee of ITSs should be set up. This Committee is for the purpose of organising General Con-

ferences of the ITSs, choosing ITS representatives to sit in the bodies of
the ICFTU, and co-ordinating the activities and efforts of the ITSs
among themselves and with the ICFTU. The Liaison Committee
consists of ten ordinary members and nine substitutes. It sends two
representatives to the ICFTU Executive Board and one representative
to its Sub-Committee. ITS representatives are also eligible to attend
the ICFTU World Congress. The senior body of the joint ITSs is the
General Conference, which usually meets each year. There is also a
Consultative Council which meets occasionally, consisting of the
ICFTU Executive Board members, delegates of the ICFTU Regional
Organisations and representatives from the ITSs. It is this body, mainly,
which has gone thoroughly into the question of joint regional activities,
and has improved co-operation.

In addition to these formal channels of ITS-ICFTU consultation,
there is an agreement that the ICFTU shall have the right to send
representatives to all the individual ITS Congresses, and to the General
Conference and Liaison Committee. Their main tasks are to observe
proceedings and give advice on ICFTU policy, where necessary.

There is every indication that relations and co-operation between the
ITSs and the ICFTU are considered to be of growing importance,
particularly by the latter. In 1957 a special ITS Liaison Officer was
appointed to the ICFTU Geneva Office. His salary is paid by the ITSs,
and his job is to maintain close contact with them and to bring knowledge of their individual experiences to each other. It is significant that
the appointment is in Geneva. This is where the International Labour
Office is situated, and a great deal of ITS activity is centred around it,
as individual Secretariats have observer status on the ILO Industrial
Committees.

The new Trade Union Executive Committee of the "Six" countries
has decided that within its own framework, the status of the ITSs within
the Community will vary from one industrial sector to another. Their
main participation will be in industrial sub-committees, and they have
already been active in those sub-committees dealing with transport,
chemicals and agriculture.

Necessary as the ICFTU-ITS co-ordination is, it is pertinent to question
whether the existing maze of consultative channels is really the most
efficient way to conduct matters. An overlap of functions between some
ITSs, also, does not ease the position. And the development of institutional machinery connected with the Common Market and Euratom will
certainly not lead to simplification unless the opportunity is taken for
thinking out the whole structure anew. There has already been some
criticism from individual ITSs, in this connection.

It is likely that questions of a European Regional nature will become increasingly prominent as the process of Western European integration goes on. There is every probability that as the problems of the various industries of the "Six" countries become more apparent under the impact of the Common Market, the more the ITSs will be required to give advice in those fields in which they specialise. The experience of the ITSs will be invaluable to help forge international trade union policies dealing with technical and specialised matters in the new "Little Europe" trade union structure.

On the other hand, the more the ITSs have to concern themselves with policy on specialised questions, the more it will appear desirable, from the ICFTU viewpoint, that there should be some European co-ordination between them. This would ensure that they were conversant with general international trade union policy, and with each others activities in the Common Market, Euratom and the ECSC. They would not, then, inadvertently work at cross-purposes.

None of the ITSs has, at the moment, a special section for dealing with European problems, and none of them seems to have thought a great deal about making such provision. When the suggestion is put to them, ITS officials are inclined to reply that ITSs have always been universal organisations and that separate regional sections would be a radical and, perhaps, unpopular departure from practice. The fact remains that there is great scope for the ITSs to do a valuable job in Europe for the trade union movement if some such innovations are made.

ITSs are centres of information and research concerning international trade union problems. They do much routine work classifying information from their affiliates and supplying them with the collated results. A great deal of this is connected with comparative wages and working conditions in different countries.

If the trade unions are to make their influence felt in the Community countries, they must have a constant flow of such classified information to help them in their representations to the European Commission, and other Community bodies. The ILO can supply a certain amount of this information, but it cannot necessarily produce the latest and most specialised industrial data at the time it is needed. Only the ITSs could do this, on information supplied by their affiliates; and it is logical that they be given a role in the European trade union structure where their potentialities could be used to the best advantage, and duplication of efforts could be eliminated.

At it happens, the ITSs, although universal organisations, have their greatest strength in Europe, and all their headquarters, too. Consequently a large proportion of their time is already devoted to European matters. With the advent of the European Communities it is inevitable that even more of their activities will be centred on this region, although several are increasing their commitments in Africa and Asia, also.

In the circumstances, European Sections would have considerable advantages in those ITSs most affected by integration. They would allow a part of each Secretariat to specialise in European questions exclusively. This would enable each organisation to have separate meetings for the discussion of European problems. It would make it unnecessary for the delegates from other parts of the world to have to sit through lengthy discussions which are of little interest to them. And it would be a recognition of the fact that it is somewhat unrealistic to maintain a universal standpoint on all issues when the needs and circumstances of the different regions of the world vary a great deal.

If the ITSs were to be encouraged to set up European Sections, the trade union movement in Europe would have to allow them a larger role than has so far been envisaged. Serious consideration might be given to inviting the ITSs to set up all their European Sections in the Community Capital. They might even share a single building. In this way, besides their close contact obviating the need for many formal meetings, they would be able to work in close harmony with the General Secretariat of the Trade Union Executive Committee of the Communities, while maintaining traditional ITS independence.

This would not mean that the ITSs would control trade union policy on industrial and technical matters. That would still be decided by the delegates of the individual national unions meeting in special industrial committees within the new trade union structure for the "Six". But it would mean that the unions would be able to take their decisions in the light of expert briefs prepared for them by the ITSs, to which most of them would be affiliated.

The ITSs will still have to carry out their studies on integration problems in particular industries, whether or not they do so in the above context, because of their own status in the "Little European" structure for trade unions. If they do not perform this work in the Community Capital, their tasks will be less easy, and their flow of information more restricted. Nor will they be as closely in touch with the general policies of the trade unions of the "Six".

At the same time, the detailed work on the specialised technical and industrial aspects of integration would still have to be performed by an enlarged secretariat of the Trade Union Executive Committee of the "Six". It would still be essential to have the detailed briefs for the individual unions to arrive at informed policy decisions. This would mean that wasteful duplication of trade union research work would take place because of the overlap with ITS work.

It is desirable that any European Sections of the ITSs should represent European opinion comprehensively, and not confine their activities to the Community countries. They would then be able to make their specialised studies in such a way that problems of any other economic association could be related to events within the Community countries. This work would be a valuable complement to the ERO's functions, which are necessarily restricted to questions of a less specialised nature.

If the international trade union movement were to decide to give the ITSs an enhanced role in European affairs, an obvious way would be to give them full status in the "Little European" trade union structure, in the ERO, and in any other body that might be set up in connection with other free trading schemes.

There has always been a tendency to treat the ITSs as the poor relations of the international trade union movement, and the situation may not easily change. It is not usual for entrenched interests, with traditional spheres of power and influence, whether in trade union organisations or elsewhere, to relinquish, voluntarily, any of their authority, or to delegate it to other bodies. But it is possible that a rational appraisal of the changing needs and circumstances may see the ITSs given a larger part to play in the region.

So far, trade union policy on integration questions has been largely concerned with general matters. But as the transitional periods of the Common Market and Euratom run their time, and as the technical complexities of harmonising these schemes with wider European co-ordination become pressing, so will the need for a more specialised trade union approach become apparent. In the changeover from the discussion of ends to the discussion of means in Europe, the trade union movement may find that the ITSs have much more to contribute than their present role will allow.

Some people have even suggested that the future role of ITSs may include international negotiations concerning conditions of employment, thereby achieving supranational agreements, to serve, perhaps, as a basis for individual national agreements. Such a viewpoint is put by Lewis L. Lorwin, the historian of the international trade union movement.[1] It raises an interesting possibility which does not appear to have been very widely entertained, so far, either by the ITSs or by prominent trade unionists working in other sections of the international trade union

---

1. *The International Labor Movement*, by Lewis L. LORWIN, published Harper & Brothers, New York, 1953, p. 315.

movement. This problem is further discussed in the concluding part of this study, in the context of the general possibilities of international collective agreements in Western Europe.

In summary, the history of the ITSs dates from the end of the last century, and since then they have performed the function of co-ordinating the activities, in different countries, of trade unionists with a common craft or industrial background, and of keeping them supplied with information about each other. There are now nineteen ITSs varying greatly in size. They are financed by *pro rata* dues from their individual affiliated unions. They work in close co-operation with the ICFTU, by exchange of delegates to each others meetings, and by special liaison bodies. They are, however, quite independent.

They support the principle of Western European integration, and two of the biggest, representing metalworkers and mineworkers, have had considerable experience of it in the ECSC. It would probably be to the advantage of the international trade union movement if the general position of the ITSs in the international trade union structure was thought out anew, with a view to giving them greater responsibilities. This may be particularly appropriate in connection with the specialised services they could offer in an integrated Europe, especially if they had their own European Sections.

CHAPTER V

THE WORLD FEDERATION OF TRADE UNIONS

The present study is primarily an assessment of the impact of Western European integration on the trade union movements in that region, and *vice versa*, and it is not necessary, therefore, to deal at great length with the World Federation of Trade Unions. Firstly, because it has only three significant affiliates in the region–big ones in France and Italy, and a very small one in the Netherlands, none of which is typical of the type of trade union comprising the mass of the WFTU's membership. Secondly, because of the organisation's opposition to European integration in principle, it has not made detailed proposals and comments of a positive nature on the Treaties, or taken any part in their formulation. Thirdly, because it is unlikely to be a party to any trade union negotiations within the structure of "Little Europe", or of any parallel association.

Nevertheless, the WFTU is not an organisation to be ignored, if only because it claims a larger total membership than the ICFTU. And the problems of integration cannot be fully considered unless this very strong voice of opposition, reflecting the views of the Eastern Bloc of nations, is taken into account. Loud echoes of the East-West conflict are always to be heard between the ICFTU and WFTU, and inside the trade union movements in France and Italy. These echoes have some effect on the direction of the policies of the ICFTU and its affiliates, which is another reason why the opposition organisations and their viewpoints must be considered.

Ever since the 1949 split in the WFTU, the section which remained, and the ICFTU, have striven to outshine each other in the exchange of uncomplimentary remarks. For its part, the WFTU has always remembered that it was the western unions which broke away, and has consequently called the ICFTU leaders "the splitters of the working class". As far as their support of European integration projects goes, this, in WFTU eyes, makes them betrayers of working class interests, and the tools of the American capitalists and other monopoly interests.

In spite of these opinions, the other main item in the WFTU's policy on international trade union matters has been the necessity for co-operation and collaboration between all other trade union organisations and the WFTU. It has repeatedly stressed that all trade union organisations, whether affiliated to the WFTU or not, are welcome at their World Trade Union Congresses. It has addressed messages and open letters to all such organisations inviting participation, whether affiliated to the ICFTU, the CISC, or not affiliated to any international.

It is claimed that this is establishing greater unity and international solidarity of the workers because of the extra representation this policy yields at their Congresses. At their Fourth World Congress, in Leipzig, from 4-15 October 1957, the Credentials Committee reported that delegates from 81 countries were representing 105,770,620 organised workers. Of these, it was said, 13,158,060 were not members, and 92,612,560 were members of the WFTU.

Of the total WFTU membership claimed, the vast bulk of it is in the USSR, Eastern Europe and China, and only about 10% in the regions of the world in which the ICFTU holds the initiative–regions, that is, associated with the Western Bloc of nations. The effect of this is that the character of the WFTU is very different from that of the ICFTU, because of the different nature of the organisations comprising it.

Trade unions in the Soviet Union, and many other countries with communist regimes, are unlike those in western countries, even though nominally performing similar functions. The unions are usually under the domination of the party leaders, and they do not have a great deal of freedom of action, but have functions to perform decided by the state, in connection with production and working conditions. They are not voluntary associations in the sense that Western unions are, because there is a considerable amount of physical or psychological pressure brought to bear on workers to join, which emanates from party sources. There is usually no right to strike in these countries.

The WFTU, reflects the nature of its main affiliates. It has its power highly centralised, and its democratic control formalised. It was decided at the last World Congress, which is its governing body, that in future it would meet only at four-yearly intervals, instead of biennially; which decision weakens its ultimate democratic control. The other authoritative bodies are the General Council composed of 147 members; the Executive Committee, composed of 74 members and the Executive Bureau, composed of the President, the General Secretary, and twelve Vice-Presidents. There is a geographically balanced Secretariat headed by a General Secretary, and eight other Secretaries.

The WFTU has been astute in choosing its chief officers. Louis Saillant, of the French CGT, has been the General Secretary since the organisation's first days. Giuseppe Di Vittorio, of the Italian CGIL, was the President until his death in November 1957, and he was replaced in April 1959, by his CGIL successor, Agostino Novella. Thus the two outposts of the WFTU in Western Europe have been allowed to hold the chief honours in the organisation, presumably for strategic reasons. It is probable that the records of Saillant and Di Vittorio did a great deal to keep up the popularity of the WFTU among trade unionists in France and Italy. Saillant had an excellent war record in the underground movement, and Di Vittorio was greatly respected as a powerful and dynamic trade union leader in Italy, even by those who opposed his principles.

The WFTU originally had its headquarters in Paris, but after the 1949 split, the French Government took exception to its activities, and it had to move to Vienna. It had to move again in later years, and now has its head office in Prague. It produces publications in twelve languages – Arabic, Chinese, English, Finnish, French, German, Japanese, Portuguese, Rumanian, Russian, Spanish and Swedish.

The WFTU has the same consultative status with the Economic and Social Council of the United Nations, and with its Specialised Agencies, as does the ICFTU. It also has similar rights in the ILO. However, it has no consultative status with any of the Western European inter-governmental organisations, with which the ICFTU maintains close contact. The WFTU would probably disdain to ask for such status, and in any case, the Western European governments, all of which are hostile to the organisation, would certainly not consider granting it.

The WFTU is heavily dominated by personalities either in, or closely associated with Communist Parties. Some sections of opinion believe that this fact, in itself, is sufficient evidence on which to condemn the organisation for not being a trade union body in a true sense.

Others wish to look a little further into the evidence and will require to examine policies, activities and statements, before drawing conclusions.

In his report to the Fourth World Congress the General Secretary was full of praise for the achievements of the "socialist countries", which he amplified with voluminous statistics. There were no words of praise, but very much criticism for the western countries and their policies – particularly the United States. Out of a total of 32 resolutions, declarations, appeals, messages etc. passed by the Congress, seventeen of them were condemnations of political policies or working conditions in western nations. One resolution saluted the "creative genius of the Soviet workers, technicians and scientists", and another message expressed "enthusiastic admiration" of the Soviet achievement with a Sputnik. There were no resolutions criticising political policies or working conditions in any of the Eastern Bloc countries.

This latter fact is notable in view of the WFTU's overwhelming membership in those particular countries. Unless one assumes that there are no political policies or working conditions deserving of criticism in those countries, the conclusion is that the WFTU is acting as a propaganda agent for those countries against the West. This is where the ICFTU allegation that the WFTU is not a genuine trade union organisation appears to have substance.

Of course, the ICFTU, itself, is a constant critic of political and industrial policies carried out in the Soviet Union and its associated countries. Few people would suggest that either the ICFTU or the WFTU were abusing their functions by making criticisms of countries in which they have little membership or influence. Where the difference between the two organisations is outstanding, and where the *bona fides* of the WFTU are called in question, are in considering the fact that it criticises only the policies of western nations, whereas the ICFTU vigorously criticises policies carried out in western as well as eastern nations.

The criticisms which the WFTU makes of political and industrial policies in the West are not necessarily unfounded. In fact they have sometimes coincided with statements which the ICFTU has made. One such case is the criticism that both organisations have made of French policy in Algeria. Both bodies have also proposed alternative policies, with much in common, to those which were carried out in Cyprus. This fact has been very much of an embarrassment to the ICFTU, and very much of a propaganda advantage to the WFTU.

Propounding the same policy and making the same protests as the ICFTU, in western countries, has enabled the WFTU to make great play of its policy for international trade union solidarity and action. If both organisations are making the same protests, why should they not unite in action, it has asked. The ICFTU's refusal to rise to the invitation has strengthened the plausibility of the WFTU taunt that the ICFTU do not want international action and true unity for the workers.

The WFTU has continuously, and persistently, pursued the policy of asking for international trade union unity. It demands it on every possible occasion at every possible conference. It produces lists of items which could form the basis of common international programmes of action, and points out that trade unionists the world over are striving for just these things. Why, then, should the international movement be split, it asks. A typical list of these common points includes higher wages, shorter hours, abolition of discrimination based on sex, age or race, extension of paid holidays, workers' housing improvements and better industrial safety measures.

On basic political attitudes, of course, the WFTU and the ICFTU are poles apart, as they were when the split took place. The intervening years have done nothing to narrow the breach, and, in fact, it has probably widened considerably.

It will be recalled that one of the main points of discussion leading up to the split was the question of whether the ITSs should have a largely independent and autonomous existence, as was traditional, or whether they should become mere trade departments of the WFTU. The ITSs did of course, maintain their independence, and their subsequent association with the ICFTU has not lessened it.

Since then, the WFTU has set up its own Trade Departments which perform a similar function to the ITSs, but completely within the organisational and political jurisdiction of the parent organisation. They are, in fact, a part of the WFTU. Nevertheless, they may accept into membership any trade union, whether it is affiliated to any national centre or trade union international, or to none. All have equal rights within the Trade Departments.

The Trade Departments are called Trade Union Internationals (TUI), and there are twelve of them, covering most of the same industries and trades as are covered by the ITSs. The TUIs speak with the same voice as the WFTU on all policy matters, and, if anything, a little more vehemently.

Nowhere are policy differences between the ICFTU and the WFTU greater than in their attitudes to Western European integration projects. The TUIs have done stout work for the WFTU in putting the case against integration in a manner lacking any restraint.

The Miners' TUI has been particularly forceful in stating its opposition to the ECSC, or the Schuman Plan, as it was earlier called. In 1953, a WFTU pamphlet entitled "Mineworkers Unite Against the Schuman Plan" was published. It was a report and general commentary on a special conference held in Berlin in April 1953, organised by the Miners' TUI. On page 13 of the pamphlet, readers are told:

"The putting into effect of the Schuman Plan is a step towards the realisation of a political and military union. Its essential purpose is the rearmament of West Germany, and the utilisation to the utmost of the Ruhr arsenal for a war against the USSR and the Peoples' Democracies whose peoples desire peace".

On page 14 the analysis is continued thus:

"The aim of the Schuman Plan is to ensure maximum profits by ruining and pauperising the country concerned; by enslaving and robbing in a systematic way the peoples of other countries, especially those of the backward countries; and finally by unleashing wars and militarising national economies, to ensure the highest profits".

The pamphlet gives the strong impression that the WFTU Miners are willing to use any stick with which to beat the Schuman Plan, even to the point of contradicting themselves. Thus on page 3, it says that the Plan is centralising capital and investment in the most profitable businesses and that the capitalists through this great cartel "will obtain the maximum profits, disregarding national interests and sacrificing national wealth". And then, a little later, on page 12, the pamphlet makes a strong attack on the workers representatives who sit on the Consultative Committee of the ECSC, for the part they play in "bringing this instrument of poverty (the Schuman Plan) into action granting subsidies to the capitalist concerns to wipe out their so-called deficits". It illustrates this by stating that the ECSC has granted subsidies to enterprises in Italy, Holland and Belgium to cover the differences in costs and sales prices of coal produced.

Thus the TUI Miners, in almost the same breath, are criticising the Schuman Plan sponsors for allowing the capitalists to make maximum profits by disregarding national interests and wealth, and then for giving financial assistance to enterprises which make no profits but contribute coal to the national wealth.

The WFTU and its TUIs have always protested strongly against attempts to increase productivity in western countries, although extolling the virtues of all schemes which do so in the USSR and associated countries. The ICFTU has always supported plans for expansion and increased productivity, and looked upon integration projects as a main means of promoting these increases.

The WFTU does not deny that integration will increase productivity, but condemns it for just that reason. A typical example of their reasoning is given in the pamphlet, on pages 7-8. It argues that under the ECSC, the theme of increasing productivity in the mines is only a further way of exploiting the miners. Time study and rationalisation get more from the worker at the expense of his health, and of increasing accidents. The argument concludes that "Increased production results in a reduction of manpower, dismissals and unemployment. We must draw the workers into the fight against time study and all systems aimed at increasing productivity".

The other main TUI which has interests in the ECSC, that of the Metal and Engineering Workers, has not handled the scheme any more gently. In its Report of Activities from 1949-1954, submitted to its Second International Conference in Vienna in July 1954, the TUI listed the consequences which it said would result, and had already resulted from the Schuman Plan. They were:

"reduction of wages and social security to the lowest possible level, while prices and profits are rising continuously; speed-up of work and lengthening of working hours which cause an increasing number of labour accidents and occupational diseases, growth of unemployment and the closing down of factories; deportation of labour from one country to another, and exploitation of the deported workers in order to lower the living and working conditions; intensification of war preparations; destruction of the independence of nations; strengthening of oppressive measures against those workers who oppose poverty and war".

The next part of this study which deals with the ECSC gives an indication of the actual results of the scheme, and allows a thorough assessment of the validity of the above statements. In the meantime it can be said that they were neither good predictions nor accurate descriptions of circumstances at that time.

The Metal and Engineering Workers TUI roundly condemned the ICFTU, particularly its leaders, for supporting the ECSC. They should be exposed for what they were "the active assistants of the warmongers and the initiators of anti-national measures directed against the workers' interests".

The ECSC, as the first European integration project, came in for the first heavy barrage of WFTU criticism. The criticism has continued as subsequent projects have been discussed whether they be the proposed Transport Pool, the Common Market or Euratom.

The TUI of the Transport, Port and Fishery Workers produced a duplicated document in November 1954, entitled "The Transport 'Pool', Its Meaning, Its Aims and Its Social Consequences". In it, the ECSC, and the Conference of Transport Ministers of Europe were condemned as the economic left-overs of the defunct European Defence Community (EDC). In a section headed "The Transport 'Pool', Instrument of Social Reaction", the WFTU viewpoint is expressed thus:

"Firstly the European transport community, as an indispensable adjunct of the ECSC is one of the instruments of NATO (North Atlantic Treaty Organisation) for the preparation of war. The first measures taken by the Conference of Transport Ministers for the organisation and co-ordination of transport show that these measures primarily serve the interests of the Ruhr magnates who, as everyone knows, have always been the fanatical advocates of a crusade against the Soviet Union."

The TUI's views are completely opposed to those of the International Transport Workers Federation (ITF), the Trade Secretariat associated with the ICFTU, whose views were examined in the previous chapter. The TUI document bitterly attacks the ITF and its leaders, and calls them "the most active agents of international reaction". It claims that in supporting a transport pool, the ITF is giving tacit approval to a levelling of wages and social costs down to those appertaining in the Community country where they are lowest.

In 1957, the WFTU was criticising the European Common Market on very similar grounds to those on which previous integration projects had been condemned. In his report to the Fourth World Congress in October, Louis Saillant indicated the opinion that his Executive Committee had expressed early in the year, in the following words:

"With the active backing of the United States monopolies, the European capitalist monopolies are using the European Common Market as a means to overcome the contradictions which stand in their way, and to co-operate in exploiting the resources of Western Europe and certain countries in Africa.

Under these conditions alignment of the economic and social policies of the six European countries concerned can only lead to levelling down of living conditions for the workers as a whole. The loss of a measure of national independence by the countries taking part, more domination by the imperialist German monopolies, along with the Americans, the perpetuation of an even more deeply divided Germany, the inclusion of African countries in the European Market and the consequently increased exploitation of these countries–all these are against the interests of the workers."

Because the WFTU has opposed the Common Market and Euratom in principle, it has not found it necessary to go into specific detail on the merits and demerits of the schemes in the way that the ICFTU and ERO have done. It has been content to condemn the whole idea of integration as it stands and the main thread of consistency throughout the successive condemnations has been that these projects were merely means to the ultimate end of building up a powerful military bloc in Western Europe–a sort of American-German capitalist condominium– which was a potential threat to the security of the Soviet Union and her allies, and to the living standards of Western Europe.

Western European trade unionists affiliated to the ICFTU have also seen the new Communities as blocs in opposition to Soviet policies, of course. The difference from the WFTU viewpoint, though, is that they look upon an integrated Europe as an economic, and subsequently, a political bulwark against communism, and not a military bloc. They believe that an economically and politically united Western Europe can better resist the internal encroachments of communism, through its sense of unity, independence and economic power; and also that it can, at the same time, look the American dollar more squarely in the eye.

One major reason why it would have been unwise for the WFTU to elaborate on the economic consequences of the Common Market is that it could not have reconciled different opinions within its own organisation if it had done so. For a split has appeared in the WFTU ranks, on the question of the Common Market, which is upsetting the whole of its campaign.

It is one thing for the WFTU to condemn a scheme which adversely affects Soviet interests, but it has to proceed with great caution when the interests of one of its important affiliates does not coincide with the Soviet Union's.

Such is the case of the Italian CGIL, the largest of the WFTU's Western European affiliates. It is often thought that Italy is a country which stands to gain more from the Common Market than some of the other members. Consequently the CGIL found that following the strict opposition line laid down in the WFTU and the Italian Communist Party, was losing it considerable support in the country. It therefore put the policy into reverse, and is now supporting the Common Market. This fact, in itself, is very embarrassing for the WFTU, as it seems to belie its arguments that the economic effects of the Common Market will all be bad.

In a letter circulated at the 1957 Leipzig Congress of the WFTU, by the CGIL, delegates were told that CGIL disagreement with WFTU policy was mainly on the grounds of trade union unity. It felt that they should throw in their weight with other trade unionists, internationally, in order to ensure that the workers could effectively press for the defects of the Treaty to be removed, and so prevent the exploitation of workers in the associated colonies.[1] The resolution of the CGIL Executive, passed the previous July, and meant for home consumption, had laid more stress on the economic benefits of the Common Market to Italy, as a reason for its support.

The rift was extremely embarrassing to the WFTU because of the fact that the General Secretary of the CGIL, Di Vittorio, was also the

---

1. The position of the CGIL relative to the Common Market is set out fully in Chapter XVII.

President of the WFTU, with the result that he was making statements on the Common Market which were entirely incompatible with those made by the General Secretary, Saillant, in his report to Congress. However, there was no motion on the agenda of the Leipzig Congress condemning the Common Market, which would have been very likely in other circumstances.

The other large affiliate of the WFTU in Western Europe, the French CGT, has not followed the lead of the CGIL in this respect. It still officially condemns the Common Market, although it has taken the same action as the CGIL in asking for representation on Community institutions. The CGT emphasises that this does not indicate support for integration – it is only done in the desire to lessen its evils. It is worthy of note that it is not generally believed in France that the country has as much to gain from the Common Market as, for example, Italians believe their country has, which may account for lack of CGT enthusiasm.

The WFTU made no official pronouncement on its attitude to the proposed Free Trade Area, but there is no doubt that it was generally against it, also, on principle. It has not pronounced on the Free Trade Association agreement either. It is possible that it will not oppose this because it may see it as a potential divider of Western Europe.

In spite of the ICFTU's persistent refusals to have any joint activities whatever with the WFTU, there are certain international organisations on which both trade union internationals are represented, and where it is not possible for them to ignore each other. Perhaps the most important of all these is the ILO, where the delegates of all three trade union internationals, and their affiliates, meet together in the Workers Groups to discuss policy, prior to the plenary sessions.

Surprisingly, when this sort of co-operation is thrust upon the organisations, they do not get along too badly together. One reason for this is that the main responsibilities at ILO meetings fall upon trade union national centres, and not the trade union internationals to which they are affiliated, which have only consultative status. One has the feeling that if this were not the case, then attitudes would probably be more intolerant.

As things are, the delegates of organisations affiliated to the ICFTU and the CISC work together with the combined majority they possess to prevent any representatives from WFTU-affiliated centres being elected on to the Governing Body of the ILO. The WFTU naturally protests against this discrimination, but does not do so with the truculence or perseverance that might have been expected.

The ILO, being a United Nations organ, is bound to give the same consideration to all organisations, no matter with which political power bloc, or which trade union international they may be associated. The WFTU has been keen to use this common meeting ground of the ILO to further its policy of common action with the ICFTU and the CISC, or at least with their affiliates. It has therefore been careful not to say or do things in the ILO which would worsen the relations between the internationals, and possibly provoke a complete severance of contact within the organisation.

To have protested with their normal vehemence against the actions of the ICFTU and the CISC-affiliated delegates in keeping their WFTU opposite numbers off the Governing Body, would have been to risk the chance of a complete freeze-out. As it is, there is a certain amount of co-operation taking place in such a manner that the ICFTU and CISC-affiliated unions cannot bring any substantial complaints about the WFTU-affiliated organisations' attitudes or behaviour.

This position suits the WFTU well, as it enables it to indicate that the three internationals can co-operate reasonably on a common programme when they set their minds to it. They consider that this greatly strengthens the attraction of their appeals for international trade union solidarity.

It actually does more than this. It enables the WFTU to cite the ILO as the ideal centre for the international trade union co-operation which it advocates. And if anybody wants regional trade union co-operation in the ILO, then the WFTU would like that also provided it is true regional co-operation. But it is against the splitting up of a geographical region, such as Europe, and treating the eastern and western halves separately. Here they are on strong ground, as the ILO would be running the risk of being accused of political partiality if it were to attempt to deal with Western Bloc nations differently to Eastern Bloc nations.

When the ILO called its first European Regional Conference in January and February 1955, it was mainly concerned with making an examination of European integration trends and possibilities. But, constitutionally, it had to be an all-European conference. The WFTU did not object to it, and its affiliated national centres took part. It will not object to any further conferences of this nature which the ILO may wish to convene, but it would object to such a conference for Western European nations only.

The WFTU claims to have no objections to proposals to harmonise social benefits and working conditions in an upward direction, as the ICFTU-affiliated organisations, and the ERO, wish to do. It does object to this being done for Western Europe only, however, and claims that it should be done for all Europe. As the ILO would probably be much concerned with any such programme, the WFTU has a convenient platform in that organisation for propounding its version of the upward harmonisation programme, if it so wishes. The 1955 ILO Regional Conference had to consider such a programme for all Europe, although there does not appear to be the faintest possibility of any scheme being implemented with a wider scope than the Common Market countries, or the OEEC countries.

To recapitulate, the WFTU is the trade union international representing mainly the Russian and Chinese trade unions, and the unions of other countries within their political orbit. Its only sizeable Western European affiliates are in France and Italy. The two main planks in the WFTU's policy platform are a condemnation of the ICFTU's leaders, and nearly all they stand for, including Western European integration, and, rather incongruously, a programme of co-operation with the ICFTU and its affiliates.

The power in the WFTU is highly centralised, and its Trade Departments (the equivalent of the ITSs) have no independent powers of policy action. The whole movement spends much time and effort on condemnations of political and industrial practices in the Western World, where it has little influence, but appears completely satisfied with everything that occurs in countries of the Eastern World.

The main grounds on which the WFTU and its Trade Departments attack Western European integration are three. Firstly, that integration schemes are mainly for the benefit of American military and capitalist policies and German monopoly interests, and so threaten the Soviet Union. Secondly, that integration would mean reduced economic standards and political effectiveness for Western European workers, and, thirdly, that the whole idea splits the geographical entity of Europe into two. The WFTU has been able to use ILO platforms to propound the last point, and also to work for its policy of common action with the other trade union internationals, but it has suffered a major embarrassment since its Italian affiliate decided to support the Common Market in principle.

CHAPTER VI

THE INTERNATIONAL FEDERATION OF CHRISTIAN TRADE UNIONS

A main feature of the International Federation of Christian Trade Unions (CISC) which distinguishes it from the other two trade union internationals is that its constitution is worded in such a way as to appeal to trade unionists of one particular philosophic outlook–that is to those trade unionists who consider Christianity to be the dominant theme of their lives. The ICFTU and the WFTU, it will be recalled, particularly avoided discriminatory clauses in their constitutions, designed to appeal more to workers of one particular outlook than another; except, of course, for the ICFTU's stipulation that the trade union organisations affiliated should "be free".

It can be said at the outset that the CISC does not aim at universality in its representation, as do the other two internationals. It feels that it has a specific job to do on behalf of christian workers, and therefore confines its activities, mainly, to organising and representing Christians. The qualification in this statement is necessary because the CISC does have a largely Buddhist organisation affiliated to it in Vietnam, apart from one or two smaller affiliations of a doubtful christian authenticity.

The CISC does not specifically appeal to trade unionists of one denomination rather than another. Neither, for that matter, do the ICFTU or the WFTU specifically appeal to trade unionists of one political persuasion or another. But in all three cases, the circumstances of their growth, and the personal persuasions of the respective leaders, have given rise to the predominance of one particular element. In the case of the ICFTU, the predominant element is social democrat. In the cases of the WFTU and the CISC they are communist and Roman Catholic respectively.

The CISC does not attempt to impose Roman Catholicism on its Protestant and other minorities in the same way that the WFTU may be said to make its communist philosophy all-pervasive. The wording of its constitution, programme and publications is designed to have a wide appeal to all christian trade union organisations and workers. But, in fact, the great majority of its affiliates, and of its chief officers, are adherents of the Roman Church.

The CISC has one fair-sized Protestant trade union centre affiliated. This is the CNV in the Netherlands. It also has a very small one in Switzerland. Apart from these, the overwhelming majority of its affiliates are Roman Catholic in composition, although some of them contain minorities of other denominations.

The CISC has a total membership of about four millions. It has affiliates in Canada, Jamaica, South America, Vietnam, Central, North and West Africa, and in Madagascar, apart from its European affiliates. Nevertheless, the great bulk of its membership, probably over three-quarters, is contained in its Western European affiliates.

Its main affiliates in the region are the French Federation of Christian Trade Unions (CFTC), the Federation of Christian Trade Unions of Belgium (CSC), the Netherlands Catholic Workers Movement (KAB), and the Netherlands Federation of Christian National Trade Unions (CNV).

Affiliations are claimed in Austria, Denmark, Germany, Gibraltar, Luxembourg, Spain and Switzerland, but they are mostly very small indeed. Affiliations from small Polish and Ukranian Confederations are also on their list, but generally speaking, France, Belgium and the Netherlands are the only countries where CISC-affiliated organisations have much influence through their industrial strength.

In the other countries, what little influence they wield is owed more to their close affinities with Christian Democrat members of Parliament than through strength of numbers. The individual national centres usually take care to state their independence of any political party, and, indeed, maintain no organic links with the Christian Democrats. But they do not deny that informal and friendly co-operation does take place; even though some of them stress that because christian political parties are usually rather conservative in outlook, it is not always easy for trade unionists to convince them of their own ideas on social progress.

In the main countries of CISC strength, the position on co-operation with christian parties varies.

In France, some informal consultations do take place between christian unionists and politicians, but the unions do not place great importance upon them. In order to maintain official independence, the CFTC has a ruling that none of its officers is allowed to be a Deputy in the French Parliament. The only exception is in Alsace, where there are special circumstances.

In Belgium there is a similar ruling about Parliament, but otherwise the trade union-political party co-operation is a little stronger than in France. In the Netherlands there is no ruling against officers being members of Parliament, and co-operation with the christian parties is stronger than in either France or Belgium. However, the situation is a little more complex owing to the existence of three different christian parties, not all of which are looked upon by the unions as being socially progressive.

The CISC, itself, has unofficial consultations with the christian groups of politicians in the Council of Europe, and in the Communities. It also has consultations, mainly on European questions, and general friendly relations with the International Union of Christian Democrats, which is a body having individual members and affiliated organisations in a number of countries.

In general it can be said that the influence of the CISC in Western Europe is not great although it is greater than that of the WFTU, in spite of a smaller membership. The main reason is that there are a number of countries where Christian Democrats either control, or have a substantial influence in Governments. This situation enables the christian trade union movement to have an accepted place in the life of these countries, and to be listened to with respect. The WFTU has to fight hard for either of these advantages in Western Europe.

Structure and Background

The CISC was founded at a Congress at the Hague in June 1920. At that time it had a large affiliated membership in Italy, and smaller ones in Hungary and Czechoslovakia, in addition to the European countries mentioned earlier. It also had a large membership in Germany.

Subsequent political events in Germany and Italy, leading up to the second world war, deprived it of nearly all its membership in these two countries.

The headquarters of the CISC was in Utrecht, in the Netherlands, from its formation until the time the country was occupied in World War II. From then until the end of the war the CISC was unable to carry on its activities. It held its first postwar Congress in Brussels, in October 1945, and since then has moved its headquarters there.

From the inception of the CISC, the post of General Secretary was held by the same man, P. J. S. Serrarens, a Dutchman, up until 1952. In July that year he resigned the position in order to take up an appointment as a member of the Court of Justice of the European Coal and Steel Community. He was replaced by the Assistant General Secretary, A. Vanistandael, who has held the post since then. The Presidency is held by Gaston Tessier, who is Honorary President of the CFTC, of France.

The organs of the CISC are a Congress, a General Council and an Executive Committee. The Congress meets every three years, normally, and is the supreme body. It is composed of delegates from affiliated National Confederations, Trade Internationals and Extraordinary Members. The Trade Internationals are the approximate equivalents of the International Trade Secretariats affiliated to the ICFTU. The Extraordinary Members are organisations which are not trade union federations but which are eligible for affiliation under Article 7 of the CISC's constitution, because of their recognition of its principles and programme.

The General Council is also a delegate body on a similar basis to the Congress, and it meets annually, or more often, if specially requested. Its members have a mandate for the period between Congresses. The Council has to establish the main lines of policy within which the Executive Committee works, and to hear its reports. It also has to consider and establish the CISC budget.

The Executive Committee is a body of twelve members elected by Congress from among its delegates for a three-year period. It is composed of at least five members representing national centres, and at least five representing Trade Internationals. It is stipulated that seats should be allotted to as many nationalities as possible. The President and General Secretary complete the membership of twelve, and both are elected by Congress, the latter upon the nomination of the Executive Committee. The two Vice-Presidents are also elected by Congress from among the Executive members.

The duties of the Executive Committee, laid down in Article 28 are, to be in charge of "directing the CISC, of instructing the General Secretariat for the performance of its task, of appointing representatives of the CISC at institutions and for meetings wherever they consider such representation desirable". The Committee meets at least every four months, and may call special meetings if it wishes, to further co-operation with the Trade Internationals.

The CISC is financed mainly by affiliation fees from members. The level of these is decided by the Congress on the basis of the financial reports and estimates submitted to it by the Executive Committee. Although both the Executive and the General Council are responsible for the financial affairs of the CISC, the General Secretary is given more latitude than is customary in most organisations, in this respect. Article 36 of the constitution authorises him to "spend money within the limits of the budget", apparently without specific permission from the Executive Committee.

Finance apart, there are a number of other indications in the CISC constitution of the great centralisation of power, particularly in the hands of the General Secretary and his assistant. First of all, the General Secretary is elected by Congress on the nomination of his Executive Committee, so that the choice of nomination is not open to anybody who does not agree with the Executive's viewpoint or past record. When he is elected, it is for an undetermined period, and he cannot be dismissed except by Congress casting a two-thirds majority vote at a special meeting, representing at least three-quarters of the ordinary members.

Article 33 of the constitution reads "The Secretary General shall represent the CISC with full powers under all circumstances". This appears to give him full rights to initiate any policy in any circumstances, without prior reference to the Executive or the Counciil.

The Assistant General Secretary is appointed by the Executive Committee, and not elected, and the constitution states that he should eventually replace the General Secretary.

The centralisation and perpetuation of power inherent in the clauses of the constitution are the subject of a good deal of criticism of the organisation by ICFTU leaders. They depict it as being rather typical of organisations connected with the Church, which tend to have a hierarchic structure rather than a democratic one which is more fitting to genuine trade union organisations. Some have even described the CISC as an authoritarian organisation, and this impression is, perhaps, not dispelled for them by references in the constitution to the General Secretary and his staff being "bound to secrecy" when they are entrusted with some mission.

Another criticism often made of the CISC, and what are frequently called "confessional" unions, by those in other camps, is that they are more concerned with propagating christian values than with obtaining the trade unionists' bread and butter. There is certainly a strong emphasis on Christianity in the constitution. Articles 2 and 3 are devoted to the principles and purposes of the CISC. Article 2 reads:

"Recognizing the principles of Christian doctrine and Christian moral teaching as the foundation of human society, the CISC shall endeavour to make them predominant in the world, trying to achieve, through its activities, a social order in conformity with Christian principles."

Article 3 then enumerates five aims and objectives in five sub-paragraphs. In two of these the intention is declared of representing the workers and their interests, but the stress is also heavily laid on promoting the interests of Christianity. However, this does not mean that the CISC does not have anything to say about trade union principles and action. In its "Programme", a number of interesting ideas come out, although they are generally rather less material and somewhat more spiritual than one would normally expect of trade union policies.

There are a number of ideas which stand out. One is the desire of the CISC to take a mid-position between state and individual, between one class and another, between owner, manager and worker. It opposes the concept of the class struggle, and believes in safeguarding people from both the abuses of excessive individualism, and of domination by the state. Co-operation between different sections of the population to achieve a Christian and harmonious social order is the keynote of their philosophy.

The programme is very much concerned with enhancing the dignity of the human being, the rights and privileges of the family, and with condemning Marxism. It is in favour of working people being private property owners, but believes all forms of ownership are linked to moral obligations. The CISC is not against limited nationalisation of industry, but states that where private enterprise does operate, it should not have profits as its sole purpose. The worker should have the rights and status of a co-operator in his job, and the level of employment should be kept high and stable, either by the efforts of the "vocational group", or by the state.

The CISC programme would give much of the work of bettering working conditions to the ILO to perform, if possible, and would make its Conventions legally enforceable in all countries. The CISC seems particularly anxious that the work of the ILO should be expanded as much as possible. This is probably bound up with its own interest in having a sound basis for co-operation with the ICFTU, which the ILO can provide. Both the WFTU and the CISC have a desire to be recognised by the ICFTU as organisations worthy of its co-operation. In the former case, such recognition would lend the WFTU respectability in the eyes of the western world. In the latter case it would elevate the status of the CISC to a level which its size cannot justify.

More specifically, the CISC has a well detailed list of aims and reforms dealing directly with the improvement of working conditions and the settlement of certain associated political and economic problems. Some of the items are of a nature usually left for decision at national level in other trade union organisations, but which the CISC thinks should come within its own field of advocacy. It recommends, for instance, that central economic bodies should be established in each country, representative of management, labour, and possibly governments, which should settle disputes between various vocational groups, and should also co-operate in the establishment of national economic policies and the harmonisation of international economic policies. At enterprise level there should be joint bodies of mangement and labour and, again, at national industrial level. These latter bodies should have the power to pass legally enforceable ordinances for their industries.

The CISC wants an eight hour maximum working day; a minimum employment age of sixteen; a minimum wage or salary fixed according to the cost of living, but also taking account of skills and the workers' own contribution to the value of the product; equal pay for equal work; a guaranteed wage or salary for all those on the personnel roll of any undertaking; and a number of other reforms and benefits.

The influence of church thinking is apparent in several of the other proposed reforms in the programme; reforms which probably would not meet with approval from other trade union sources. Such proposals include those to apply four-shift systems to all industries with continuous processes, so as to allow all workers two free Sundays per four weeks; and the stoppage of all production from Saturday night to Monday morning where there are "semi-continuous" operations performed. Many trade union organisations would believe this to be over-rigid, and would prefer to leave such arrangements to the needs and inclinations of workers and employers at local levels. There are very many workers who do not feel badly treated if they are asked to work on Sundays, and some who even prefer to do so.

The CISC also aims at the "gradual elimination of the employment of married women in gainful occupations", a suggestion that many trade unionists resent as being an attempted interference with the rights of the individual to regulate his or her own life. Neither do many sincere and righteous trade unionists, outside the Christian movement, approve of the CISC's determination to improve and extend legislation "concerning morals, health and security". The two latter items, perhaps. But there are very many who consider that legislation is not the appropriate way to raise moral standards, even if there could be agreement as to what were "improvements" in this respect.

Attitude to Integration

One small but important section on page eleven of the CISC's published "Programme" gives the basis of its attitude to European integration questions. It says:

"In certain areas, especially in Europe, a close and organised co-operation of the various national communities is an urgent need. In the economic field every national community depends, somehow, on other national communities. Therefore any policy of self-sufficiency will doom such nations as resort to it to indigence, and foster envy, hatred and war."

This policy is generally stated, without specifically mentioning Western European integration projects. Nevertheless, other documents of the CISC show clearly that it has supported integration from the outset, and that its policies and attitudes in this respect do not differ radically from those propounded by the ICFTU. It supported the setting up of the ECSC, in principle, and since then has supported it in practice.

In the case of the ICFTU it will be recalled that one of the origins of its support for integration was political ideology. Not that it believed that integration would necessarily promote the interests of its favoured political group, the Social Democrats. The prospect of a united socialist Europe is too idealistic for trade unionists to adopt as a serious goal at the moment. They aim at the slightly more attainable goal of replacing fifteen, or so, national administrations with one comprehensive one, competent, at least, in some fields of European endeavour.

There is also a political foundation in the CISC's support for integration, and probably a religious one. For christian trade unionists, the prospect of a Western Europe united on the basis of one political ideology may not seem as far off as it does to socialist trade unionists. Among the six Community countries, there is sufficient strength in political and church circles to make the possibility of Roman Catholic hegemony in a united Europe a factor to be seriously considered. The CISC leaders would be hardly human if they had not allowed these considerations to influence their attitude to integration.

Like the ICFTU, the CISC wants an integrated Europe to have as its basis an expanding economy, rising living standards, full employment and full representation of the workers at all levels where economic and social policies are decided. It believes, particularly, that the participation of workers in management, at all levels, is essential, that social policy should not be subordinated to economic policy, and that there should be an upward levelling of social conditions.

The CISC also wants mobility of labour, provided that workers who emigrate do not suffer any social disadvantages in regard to freedom to choose their job, to receive social benefits, or to have the right to organise freely in trade unions. Mobility of labour must not mean that schemes for the readaptation and reabsorption of displaced workers should go by the board. They must be maintained, and improved upon.

Again, like the ICFTU, the CISC has a liking for strong supranational institutions to ensure the administration of the integration projects along truly international lines.

The international outlook of the Community countries must be strong enough to ensure that investment funds are controlled by international bodies, particularly so that aid can be awarded to underdeveloped areas of Europe. The CISC will not consider European integration to be complete until such time as the political and ideological barriers dividing the area are finally removed, and all countries have the chance of working together.

As far as the proposals for Euratom are concerned, the CISC found itself at one with the ICFTU in stipulating that the Treaty should encompass only specifically peaceful purposes for atomic energy. It believes, also, that the ownership of fissionable materials should be acknowledged to Euratom, otherwise it would be difficult to have the necessary common supply.

Although the CISC tried to avoid making official statements on its attitude to the original Free Trade Area proposals; generally, it supports the principle of an extension of Western European integration and co-operation, but has felt it difficult to commit itself specifically on proposals of such an elastic nature as those discussed at the OEEC. It believed that some organisation in addition to the OEEC would have been necessary to supervise the functioning of a FTA, but it would not necessarily have had to be similar to European Economic Community institutions.

European integration is not a problem which the CISC believes can be treated in isolation from the rest of the world. The essence of how Europe fits into the world picture, from their viewpoint, is given in an article in its official publication "Labor", for February 1957. It is signed by the General Secretary, Vanistandael, and says:

"Not until European solidarity has ceased to be a vain expression, imprisoned within the narrow view of national interests, will the European countries be able to forsake their short-sighted policy and grotesque concern for balancing ill-understood interests. Nor will it be possible to speak with force and pride of Europe and her mission in the world, so long as Europe does not understand that her centuries-old experience in the economic and political field, no more than her cultural patrimony, are of any value if they are not placed at the service of the other continents with a view to raising them to a higher level, instead of being wrongly used to hamper their development."

On the organisational side the CISC has not been inactive in considering the changes in its own structure and practices, necessary to meet the challenge of integration. A new European Organisation has been set up within the CISC, with a three tier structure, which will be competent for the Common Market, and possibly any other association in Europe, but not for the European Coal and Steel Community, which has its own Christian Trade Union Federation. The new European Organisation is described in Chapter Twelve.

There are, altogether, eleven Trade Internationals associated with the CISC. They cover very much the same industrial groupings as the International Trade Secretariats affiliated to the ICFTU, and the Trade Union Internationals of the WFTU. The CISC and their Trade Internationals have a rather more closely linked relationship than do the ICFTU and its affiliated ITSs.

In other words, the Trade Internationals are partly independent of the CISC, while maintaining close relations and co-operative action with it. They take an important part in actual policy making within the Federation, as they directly nominate five of the twelve members of the Executive Committee, all of whom have full voting rights. The ITSs have only consultative status in ICFTU bodies. Thus a greater co-ordination of policy is achieved between the CISC and its Trade Internationals. It is usual for the CISC to speak on behalf of the Internationals in all general policy matters, including Western European integration. The Trade Internationals are, themselves, only very small organisations by comparison with their opposite numbers attached to the ICFTU and the WFTU.

Relations with other Organisations

The CISC has consultative status with all the United Nations organs, and other international bodies which the ICFTU has, and on the same basis. That is: the Economic and Social Council of the U.N., the ILO, UNESCO, the Food and Agriculture Organisation of the U.N., the U.N. Children's Emergency Fund, the Intergovernmental Committee for European Migration, the OEEC and the Council of Europe. Naturally, owing to its smaller size, it does not have the same influence with these bodies as the ICFTU.

The policy of the CISC is to work together with the ICFTU in liaison committees wherever possible. The ICFTU does not share this aim, generally speaking, but the place where regular and official co-operation does take place is in Paris, in the Joint Trade Union Advisory Committee to the OEEC. The OEEC deals only with representations made through this Committee, or its joint Secretariat, which consists of representatives of both Internationals. The co-operation here is reasonably good, and the CISC, for its part, wholeheartedly approves of the arrangement. The ICFTU does not positively disapprove of it, but the initiative for the JTUAC came not from the ICFTU, but from the

OEEC, itself, which insisted that it could not continue its old practice of consulting two trade union internationals separately.

The CISC has good relations with the ILO and its Workers Relations Service. With the co-operation of the ICFTU it holds one out of the twenty seats reserved for Workers delegates and substitutes, on the Governing Body of that organisation. The ICFTU holds the other nineteen, and the WFTU holds none. The CISC is a great believer in working for improvements in industrial conditions through the ILO, and it would like to see the organisation hold separate and regular Conferences for the European Region. It would favour such Conferences passing Conventions which would be effective in Europe only, in addition to the general Conventions passed in the General Conferences.

There are occasional informal consultations between the two western trade union Internationals in some of the other international organisations where both are represented, such as the Council of Europe. However, they are not regular, and the desire for them comes mainly from the CISC. The CISC has, in fact, suggested that joint liaison committees with the ICFTU should be set up, along JTUAC lines, as in Paris. There should be one for each organisation where both Internationals are represented, especially in Europe, to co-ordinate policies at that level.

ICFTU circles, however, are opposed to closer co-operation with the Christians, as they cannot get them to agree on suitable terms. What the ICFTU has in mind is that the Christians should lose their separate organisational identity where such co-operation takes place. This is not acceptable to the CISC. Thus the relationship between the two organisations has not improved much over several years, because neither side will make concessions to the other's viewpoint.

The root of the matter is that relations in the separate countries are generally strained, as between the affiliates of the ICFTU and the CISC, often because of their collaboration with different political parties. This is reflected at international level. What has annoyed the ICFTU and its affiliates more than anything else has been the attempts of the CISC to set up new national centres in countries where it had no membership, thus trying to split hitherto united movements. Germany is the particular example most quoted to illustrate this.

There, the CISC set up a Christian national centre, perhaps thinking, nostalgically, of its large pre-Hitler membership; at a time when the postwar trade unions were all united in the DGB, the German Trade Union Federation. The new centre lost members and money rapidly, and has been proved a definite failure; but the ICFTU has not forgiven the attempt. Another instance cited is in Austria, where, although the Trade Union Federation, the ÖGB, is still united at national level, the Christians, at a lower level, have persuaded sections of the membership to affiliate to the CISC. Most of the ÖGB membership is affiliated to the ICFTU. The CISC's answer to the charges maintains that there is a separate need for Christian trade union centres, and that it must do its best to help set them up where there is a demand.

It seems unlikely that the ICFTU will ever agree to closer co-operation unless the CISC ceases to recruit in the former's spheres of influence. ICFTU representatives tend to dislike the authoritarian basis which they say exists in the Christian movement, and emanates from the Church. They also feel that the CISC is out to score cheap propaganda victories concerning certain achievements, which the ICFTU claims to be largely its own doing. It is feared that this tendency would increase if co-operation were closer.

As far as relationships with the WFTU are concerned, the CISC and the ICFTU appear to have been competing with each other for some years to prove that each has the best anti-communist record. Neither organisation has the slightest hesitation in condemning the WFTU as a tool of communist political policies.

The General Council of the CISC adopted a resolution in November 1951, giving reasons why co-operation with the WFTU was out of the question. There were two main ones. First, that the respective creeds of the CISC and the WFTU were incompatible, i.e. Christian social concepts and materialistic Communism. Second, like the ICFTU, the CISC champions trade union freedom and maintains that most WFTU unions do not allow freedom, and have become, in fact, instruments of oppression.

The CISC has strongly condemned the WFTU for failing to speak out against the forceful suppression of workers revolts in Hungary and elsewhere, and has said that its attitude makes co-operation with it impossible.

Nevertheless, the CISC is generally less rigid than the ICFTU and its affiliates when practical issues of joint action arise. It is sometimes the case in France that the Christian Trade Union Federation will co-operate with the CGT (affiliated to the WFTU) where their individual policies coincide. The ICFTU-affiliated *Force Ouvrière* will never co-operate with the CGT. These same tendencies have occurred at international level.

For example, after the Hungarian revolt the CISC proposed to the ICFTU that the two organisations should issue a joint statement that their General Secretaries were willing to go to Budapest. It also suggested that, should the occasion arise, the WFTU General Secretary should be invited to accompany them. Doubtless the CISC believed this to be a good way of indicating to the world where the WFTU's sympathies really lay—a matter which could be easily ascertained by the nature of its reply to such an offer. But the ICFTU appeared horrified at the thought of communicating with the WFTU, and dogmatically condemned the CISC for its heresy.

In such situations as these, the CISC sometimes outshines the ICFTU in its ability to conduct a flexible and expedient policy without compromising its general principles. In this, it has, perhaps, the same advantage as the WFTU has over the ICFTU. Because of a greater centralisation of authority and policy making powers, both can score tactical points off their competitors by bending their dogma without breaking their prime loyalites.

In summary, the International Federation of Christian Trade Unions is much smaller than the other two Internationals, but as it has the bulk of its membership in Western Europe, it is not unimportant for the purposes of this study. It aims to organise christian trade unionists of all denominations wherever there is a demand for its services, but its compposition is predominantly Roman Catholic. A number of paragraphs in its constitution and its policy programme show a distinctive approach to trade union structure and industrial problems which reflect the thinking of the Church, and, to some extent, Christian Democrat politics. These latter factors incur the suspicion, and even hostility, of the ICFTU.

Founded in 1920, the CISC originally had its main strength in Germany and Italy, where it now has hardly any. It lost this strength during the political events of the 1930's, and it had to cease functioning for a period during the war. The CISC has a Congress, a General Council and an Executive Committee, and its powers are concentrated more at the top than is the case in the ICFTU. The Trade Internationals associated with it are really an integral part of its structure, and accept its policy. Finance is raised chiefly through affiliation fees.

The CISC fully supports European integration, and its more detailed observations on it are, in most respects, very similar to the ICFTU's viewpoint. The CISC can hardly fail to appreciate that the integrated Europe which it supports has promising prospects for Christian organisational interests in several spheres, and this is likely to be a factor supplementing its enthusiasm for integration. It has set up a European Organisation to deal with integration problems.

The CISC is keen on co-operating with the ICFTU on European and other questions, and would particularly like to do so where they are jointly represented on international organisations–especially at the ILO, which it considers should have an enhanced role in affairs. The ICFTU does not usually respond to the Christian invitations to co-operate. The CISC strongly disapproves of the WFTU, but is not as rigid in opposing contact with it in all circumstances as is the ICFTU.

THE EUROPEAN COAL AND STEEL COMMUNITY

CHAPTER VII

ECSC-THE FIRST INTEGRATION PROJECT

Since 1952, when the European Coal and Steel Community was set up, many people and organisations representing the widest range of interests have been following its progress keenly. As the first integration project, and the one on which the European Economic Community and Euratom have modelled themselves to a substantial degree, there is much to be gained in examining its experiences in the economic, political and social fields.

The ECSC should be as much of interest to trade unionists as to anyone, and probably moreso than to most. This second part of the study examines in some detail the impact which the trade union movements and the ECSC have had upon each other in a number of different ways. The development of trade union liaison with the organs of the Community, and the modifications that the trade union organisations have made in their own structure and practices are a study in themselves.

ECSC experience has had a very direct bearing on attitudes and activities relating to Europe's newer integration projects.

Before dealing with these attitudes and activities in detail, however, it is necessary to make a brief examination of the broad outline of the ECSC, including its background, structure, aims and achievements.

The Idea and its Implementation

Proposals to integrate the countries of Western Europe politically and economically were by no means new when Robert Schuman proposed his "Plan" on 9 May 1950, on behalf of the French Government. Integration proposals had been thought about and talked about by many statesmen for many years, but never before had the time been so propitious as when M. Schuman took the initiative. The feeling in France was that wars might have been avoided in the past, and could be avoided in the future if she and Germany were to unite in common effort in specific fields. Coal and steel were not only the basic products of Europe, but were also the basic products for a war potential. The integration of the economies of Europe could find no better starting point than with these two products.

Thus it was that the Schuman Plan, as it became known, and is often called, still, was proposed, by the pioneer of European integration, as a scheme which would bring the entire French and German production of coal and steel under a joint High Authority with other European nations invited to participate.

The following month a conference opened in Paris to consider a treaty for a European Coal and Steel Community. Germany, France, Italy and the Benelux countries decided to go ahead, and in the short time of ten months the Treaty was signed by the six countries, on 18 April 1951. Within a further fifteen months the ratification processes in the separate legislatures had been completed, and the Treaty came into operation on 25 July 1952. The following month Luxembourg was selected as the international headquarters of the new Community.

The British Government, in spite of its great interest in matters affecting coal and steel, decided that it could not become a party to the Plan; mainly because it could not bring itself to accept the loss of national sovereignty–for the Plan made provision for the ECSC to have supranational authority in some respects. Nevertheless, Britain announced her intention to send a permanent delegation to the new High Authority, for purposes of observation and close consultation. An Agreement of Association between Britain and the Community was signed in December, 1954; its intention being to co-ordinate, closely, action on long-term development, and to lower trade obstacles through a Council of Association established for high-level consultations.

Several other European countries send delegations to the High Authority, but without the special form of association, as negotiated by Britain. They are Sweden, Norway, Denmark, Switzerland and Austria. The United States Government has always been very interested in the project, and it sends a large delegation. Japan also decided to send one in 1954.

Shortly after the Schuman Plan, came proposals for European integration in other, wider, fields. These were the Treaties for the European Defence Community (EDC) and the European Political Community. Both were signed, but never fully ratified–probably an indication that they were before their time, or tried to do too much at once. Enthusiasm for integration was at a peak at that time, but after the failure of EDC, in particular, it waned for some years. The success of the ECSC is one of the factors that has increased the tempo in more recent years, culminating in the Common Market and Euratom Treaties.

The Community was never intended as an *ad hoc* commercial arrangement, but rather as an enduring system which would not only help to unite the countries of Europe on a peaceful basis, but would improve their material well-being in the process. The idealism of the scheme was written into Article 2 of the Treaty, which sets out the Community's general aims and aspirations. It states that its mission is:

> "to contribute to the expansion of the economy, the development of employment and the improvement of the standard of living in the participating countries through the creation, in harmony with the general economy of the member States, of a common market"

it goes on:

> "The Community must progressively establish conditions which will in themselves assure the most rational distribution of production at the highest possible level of productivity, while safeguarding the continuity of employment and avoiding the creation of fundamental and persistent disturbances in the economies of the member States."

This concern with the far-reaching social effects that the Community would have was one of the factors that made it attractive to trade unionists. Subsequent events have not caused them to lose faith, although, inevitably, social policies do not go far enough to meet the trade union ideals one hundred per cent.

Structure and Powers

The Community has four main institutions–the High Authority, the Common Assembly (now replaced by the European Assembly, common to the three Communities), the Council of Ministers and the Court of Justice (also replaced).

The High Authority is the Executive Body of the Community, with a membership of nine. Eight of these are appointed in agreement by the member governments.

The ninth is co-opted by the other eight. There may not be more than two members of the same nationality on the Authority, and this, along with a declaration that they may not accept instructions from any government or organisation, ensures its lack of national bias. To ensure a lack of personal bias, it is stipulated that the members must not have any business or professional activities or interests, whatever, related to coal and steel, either during their six-year period of office, or for three years after it ceases. One third of the membership of the High Authority is renewed every two years. The President and Vice-President are appointed from among the members of the High Authority by agreement among the six governments who must, however, consult with the High Authority concerning the appointments.

The High Authority is assisted in its decisions by a Consultative

Committee, representing producers, workers, and consumers and dealers in the Community.

The High Authority is the dominating power in the Community, and the other three institutions wield a democratic but fairly distant supervision over its activities.

The High Authority is an entirely new type of international institution which deals directly with coal and steel enterprises in the Community without reference to the national governments. Furthermore, the decisions it makes are binding.

The High Authority is responsible for implementing the provisions of the Treaty, and instituting a common market for coal and steel by removing all tariff barriers between the Community members. These restrictions were removed over a five-year period ending on 9 February 1958. During the same period the High Authority erected a common tariff barrier against outside countries which is considerably lower than the average of the previous individual tariffs.

The fixing of production targets is within the competence of the High Authority, and it aims to back up its programme by facilitating investment and technical research to help enterprises achieve the targets. However, it does not normally interfere in the general management of enterprises in any way, and it is a matter of no consequence to the High Authority whether industries are publicly or privately owned, or whether controlled by public or private bodies.

Decisions of the High Authority are binding on enterprises. It may issue recommendations which are binding with respect to its objectives but which leave the means to be employed to the choice of those affected. Opinions are also issued, which are not binding. All these declarations must state the reasons for their issue. Fines may be imposed on enterprises which do not comply with the Treaty or the High Authority's decisions, and the High Authority has means of putting pressure on any member state which does not keep faith with the Treaty.

The High Authority has to carry out studies concerning the future prospects for ECSC products and to publish its general objectives. Enterprises then use this information as guidance for their own plans. In addition to this, as the one-time head of the U.K. delegation to the High Authority, Sir Cecil Weir, has pointed out[1]:

"the High Authority has certain powers over investments to assist in the attainment of the general objectives. The plans for new and extended production units have to be submitted to the High Authority

1. *The First Step in European Integration*, p. 10. Pamphlet published by Federal Educational and Research Trust, 1957.

which issues an opinion on them. This clearly influences the ability to raise capital from public sources. The High Authority itself can grant loans to enterprises to help carry out approved investment programmes, or can guarantee loans obtained elsewhere by the enterprises. It also has certain limited powers to restrain enterprises from embarking upon uneconomic projects. In this way, through the publication of its general objectives reinforced by its investment powers, the High Authority can exert a positive influence on the future development of the Community's coal and steel industries."

The Authority raises its finance in a novel way, provided for by the Treaty. This permits a levy to be imposed on coal and steel production in the Community up to a maximum of one per cent of output value. In fact, the levy was fixed at 0.9% in 1952, and has been progressively reduced to the level of 0.35%.

This does not mean that the High Authority is doing less–on the contrary the scope of its work has been expanding, particularly in the fields of technical and social research. But the initial heavy levy was found to be an overestimate of long term requirements.

The High Authority has the duty of enforcing the provisions of the ECSC Treaty, which prohibit cartels in the Community. Fines of up to ten per cent of annual turnover may be imposed on violators of these provisions.

Another main power of the High Authority, which is dealt with fully in a subsequent Chapter, is that of pursuing its own active social policies. Where there are disruptions in employment owing to the operation of the common market in coal and steel, the High Authority may, and does, finance technical retraining, removals to new areas, "tiding-over" allowances and the setting up of alternative industries to provide employment. It also has its own building programme for workers' housing.

The supreme body of the ECSC, the Common Assembly, met for the last time in Strasbourg in February, 1958. It has now been replaced by a new Assembly which is the supreme body for all three integration schemes, the European and Coal and Steel Community, the European Economic Community and Euratom. The old Assembly had a membership of 78; the new one has 142 members.

The Common Assembly had annual sessions, to which France, Germany and Italy sent eighteen delegates each, Belgium and the Netherlands ten delegates each, and Luxembourg four delegates. They were appointed from the national parliaments. Its main task was to receive the annual report and financial statement of the High Authority. The chief power of the Assembly was that of a vote of censure on the

High Authority if it was not satisfied with its record. If such a vote had been carried by a two-thirds majority, the High Authority would have been compelled to resign as a body. The Assembly had certain permanent committees which discussed specific problems and maintained a close working relationship with the High Authority.

These special committees reported on the work of the High Authority, to the Assembly, which was kept well informed by this and other means. It was thus able to exert a rather stronger influence over the direction of policy, and over the High Authority, than many people had expected. The Assembly had begun to act in some ways as an effective European Parliament, which was, of course, the original intention. One thing which indicates this clearly was the way that national distinctions in the Assembly had become relatively unimportant to the delegates who had aligned themselves more and more on party political lines of an all-European character.

The Council of Ministers of the ECSC has six members, one from each Community country. They are usually either Foreign Ministers or Economic Affairs Ministers. The main purpose of this Council is to harmonise the activities and outlook of the High Authority with those of the national governments, but during 1959 serious disagreements over surplus coal production problems tended to drive the High Authority and the Governments apart. The High Authority usually consults the Council before taking important decisions, and in certain cases is obliged to do so.

The Council can take decisions by a majority vote on most issues – an unusual feature for such a body. Minister's meetings in other international organisations often require unanimous votes for effective decisions to be taken.

The differing practice in the ECSC is an indication of the special supranational character of the Community, and also of the fact that this particular Council was not intended to be the dominant power in it. For although the High Authority usually consults the Council, the latter's opinion is not binding.

The Presidency of the Council rotates among its members, with a change every three months. It is the President's duty to call meetings of the Council at the request of either the High Authority or of a member state.

The Court of Justice in the ECSC was composed of "seven judges appointed for six years by agreement among the governments of the member States from among persons of recognised independence and competence". This was laid down in Article 32 of the Treaty, which went on to say that every three years a partial renewal of membership should take place, affecting, alternately, three members and four members. The judges, themselves, appointed one of their number as the President of the Court. The Court has been replaced by a Court of a similar nature which is common to the three European Communities. In its later days, the original Court was composed of one judge from each of the Community countries, plus one Dutchman.

The Court had jurisdiction in fields where no national Court was competent. Its decisions had the force of law in all six countries, and there was no appeal. It could decide whether decisions of the High Authority should stand or be overruled, whether an appeal was made by an individual, an enterprise or a government. It was the sole arbiter of disputes arising in connection with the interpretation of the Treaty.

In practice, the Court showed itself to be an effective and truly independent body of arbitration. Its judgements have been respected by industries, governments and High Authority, alike.

Community Achievements

As far as the institutions of the Community are concerned, it can be said that their work has developed along the lines predicted, and in some cases has exceeded expectations. Particularly valuable has been the policy of close consultation between the various organs and the High Authority. Consultations with both the Council of Ministers and the Consultative Committee have not been confined to circumstances prescribed by the Treaty, and this has led to a growth of mutual confidence, and a decline of purely national outlooks. Similar close co-operation has been achieved between the High Authority and the special committees of the Common Assembly.

Most people will consider the outstanding achievements of the European Coal and Steel Community to be the economic ones – the clearing away of all the obstacles to a free common market, within a customs union. The achievement is an impressive one. Within the five-year transitional period, beginning on 10 February 1953, all customs barriers, quota restrictions, currency restrictions, national subsidies, double-pricing and transport discriminations connected with coal and steel were abolished, except for a small number of special temporary measures.

The increases in production indicated are a significant guide to the success of the Community up until 1957, when the whole of its activities had been in the fortuitous circumstances of a general expansion of the West European economy.[2]

2. All the statistical data in this section is taken from the March 1958 edition of the Community's English language *Bulletin*, prepared by the High Authority's Information Service in Luxembourg.

	1952 figure (metric tons) (millions)	1957 figure (metric tons) (millions)	% increase
Coal	238.9	247.8	3.8
Coke	62.4	77.2	23.7
Iron Ore	65.3	87.4	33.8
Pig Iron	34.7	45.0	30.0
Steel	41.8	59.8	42.6

Over this period, from 1952 to 1957, the Community's share in world steel production rose from 19.8% to 20.5%.

Trade in Community products also increased considerably, both within the six countries, and between them and the outside world. Between 1952 and 1957 internal trade increased by 21% for hard coal, 14.8% for coke, 25.5% for iron ore, 175% for scrap and 157% for steel products. Trade with the rest of the world in all these products also increased considerably during the same five-year period, but with the percentage increase in imports exceeding that in exports, in most cases.

The general productivity figures in the Community's coal and steel industries show an improvement since 1952, as the increase in the number of workers employed was not as great, proportionally, as the increase in production, up to 1957. The total employment figure went up from 1,600,000 to 1,680,000 – a five per cent increase.

From 1957 to early 1959, economic circumstances were not as favourable for the Community's industries, because the expansion rate of European economies eased up. Serious problems of surplus production in coal threatened to make the High Authority's task far more difficult than previously, and there was the possibility of widespread unrest among trade unionists, as occurred in Belgium, if full employment policies were threatened with serious breakdown.

Another important factor for the common market in coal and steel was the rationalising of transport costs within the Community. Whereas, previously, a trainload of coal or steel crossing a national frontier was considered as having started a new journey, for freight charge purposes, this discrimination has now been abolished. The new rates taper off according to the greater length of the journey, irrespective of frontiers. They previously tapered only as far as frontiers. The effect has been to allow fairer competition between the producers of coal and steel in the different countries.

In some cases, the formation or maintenance of cartels, has been prevented by the High Authority, with ultimate benefit to the consumer. All agreements of a cartel nature have to be submitted to the High

Authority unless severe penalties are to be incurred. The High Authority may allow the agreements if they do not unduly restrict competition, or work against the public good in other ways. In other cases they are banned. In steel production, particularly, it has often been found that maximum efficiency cannot be attained unless the production unit is large. The High Authority, therefore, has usually allowed mergers and concentrations which are not of a restrictive nature. There has been mounting concern, however, particularly in trade union and left-wing circles in Western Europe, at the apparent unwillingness, or inability of the High Authority, to prevent huge private empires blossoming in the German steel industry, and allegedly under the control of people with dubious records.

There has been a period of price stability in the Community countries in coal and steel products since 1952. This may be partly owing to the policies of individual governments in trying to keep down the prices of basic commodities in the campaign to prevent inflation. But it is probable that the abolition of dual pricing in coal and steel, due to the common market, has also played a large part in price stability.

What is of more direct concern to the trade unions in the Community is that a good deal of progress has been made on matters of close interest to labour. Chapter Nine deals with the trade union views on Community working in labour questions, but it may be useful here to make a brief appraisal of the picture.

Firstly, there has been an upward trend in real wages in all Community countries. In other words, the purchasing power of workers in the coal and steel industries has increased. Secondly, there has been no mass unemployment as a result of the implementation of the common market. Where there has been localised and temporary unemployment, the High Authority has made full use of its powers to grant special sums for the "readaptation" of the workers. Money has been used for special unemployment payments, for retraining displaced workers and for removal allowances. Some 20,000 workers had been affected by these provisions up to 1957.

From September 1957, there has been freedom of movement within the Community for most skilled coal and steel workers, who may be issued with a special card, serving in place of a passport. This allows them to take up work freely in any of the six countries. Since then, arrangements have been made to bring into being a European Social Security Convention, which will co-ordinate national social security systems. The effect will be that no worker in any industry of a Community country will lose benefits by moving to another country.

Loans and direct payments have been made by the High Authority, on an extensive scale, for the building of workers' houses. Over 10,000 had been completed by 1957, and it was estimated that by 1960, another 28,000 would have been added, using up some 180 million dollars. About 45 million dollars of this will have been advanced by the High Authority.

A great deal of social and industrial research has been undertaken by the Secretariat of the High Authority. This includes surveys of employment levels, earnings, family budgets, working conditions, readaptation, labour legislation and a number of other items. The results are published and widely circulated. There has also been a good deal of research into industrial hygiene and safety, and a very close watch is constantly kept on mine safety problems.

To sum up, the ECSC came into existence in 1952, following a proposal of M. Schuman, on behalf of the French Government. Only the three Benelux countries and Germany, France and Italy joined, although it was open to other Western European nations. Britain has maintained a special association with the Community, and the U.S. and several other countries send observers. The project was intended to be, and is, supranational in character, and it dedicates itself to full integration, and to social and economic progress.

The supranational nature of the Community is reflected in the wide powers given to its main institution, the High Authority, which can overrule national interests in many matters connected with coal and steel. It is assisted by a Consultative Committee. The other main institutions are the Common Assembly (now replaced by a wider Assembly) composed of representatives from national Parliaments; the Council of Ministers, which co-ordinates High Authority and national policies; and the Court of Justice, which, until replacement, was the final arbiter for all interpretations and disputes.

Since 1952 progress has been made in many directions, notably by increases in production, productivity and the internal and external trade of the coal and steel industries, although 1958 and 1959 showed an excess of capacity, and difficulties ahead. During the transitional period, virtually all restrictions and barriers in the Community were removed, and a common outside tariff has been brought into being. Cartels have been restricted, transport rationalised, investment guided and supplemented, and prices kept stable. In the social field, money has been provided for workers' readaptation and for housing schemes, and skilled men have been enabled to seek work freely in any Community country. Social research has been undertaken, with the stress on safety measures in industry. The record of the Coal and Steel Community has been generally pleasing to Western European trade union organisations, and has confirmed their original faith in the launching of integration schemes.

The predictions of the World Federation of Trade Unions that the Schuman Plan would bring about reductions in wages and social security benefits, and would lead to higher unemployment and a lengthening of working hours, have been proved wrong. But although the ICFTU unions and the Christian unions are generally pleased with the results, naturally they do not believe that everything is perfect. They have made detailed criticisms and suggestions which are examined a few pages hence. But first it is necessary to look at the work the trade unions have been able to perform inside the Community during its Transitional Period.

CHAPTER VIII

TRADE UNION REPRESENTATION IN THE COMMUNITY

The right of trade unions to organise freely and to be consulted by the authorities is a widely recognised factor in industry nowadays, and would seldom be contested in principle in most Western European countries. In many countries it is also accepted in the order of things that the trade unions be consulted at an appropriate level on social and economic policy matters which only indirectly affect the industries in which they have interests.

Frequently the national trade union centres, or federations, rather than individual unions, are consulted on these matters of a general nature. This is an indication of the influence and prestige of trade unionism as a factor in present day society. It is recognised that trade union organisations, as bodies which represent a very substantial section of public opinion, should be allowed to speak in their own right on general social and economic questions of the day, as well as on industrial matters of special interest to them.

The High Authority of the ECSC has never underestimated the importance of close co-operation and consultation with trade union organisations. For this reason relationships at the Community level have been harmonious, even when differences of opinion have been prominent.

The High Authority, of course, is not an employer, and the question of trade unions negotiating with it on normal industrial matters does not arise. Wages, and most conditions of employment are still the subject of agreement between unions and employers in the different countries. What does happen at Community level is that trade unions and the High Authority make representations to each other, and consult through the medium of the Consultative Committee, as well as through the separate liaison bureaux in Luxembourg of the ICFTU-affiliated unions and the Christian trade unions. The unions affiliated to the WFTU are not represented at Community level.

The High Authority is also kept abreast of trade union problems by the three trade unionists among their nine members.

Before attempting to make a general assessment of the effects of trade unionism on the Community, and *vice versa*, it is profitable to examine the separate ways in which trade union organisations and individual trade unionists have had their effect.

The Trade Union Committee of Twenty-One[1]

When the European Coal and Steel Community was set up, the unions concerned were faced with the problem of how they were to organise themselves on a Community level, in order that one coherent policy could be formulated for all the national trade union organisations involved. It was also necessary for some representative in Luxembourg to be available to make representations to, or be consulted by, the High Authority at any time, and on any question.

The trade unions affiliated to the ICFTU, and those affiliated to the CISC, were all faced with the same problem, but each group decided that it would go ahead with its own structure, and no form of official liaison or joint policy-making has been entered into. The Committee of 21 became the co-ordinating body of the ICFTU-affiliated unions, and was far more representative and influential in the Community as a whole, than the equivalent body of the Christian unions. This is because ICFTU-affiliated unions have a monopoly of Italian trade union organisations interested in the ECSC, and a near-monopoly in Germany. They also represent the great majority of trade unionists in Luxembourg. Only in France, Belgium and the Netherlands are the interested unions divided more equally between ICFTU and CISC affiliation.

Originally, the ICFTU's European Regional Organisation had wanted to be responsible for trade union co-ordination in the ECSC, but the mineworkers and metalworkers organisations of the six countries decided that they would set up their own co-ordinating committee. Later, the national trade union centres, because they considered that the ECSC was the beginning of an overall integration process, joined them on the new body, which became known as the Committee of 21.

Strangely, the Committee never had exactly 21 members, but it had representatives, in respect of ICFTU-affiliated organisations in the six countries, from all the mineworkers and metalworkers unions, from each of the national trade union centres and also from the international mineworkers and metalworkers federations. The ERO was represented, in the person of Walter Schevenels, its General Secretary. In addition,

1. This title is no longer used, officially, for the new committee which has replaced the original. The new committee performs a very similar function to the Committee of 21, but has not the same autonomy, being a sub-body of the Trade Union Executive Committee of the "Six", which covers all three integration projects.

observers from various interested trade union organisations in Britain, Austria and the United States attended the meetings.

There was an Executive Committee of eight members, on which the ERO was again represented by Schevenels. Thus the ERO was closely in touch with all developments inside the Community affecting trade union interests. The Committee's Executive met as required, and could take policy decisions on its own initiative which were later confirmed by the full Committee. The Committee, itself, met only three or four times a year, normally.

Although it was not provided for in the constitution, the practice became established of having a conference, every two years, or so, at which three delegates from each organisation attended, instead of the usual one.

Some trade unionists have criticised the Committee of 21 on the grounds that they could not see that it performed any great function. They argued that as the Committee was in no sense an executive organ of international trade union policy it could not have much utility. Furthermore, they said that it was not in a position to negotiate improved pay or conditions with anybody, and it had no official status in the eyes of the High Authority.

While the latter two points may be true, the first criticism that it performed no great function does not stand up well to close examination. The merits of the Committee lay in its effectiveness as a co-ordinating body, rather than as a virile organ for policy implementation. Its main virtue, perhaps, was that it allowed the trade unionists of each of the Communtiy countries to draw directly on the experience of their opposite numbers. This had the effect of harmonising policies fairly closely, and has resulted in a tendency for wages and conditions of employment to move towards the highest levels to be found in the Community countries.

While the Committee of 21 was, to some extent, a policy-making trade union body in its own right, the scope for extensive policy-making was limited by factors which have already been mentioned. Nevertheless, there is a large range of matters falling outside the fields of wages and conditions of employment, which can be, and are, decided at Community level; frequently those concerned with the High Authority's various social policies and their implementation. A single trade union opinion on these subjects, collectively arrived at, is an asset to both unions and High Authority.

The General Secretary of the Committee of 21, until 1958, was Harm G. Buiter, a Dutchman.[2] He was also the chief liaison representative

2. Since February 1958, BUITER has been General Secretary of the European Trade Union Executive Committee of the "Six".

with the High Authority. Buiter had two assistant secretaries in the Committee's permanent Luxembourg offices, one of whom was a specialist on steel questions, and the other on coal.

The General Secretary was frequently consulted by the High Authority in order to ascertain the trade union viewpoint on this or that subject. Matters of day-to-day policy could be decided on the General Secretary's own initiative, although in major decisions he had the guidance of the Committee and its Executive. This enabled him to be constantly in touch with opinion in all Community countries and avoid taking decisions which would not be acceptable to them.

The High Authority, for its part, recognises the value of having a permanent liaison representative who can keep it in touch with trade union feeling in the Community. ECSC policy has always been to take full account of the trade union viewpoint, and co-operation and relationships have been generally good. The unions, themselves, are reasonably satisfied with the position.

The Committee of 21 could, if it wished, make representations direct to the High Authority on matters where it believed it was competent. The High Authority was not bound, constitutionally, to lend its ear to them, but in practice it was quite willing to do so, perhaps because of its sitting trade union members.

There are at least two other main ways of influencing the policy of the High Authority in a rather less direct manner. Firstly, by unofficial representations to, and consultations with, the trade union members of the official Consultative Committee, which advises the High Authority. The Secretariat of the Committee of 21 has acted also as the secretariat of the workers' group of the Consultative Committee. Apart from the co-ordination achieved in this manner there are other, less formal contacts. There are usually twelve trade unionists representing organisations affiliated to the ICFTU, on the Consultative Committee, out of a total of seventeen trade unionists.

In the ECSC, as in other international trade union work, the overlap of personalities is quite considerable, and this includes Committee of 21 members and Consultative Committee members. It is a frequent occurrence for the same two trade unionists to meet each other in different places in successive days or weeks, each acting in quite different capacities on each occasion. In such circumstances, assimilation of each other's viewpoints on many matters is likely to take place, without either trade unionist feeling that he has consulted the other, in any official sense. This is one of the factors which ensures a well co-ordinated trade union policy in Luxembourg.

Secondly, unofficial exchanges of viewpoint took place from time to time between the Committee of 21 and the Socialist Group of deputies in the old Common Assembly of the ECSC, and they will doubtless continue with the new European Assembly.

Co-operation in this field was good, and many matters of common interest were discussed. The proposals of the Committee of 21, and of the Socialist Group of the Assembly, were frequently very similar, particularly in the case of proposed Treaty revision. The Socialist Group at Luxembourg had trade unionists among its own members, which was another reason for its close sympathies. These trade unionists were naturally in touch with their own national centres, as well.

However, there is one limiting factor in this type of co-operation at Community level, as far as the ICFTU-affiliated unions are concerned. They must be careful not to associate themselves too closely with the politicians of the Socialist Group because of possible repercussions on their non-socialist memberships. The largest trade union centre in Italy, affiliated to the ICFTU, is predominantly Christian Democrat in sympathy, and a sizeable minority of the German Trade Union Federation membership has similar political inclinations. Indeed, some of the prominent trade unionists in these two countries are Christian Democrat Deputies in their own Parliaments.

Fortunately for the ICFTU unions, differences between them and the Christians are not great, so that collaboration with the socialists has not so far caused much observable friction. But they have to continue to tread warily, unlike the Christian trade unions at Luxembourg, which do not suffer from the same limitations in their relations with Christian Democrat politicians.

Although the official functions of the Committee of 21 were fairly strictly limited, its influence, nevertheless, was widespread through many diverse channels, all of which had some effect on the High Authority, and consequently upon ECSC policy. But because of the informal, and even unpremeditated manner in which this occurred, it is almost impossible to evaluate the relative effectiveness of one channel of influence as against another.

Those trade unionists who criticise the Committee of 21 on the grounds that it did not get very much done, or did not hold great power, are probably missing the finer points of the trade union scene in Luxembourg. The Committee's influence was felt more in the corridors of the High Authority headquarters, than in its own formal sessions. It provided a stable basis on which the valuable work of trade union lobbying could be carried out, in its broader sense; that is by maintaining a secretariat and full-time representatives who could keep up a continuous flow of information on trade union viewpoints and attitudes, which was dispensed to those in a position to influence the course of events in the Community.

There is a great deal to be said for the merits of this type of activity, from the trade union viewpoint. Its efficacy is greater than if the activities consisted of formalised negotiations, in which each side tends to "dig itself in", and make no concessions if it can possibly help it. The new process is not at all in line with traditional trade union practices, and it may take some time before trade unionists with a predilection for institutionalising all their activities are prepared to accept it fully. But then the High Authority is not in the position of an employer, but almost of an independent advisor, listening to each side on questions of industrial negotiations. A modified trade union approach is therefore fitting.

In certain circumstances, the High Authority has deliberately taken on an independent role in bringing together representatives of trade unions and employers in an *ad hoc* consultative committee to discuss common problems, with a High Authority representative in the chair. This has proved very useful, all round.

It is sometimes asked whether the Committee of 21, or its successor, should not have full supranational powers, and be able to take on the task, for instance, of making international collective agreements with Community employers, concerning wages and conditions of employment. The answer to this question, broadly, is that the trade unions do not believe that international collective bargaining on any substantial scale will come about in the near future.

There are two main reasons for this. First, the national trade union organisations are rather conservative about delegating their traditional powers to supranational, or any other bodies, and secondly, it seems uncertain that international collective bargaining would bring greater benefits for the majority. The interesting point here is that the one noticeable exception in the general lack of enthusiasm for international bargaining is Italy. Real wages in the Italian steel industry, and in coal, have been rising in recent years, but they have not been rising as fast as in the other countries of the Community. Heavy unemployment in the economy, generally, and comparative lack of trade union strength are two of the reasons for this.

Italian trade unionists feel that if international collective bargaining were to come about, they would gain a good deal from it by being levelled up to the standards of other countries. To a certain extent, the opposite case applies to the other Community countries. A good number of their trade unionists feel that, although international collective bargaining may not actually lower their standards, it may act as a drag on their present ability to push a little ahead of the average of wage improvements.

One indication of trade union doubts about the effectiveness of supranational bargaining was given in May 1956, at a special conference for trade union organisations associated with the ECSC. One of the major topics discussed was the implementation of a 40 hour week–one of the few industrial conditions with which the international trade union movement has concerned itself very directly. The conference did not believe that purely international action could bring about the 40 hour week. It thought international endeavours were only a useful complement to the main action which must be taken at national level, and that the national trade union organisations must use their influence on the ECSC representatives from their own countries.

Whatever the differences in ideas as to the appropriate range of functions of the Committee of 21, there is general agreement that the organisation was a very necessary and useful one, even though it could never be spectacular. It can be said with certainty that if it had not existed in its actual form some such body would have had to be created. Its structure proved to be well-balanced and democratic, and if imitation is a form of flattery, then its members can feel justifiable pride that it has served as the model on which the new European Trade Union Committee has been created, for the three integration projects together.

The Federation of Christian Trade Unions in the ECSC

The Christian trade unions were faced with very similar problems to the ICFTU-affiliated unions when the European Coal and Steel Community was set up. Consequently, they, too, decided to set up their own Liaison Bureau in Luxembourg. But they found that the fairly loose sort of organisation which served the ICFTU well, was not sufficient for their own needs; and their preference for strong central institutions gave rise to the Christian unions at Luxembourg federating, in March 1955.

The Federation of Christian Trade Unions in the ECSC, as it has called itself, has a much smaller affiliated membership than the Committee of 21 had. It draws its strength from the trade union organisations of the Netherlands, France, Belgium, Germany and Luxembourg. All but a tiny proportion of the strength is contained in the first three countries mentioned. In spite of the huge differences in size between the affiliates of the Federation, all have equal representation and voting power, and all pay the same financial contribution to Luxembourg.

As with the Committee of 21, the national centres, and the individual metalworkers and miners unions from each of the five countries, are represented by one delegate on the Committee of the Federation. As these unions are duplicated in the Netherlands, this brings the total number to eighteen. Another five members represent the white-collar workers' organisations–two from Germany, and one each from the Netherlands and Belgium. This makes a total of 23 members, plus one representative of the Christian International, the CISC, in Brussels, who sits in a consultative capacity. The Trade Internationals are not separately represented on the Committee, as the ITSs were on the Committee of 21.

The Committee has its meetings not less than once every three months, and it is responsible for directing the general policy of the Federation. There is an Executive Board consisting of six members–the President, three Vice-Presidents, the Treasurer and the Secretary.

Unlike the Committee of 21, the Statutes of the Christian Federation make provision for a General Assembly, which has the same basis of representation as the Committee, but in duplicate. It meets not less than every two years. The President and Secretary of the Executive Board occupy the same positions in the General Assembly of the Federation.

The Committee is the main guiding organ of the Federation, and decisions reached, usually requiring a two-thirds majority, are binding on all affiliates. There is, however, provision for appeal to the CISC in Brussels, in certain circumstances. Decisions of the Committee or the Assembly which affect the religious convictions of members require a unanimous vote of approval.

The Christian Federation has its own offices and Secretariat in Luxembourg, controlled by the Secretary, A. C. de Bruijn, a Dutchman. He, together with the President and the Treasurer, have full powers to represent the Federation in the ECSC. The Federation has a Commission of Experts whose job is to study ECSC problems, and draw up studies which will enable effective Community policies to be adopted on development and labour questions.

The aims and objectives of the Christian Federation, as stated in its Statutes, differ little from the aims and objectives of the Committee of 21, except that the Federation states that the basis of its activities must be in accordance with the christian principles laid down in the CISC constitution. The Federation, generally, has performed very similar work to that of the Committee of 21.

The more centralised structure of the christian trade unions in the ECSC does not mean that they believe their Federation may become a collective bargaining agency, to replace the national organisations, in any form. The christian trade union viewpoint on this question is similar to the ICFTU's. As far as conditions of employment are concerned, it is believed that national trade union pressures are, at present, more effective than international ones, although the possibility of a change in the method of negotiation in the future is not ruled out. The Christian trade unions believe that some conditions and hours of work may be decided internationally, in due course, but not wages.

The Christian Federation, like the ICFTU-affiliated unions, has found that the personal contacts of its representatives among High Authority personnel are an excellent way of spreading influence. Its representatives are in close touch with the christian trade unionists on the Consultative Committee, and the more recent appointment of a christian trade unionist to the High Authority, itself, will doubtless ensure a sympathetic ear on that body.

The Federation had close and friendly contacts with Christian Democrat Deputies who attended the Common Assembly, and will certainly continue to pursue this frutiful collaboration in the new European Assembly.

In view of the close similarities of purpose, structure and ideas of the ICFTU-affiliated and CISC-affiliated unions in the ECSC, it may seem surprising that they have not joined forces in Luxembourg. It is inevitable that some unofficial exchanges of ideas, and some consultations, should take place between the representatives of the two organisations, if only because they are bound to meet each other about their business. But when this does occur, it is certainly not because of the enthusiasm of the Committee of 21 representatives, or their successors. In accordance with general ICFTU policy, they remain fairly aloof from an organisation which they accuse of trying to split the united trade union movements in Germany and Austria.

The Christian representatives, in accordance with the policies propounded by their International, advocate co-operation with the ICFTU unions, and believe that the potentialities for such an association are greater in the ECSC than anywhere else. It is their view that one of the main causes of aloofness between the organisations is that the various national centres are in close, if informal, collaboration with Social Democrat or Christian Democrat political parties, and this exaggerates the differences between the trade unionists.

Representatives of the High Authority say that they have found no major difficulties in maintaining contact with two trade union liaison offices rather than one, so it does not appear likely that there will be much pressure from the High Authority for a joint organisation, as there was from the OEEC, in Paris, for a Joint Trade Union Advisory Committee. There is, therefore, little prospect of close collaboration, unless the general relationships between the two Internationals in Brussels improve considerably.

Unions not represented in the ECSC

There remains a section of organised workers who have no representation at all at the ECSC, but who earn a livelihood in the Community's coal and steel industries. These are members of trade union federations such as the CGT, in France, the CGIL, in Italy the very small EVC in the Netherlands, plus a sprinkling of trade unionists in Luxembourg. All these national trade union centres are affiliated to the World Federation of Trade Unions, the WFTU, which is, of course, completely opposed on political grounds, to the ECSC.

The three national centres concerned did not ask for representation on the Workers Group of the ECSC Consultative Committee, and it is fairly certain that had they done so, the Council of Ministers would not have been willing to nominate them. It is an established practice among the governments of Western Europe that they do not nominate communist, or WFTU-affiliated, trade union organisations, to any of the various public positions or delegations, internationally, to which it is their prerogative to send union representatives. The Council of Ministers would, naturally, have taken a similar attitude.

The WFTU and its affiliated organisations in Western Europe have not sought to set up their own Liaison Bureau in Luxembourg to co-ordinate their activites, or to maintain contact with the High Authority, presumably upon the grounds that one does not associate with organisations of which one disapproves, or talk with their controlling bodies.

Although the CGIL, and the CGT have asked for representation on the organs of the European Common Market, they have not felt able to reverse their previous stand against the ECSC. They have not made any move to represent their steelworking and coalmining members at Luxembourg.

The WFTU-affiliated organisations have suffered only minor disadvantages, as far as their members are concerned, in not being represented at Luxembourg. They are, after all, still fully competent to negotiate on behalf of their members, at local and national levels, with the people who are their employers. If they were represented at Luxembourg it is difficult to believe that they would achieve anything for their members, in addition to what has been obtained for them, already, by the efforts of the other trade union organisations, and individuals. Any policy that is decided upon affecting the Community's employees will be applied, equally, to all of them irrespective of the trade union organisations to which they belong.

In these circumstances, the WFTU appears to have considered it expedient to allow its members to benefit from the efforts of other trade unionists, where these brought results, and to criticise where no benefits were apparent; at the same time disclaiming responsibility for anything which it considered worthy of criticism. The idea of pursuing a militant, but non-responsible policy, of this sort, is not without its attractions to the rank-and-file members.

The Consultative Committee of the ECSC

The Consultative Committee was an entirely new form of organisation which had no close parallel in any other international institution until the advent of the Economic and Social Committee of the Common Market. In the present study, the main purpose is to examine the various methods of trade union representation, but in the case of the Consultative Committee, this is not a practical possibility unless the wider implications of it are appraised. The Consultative Committee has served, in most respects, as a model for the Economic and Social Committee of the Common Market and Euratom, and this form of consultation with interested parties is a significant new factor in international institutions.

The general picture of the Consultative Committee is drawn fully, and concisely, in the Treaty, and it is valuable to examine the full text of Article 18, and part of Article 19.

"Article 18

There shall be created a Consultative Committee, attached to the High Authority. It shall consist of not less than thirty and not more than fifty-one members, and shall include an equal number of producers, workers, and consumers and dealers.

The members of the Consultative Committee shall be appointed by the Council.

As concerns producers and workers, the Council shall appoint the representative organisations among which it shall allocate the seats to be filled. Each organisation shall be asked to draw up a list comprising twice the number of seats allocated to it. Appointments shall be made from this list.

The members of the Consultative Committee shall be appointed in their individual capacity for a period of two years. They shall not be bound by any mandate or instruction from the organisations which proposed them as candidates.

A President and officers shall be elected for periods of one year by the Consultative Committee from among its own members. The Committee shall make its own rules of procedure.

The allowances of members of the Consultative Committee shall be determined by the Council on the proposal of the High Authority.

Article 19

The High Authority may consult the Consultative Committee on all matters it deems proper. It shall be required to do so whenever such consultation is prescribed by the present Treaty.

The High Authority shall submit to the Consultative Committee the general objectives and programmes established under the terms of Article 46, and shall keep the Committee informed of the broad lines of its action under the terms of Articles 54, 65 and 66".

It can be seen from the wording of these Articles that the Consultative Committee was not intended to be merely a body on which the High Authority could bestow its patronage as it felt inclined. It was intended to be what it has become–an organisation genuinely representing the viewpoints of parties interested in the working of the Community, and one which has a quite definite influence on the policy decisions of the High Authority. Furthermore, the High Authority has welcomed the opportunity of hearing the Committee's views, and has not confined itself to consulting it only when the Treaty provisions made it obligatory.

In practice, the number of members on the Committee has been fixed at 51; that is seventeen representing producers, seventeen representing workers and seventeen representing consumers and dealers.

The representative workers organisations which the Council of Ministers has nominated for entitlement to seats, under the terms of Article 18, are divided as fairly as possible between ICFTU-affiliated and CISC-affiliated trade union organisations, in proportion to their relative national strengths, bearing industrial strengths in mind.

Thus it has become the practice to seat eleven or twelve representatives of ICFTU-affiliated organisations, four or five CISC-affiliated representatives and one representative of the independent white-collar workers' federation in France, the CGC. When there are eleven representatives of ICFTU allegiance, there are five of CISC allegiance, and when twelve of the former, there are four of the latter. The position normally changes every two years, but the balance is, in any case, redressed by the presence of a special observer nominated by the Council.

The national strengths are reflected by the following example of the composition of the Workers' Group of the Consultative Committee from 1955 to 1957.

Germany: five representatives (all with ICFTU affiliations)
France: five representatives (two each with ICFTU and CISC
             affiliations, and one independent)
Belgium: two representatives (one each with ICFTU and CISC
             affiliations)

Italy: two representatives (both with ICFTU affiliations)
Netherlands: two representatives (one each with ICFTU and CISC
                    affiliations)
Luxembourg: one representative (ICFTU affiliation)

The Consultative Committee has a Bureau of six members. This is composed of the President and the two Vice-Presidents of the full Committee, plus three other members, and it holds a mandate for one year. Its composition is always divided equally between the producers, the workers, and the consumers and dealers. The practice is well established of having one representative of each of these Groups as the President or a Vice President. The Presidency rotates, annually, to give a representative of each of the Groups, the position for one year.

The Presidency of the Consultative Committee has been held by a workers representative on two occasions up to 1958. In 1954-5 A. Renard, a Belgian, occupied the position, and in 1957-8 it was held by a German, F. Dahlmann.

There are three Commissions of the Consultative Committee, for dealing with special problems. They each have six members–two from each Group. The particular subjects with which they concern themselves are General Objectives, Markets and Prices, and Problems of Work.

It is usual for trade unionists who are members of the Consultative Committee to be full time officers in their own trade unions or national centres. Their ECSC jobs are not full time, and they must earn a living elsewhere. This is valuable in that it ensures that those consulted are closely in touch with the day-to-day problems of the industries on whose behalf they tender advice.

The range of subjects on which the High Authority is under obligation to consult the Consultative Committee, under the terms of the Treaty, is surprisingly large. Trade unions are kept closely acquainted with the day-to-day problems of the administration of the Community through the Consultative Committee, and any member of that Committee has full opportunity to acquire detailed knowledge of practically any aspect of the Community's working.

The Workers' Group of the Committee has tended to bring a more concerted, and therefore a greater influence to bear in the Committee, than either the Producers' Group or the Consumers and Dealers' Group. Perhaps it is that trade unionists find it easier to arrive at common policies, along lines of common interests, than do producers or consumers.

When the Committee does divide over an issue, it usually does so along the lines of its tripartite composition, rather than on national or industrial lines. But there are some exceptions to this.

From the point of view both of the trade unions and of the High Authority, the Consultative Committee has functioned fairly well, and performed valuable service to the Community. The trade unions have some criticisms of the operation of the Committee, and the High authority has felt, at times, that the members of the Committee were attempting to exercise an undue influence over their senior body. But grievances on either side have not reached major proportions, and have not detracted from the high value each has placed on this form of consultation.

The main reason for this examination of the trade unions' role in the Consultative Committee is to enable an assessment to be made of the value derived from their experience in it. In the light of this, the trade unions have been able, as will be seen later, to make comments and suggestions for improvements in consultative methods, and to appraise, critically, the provisions that have been made for consultations in the European Economic Community and Euratom Treaties. ECSC experience will be a valuable grounding for the unions in exercising pressure for appropriate consultative methods in any free trading scheme which is set up in the wider Europe.

Other Trade Union Influences in the Community

The exercise of national partisanship, or the receipt of a mandate from any organisation, for members of the High Authority, and also for members of the Consultative Committee, is forbidden by the Treaty. It is right and proper that this should be the case. But having said that, nobody believes, and nobody would expect, that any man who has spent many years in public life in the sincere advocacy of some partisan or national cause, could suddenly become a non-opinionated and passive onlooker of the scene which he has vacated, when accepting a High Authority nomination.

In appointing members of the High Authority, the six Community Governments made allowance for a balance of interests, realising that this was the case. The Treaty, itself, states that not more than two members of the High Authority shall be of the same nationality. Since the Community's inception, two of the nine members have been trade unionists, and for the reasons outlined, it must be assumed that the trade unions benefit directly by having members there, whose nature it is to consider trade union interests with a large measure of sympathy. It is therefore legitimate to mention the trade union members of the High Authority when dealing with trade union influence in the Community.

The most outstanding trade unionist with High Authority service is the ex-President, Paul Finet. He succeeded René Mayer in the post in January, 1958. Finet was the ninth member of the High Authority (co-opted by the other eight under the constitution) after it was set up. He was chosen at that time because of his special knowledge of labour problems, and he has given faithful service to the Community since. He is an ex-President of the ICFTU, and he continued to hold his appointment as Secretary-General of the Belgian Trade Union Federation for some years. He has wide experience of the International Labour Organisation.

As a member of the High Authority, Finet gave special attention to social policy, and relations with Community trade unionists; and has done special work, also, in connection with mine safety in the Community, particularly in helping to set up a special Mine Safety Commission. There is no doubt that his appointment, as President, gave Community trade unionists a feeling that this was a great chance to establish fruitful relationships with the High Authority.

The other trade unionist with a seat on the High Authority, from the outset, is Heinz Potthoff, a German, who was one of the appointees agreed on by the six governments. He was previously an official of the DGB, the German Trade Union Federation, in the Ruhr, and had a good deal of experience of the German system of co-determination in management for heavy industry. He holds a doctor's degree.

In January 1958, a new trade union member was appointed to the High Authority. This was Roger Reynaud, a Frenchman. He has held the post of Secretary-General to the Christian Trade Union Federation, the CFTC, in France, and has been its economic advisor. He has also been a member of the CISC General Council. Reynaud has a good deal of experience in other forms of public life, having held the position of inspector in the Ministry of Finance, and having had membership of the *Conseil Economique*, or French Economic Council. The Christian trade union movement was naturally jubilant in having somebody so closely associated with them on the High Authority for the first time.

There is little doubt that the concern the High Authority has shown in matters relating to the working and living conditions of the Community's miners and steelworkers, and their enlightened approach to social questions, is, in good measure, owing to the influence of the trade unionists who sit on it.

There were a good number of trade unionists among the delegates to the Common Assembly, as there are among the delegates to the new Assembly. Their influence, in addition to influences working through other channels, has ensured, and should continue to ensure, that the legitimate aspirations of people whose livelihoods are bound in with the Community, are brought to the notice of those in a position to control the future course of events.

In summary, it may be said that there are a number of ways in which trade union competence is recognised, and its influence made effective, in the European Coal and Steel Community. The unions affiliated to the ICFTU and the CISC maintain their separate Bureaux at Luxembourg, and although they do not officially co-operate, in practice their policies and viewpoints in the Community are very similar.

The Committee of 21, now replaced by a similar body, was the official organ of the ICFTU-affiliated unions, and was composed of representatives from national trade union centres, national mineworkers and metalworkers unions, and the International Trade Secretariats catering for those trades. The ERO was also represented. The Committee had an Executive of eight, and maintained a small Secretariat in Luxembourg. The Secretary was the main liaison representative with the High Authority. The Committee was able to make policy on many issues, although its member organisations maintained their independence. Its influence was certainly felt in the Community, and although it did not have bargaining powers in respect of wages, and most conditions of service of the workers, it was able to influence and co-ordinate individual national efforts in this direction, with beneficial results. It had the ear of the High Authority, particularly on questions of social policy.

The Christian Trade Union Movement has its Federation of Christian Trade Unions in the ECSC, representing a much smaller number of trade unionists, but performing a very similar function to the Committee of 21. The main difference between the two is that the Federation's decisions are binding on all members, and its powers are more centralised. Also, each affiliate is treated alike, irrespective of size, as far as financial dues to the Federation are concerned. There is little official co-operation between the two trade union organisations, and liaison with WFTU organisations does not arise, as they are not represented, at all.

Other methods of promoting trade union influence in the Community are through the official Consultative Committee, which advises the High Authority, and is composed usually of producers, workers, and consumers and dealers; and through unofficial exchanges of viewpoint between the organised trade union Bureaux, and favourably inclined politicians, who are delegated to the Community Assembly, a number of whom are trade unionists themselves. The trade union viewpoint has been given recognition on the High Authority, which has contained at least two trade unionists since the Community's inception – one of them, Paul Finet, was made President in 1958; retiring with the rest of the High Authority in September, 1959, but again being co-opted as the ninth ordinary member after the new High Authority was appointed.

The picture, in perspective, is that trade unions and trade unionists have been given a full part to play in the Community, and all sides have appreciated the mainly harmonious relations which have resulted, no less than the enlightened social policies of the Community. The experiment has provided valuable experience for trade unionists considering forms of association with new integration projects. While the trade unions have been fairly pleased with their experiences in the Community, they are not without criticisms, and suggestions for improvements, and it is valuable to make a study of these, before considering the unions' role in other integration schemes.

CHAPTER IX

THE TRADE UNIONS AND TREATY REVISION

Article 96 of the Treaty of the European Coal and Steel Community makes provision for the amendment of the Treaty after the end of the transitional period. This would be done by a conference of representatives of the governments of members states, if the Council of Ministers agreed to such a conference. Amendments approved would have to be ratified by all member states in their national legislatures. There is a separate and simpler procedure for minor amendments.

The transitional period ended in February, 1958. Article 96 only makes provision for member states, or the High Authority to propose Treaty amendments, but the two trade union movements at Community level have felt it necessary to publish their own proposals,[1] and have solicited support for them by several methods, including circularisation of them to High Authority Departments and personalities, national governments, political groups in the Assembly, and other influential sources. The unions have not confined their proposals to questions of social policy, but have felt that the economic and institutional provisions in the Treaty should also come within their critical range. As social policy is of the most direct concern to trade unionists, however, it is dealt with, first, in this Chapter, and in more detail than the other, general, proposals.

Readaptation

The word readaptation is a new one which came into vogue through the special scheme in the Coal and Steel Community, which makes necessary provisions for re-employing workers displaced in the coal and steel industries. Readaptation has come to mean a combination of several measures to ensure such a smooth changeover. First, there are "waiting allowances" which are paid to workers in the period between losing one job and starting the next. They are based on previous remuneration, are much higher than ordinary unemployment benefits, and continue

1. An *ad hoc* committee was set up by the Committee of 21 to prepare these proposals for the ICFTU-affiliated unions, consisting of representatives of organisations affiliated to the Committee of 21. For the sake of convenience the proposals will be referred to, throughout, as "Committee of 21 proposals".

for up to fifteen months. Next, there are retraining facilities, to allow workers to acquire new skills. Third, the expenses of removal and rehousing are paid if the worker is encouraged to move to a new area; and, finally, there are provisions for investment, in some circumstances, to provide new industries which can absorb workers laid off from coal and steel employment.

Readaptation is a new idea—a main provision in the hands of governments and High Authority for overcoming employment difficulties, and is a milestone of progress on the social side of industry. It is supplemented by certain other measures, such as the issue of a Labour Card to skilled workers allowing them to move freely in the Community, and large scale housing schemes sponsored by the Community. Readaptation is still in its infant stage, and up to November, 1957, had only affected 24,583 workers—most of them in Italy and France. Not all the schemes have been successful, but where they have not, valuable experience has been gained, which should prevent other miscalculations occurring in future.

Readaptation powers can come from two sources. Firstly, from Section 23 of the Convention containing the Transitional Provisions of the Treaty, and, secondly, from Article 56 of the Treaty, itself. Only Section 23 had been invoked up to 1958. This makes provision for the forms of assistance outlined above to be given during the transitional period, and for two years after that, if the High Authority and Council of Ministers so agree. The High Authority cannot inaugurate readaptation schemes without first receiving a request from the government of the country concerned; and where a scheme is carried out the High Authority and the government normally take equal shares in the financial burden. All the assistance so given to workers is non-repayable. A condition of applying readaptation provisions is that the need for them shall be a consequence of coal or steel enterprises ceasing to operate, or changing their activities, owing to the introduction of the common market in those industries.

Article 56 makes similar powers of intervention by the High Authority permanent, but limits, more severely, the circumstances under which they can be used, by confining them to cases where "the introduction of technical processes or new equipment, within the framework of the general objectives laid down by the High Authority, should lead to an exceptionally large reduction in labour requirements in the coal or steel industries, making it especially difficult in one or more areas to re-employ the workers discharged".

In their Treaty Revision proposals, the Committee of 21 (consisting of ICFTU-affiliated union delegates) has pointed to the more restrictive nature of Article 56, and expressed the opinion that it will not be adequate to meet the circumstances after February 1960, when the provisions of Section 23 of the Transitional Convention can no longer be invoked. It would have liked to have had the provisions of Section 23 written into the Treaty, so that readaptation schemes could be operated wherever there was unemployment as a result of the common market. But it was realised that, as time went on, it would become increasingly difficult to decide what was, and what was not, a result of the common market, and so it proposed, instead, that the High Authority be given powers to take action on any occasion when unemployment occurred.

The proposed new clause would have the restrictive phrases of Article 56 removed, and would simply allow the High Authority to act "If the introduction of technical processes or new equipment should lead to a reduction in labour requirements in the coal or steel industries, making it especially difficult to re-employ the workers discharged." The proposal also makes clear, perhaps with an eye on changes which may be brought about by the Economic Community, that the unions would wish to see action if unemployment arose through modifications of the economic structure.

The Committee of 21 proposals would give more power to the High Authority to intervene, without the government concerned having specifically requested this, and if the request was not made within a reasonable time of unemployment difficulties arising. To make this workable, local or regional organisations should officially be given competence to approach the High Authority, themselves, if the governments did not. And the High Authority should have the right to make its own investigations in the areas affected. The provision whereby the government concerned normally has to pay half the cost of a readaptation scheme, at present, should be abolished, and the High Authority should be competent to decide what proportion of the expense should be borne by government or local organisations, or whether the High Authority should foot the whole bill, itself. The High Authority should have full rights to control readaptation schemes which are Community-subsidised.

The Christian Trade Union Federation at Luxembourg has since published its own Treaty Revision proposals, which are, in many respects, similar to those of the Committee of 21. On readaptation, it also believes that the High Authority should have extra powers–particularly to make investigations into possible schemes at the request of local organisations and trade unions. It should apply readaptation schemes in collaboration with interested governments when a reduction in manpower requirements is brought about, either through technological or structural causes, or when agreements on specialisation or concentration of industry cause employment difficulties.

Support for the trade union point of view on readaptation has come from two other influential sources. One of them was urging similar reforms well before the trade unions made their own proposals. This was the Bertrand Report, a document drawn up for the Common Assembly's Social Affairs Committee in 1956. The second influential source was the Common Assembly, itself. At its final meeting in February 1958, it adopted a number of proposals for Treaty Revision, some of which had been suggested in a report prepared by Gerhard Kreyssig, a German Social Democrat.

The Assembly has no power to amend the Treaty, but can make suggestions to the High Authority and member governments. The amendments it suggested on readaptation follow trade union proposals fairly closely. Both reports stressed particularly that the High Authority's powers should not be lessened in the field of readaptation, and that it should be given the right of initiative in those cases where governments, themselves, did not act, or did not act with sufficient speed.

Particular concern has been felt by the trade unions, and expressed in the Bertrand Report and by the Assembly, that a sense of false confidence could possibly obscure the fact that readaptation provisions and powers would be very inadequate if a major recession should occur. The Treaty should be amended so that the High Authority could act quickly, and effectively, to relieve heavy unemployment if less favourable economic circumstances should prevail. This would mean eliminating certain restrictive Treaty clauses which confine readaptation projects to situations which are the result of the introduction of the common market, or of technological re-equipment.

It can be said, with assurance, that the trade union viewpoint on readaptation has had a very real influence, through a number of channels, on the thinking in the Community as a whole. The Common Assembly has reached very similar conclusions concerning Treaty revision on a number of proposals in the social field–perhaps because of close contacts with the unions.

Although they have made suggestions for improvement, the trade unions at Community level have not been entirely dissatisfied with the progress of readaptation so far; and they consider that in spite of some failures, the system has not worked too badly in its trial period. There is some feeling in High Authority circles, however, that the trade unions in the localities concerned have not always taken the interest in readaptation that they might have done.

It is felt that trade unions in the countries affected by unemployment in coal or steel could, if they used initiative, surmount some of the shortcomings of the Treaty, concerned with High Authority intervention. If, for instance, a government does not take action on unemployment, it is sometimes because the situation is not brought to its notice sufficiently strongly. Trade unions have it within their power to act as effective agents for this purpose and to persuade their governments to approach the High Authority on the matter. Alternatively, and unofficially, trade unions can write direct to the High Authority stating their complaint, and the High Authority will then pass the communication on to the appropriate government, and gain its interest in this way. Neither of these methods are used, at present, as widely as they could be.

The main trade union national centres in Italy and France, the countries most affected by readaptation, feel that though improvements can be made, readaptation, so far, has not worked too badly in practice, and that the situation is certainly better than if the ECSC had not been operating at all. This opinion prevails in spite of some natural cynicism in France concerning the failure of the largest scheme of all, which envisaged the transfer of some 5,000 miners from the uneconomic Centre-Midi coalfields to Lorraine. Only a small fraction of this number eventually went, and for reasons which ought to have been forseen. High Authority opinion, in consequence, has hardened against the large-scale movements of labour to new regions, and the emphasis is now more on creating new employment in the regions where the difficulties occur.

There seems reasonable prospect that with the gaining of Community experience in readaptation, and with the climate of opinion moving in favour of improvements, further progress and innovations may be made in the not too distant future.

Community Housing and Social Investment

Another direction in which the High Authority's powers ought to be extended, according to the Committee of 21 proposals, is in the domain of workers' housing. The proposals favour the High Authority being able to take the initiative in housing projects, which would not necessarily be tied to readaptation schemes. It should have powers to finance regional and local authorities, which could then build and let houses to the Community's workers. The Committee of 21 would also have liked to have seen the inauguration of constructional co-operatives, to which the High Authority would be allowed to make loans. Ownership of the property, for those who desired it, could be arranged through the co-operatives, and the system would be a safeguard against the houses becoming a vested interest of the enterprises with which they were associated.

The proposals make it clear that funds for social investment, for housing, and for other purposes should be regarded in the Treaty as equally important as funds for technical investments. Health and safety measures should be eligible for High Authority finance. The High Authority already has lending powers in these fields, but only from monies which it has, itself, borrowed. The Committee of 21 wanted funds derived from the levy on coal and steel production to be available for these social investments. Part of this levy should be available, also, to enable the High Authority to lower the rate of interest on loans which it makes from its own borrowings.

It is suggested that Article 55 of the Treaty, which sets out the duties of the High Authority in the field of promoting technical and economic research in coal and steel, be amended to allow the Authority to conduct researches in the social field also–presumably under the same conditions as prescribed by the Article for other forms of research. That is, the financing of such researches jointly with enterprises, by the earmarking of grants received, or, by agreement with the Council of Ministers, from funds derived from the levy on production.

The trade union statement recalls that, following a resolution of the Common Assembly in November 1956, the High Authority agreed to publish its general social objectives. It is felt that, welcome as this may be, it would be better still if such an obligation for the High Authority were written into the Treaty, as it is concerning the economic objectives of the Community, in Article 46. Paragraph three of this Article requires the High Authority to "periodically set out the general objectives with respect to modernisation, the long-term planning of production and the expansion of productive capacity". The Committee of 21 would have added to the paragraph "and the improvement of living and working conditions of labour in each of the industries within its jurisdiction".

The proposals of the Community's Federation of Christian trade unions have largely reiterated the points made in the Committee of 21's document, on questions of housing, social investment, objectives and research. The trade unions in Luxembourg are at one on Treaty modification as regards major social questions and readaptation.

Collective Bargaining, Workers' Standards, and Employment

Article 68 of the ECSC Treaty states that traditional national methods of fixing wages and social benefits shall not be affected by the Treaty except in special circumstances. This latter phrase means, broadly, when governments or enterprises attempt to obtain unfair competitive advantages for the coal or steel industries by arbitrarily reducing wage levels. The High Authority may then intervene with a view to bringing the erring parties into line, after consulting the Consultative Committee and the Council of Ministers.

The Committee of 21 is not completely satisfied with these provisions. It agrees that the negotiating of wage and social security levels, and the length of working time, should remain national prerogatives; but believes, nevertheless, that the High Authority should have a specifically defined duty to promote improvements in the living and working conditions of the Community's employees. It is felt that some interested parties, holding opposite viewpoints to the trade unions, are invoking the present wording of Article 68 in support of their viewpoint that the High Authority should not take any part in the determination of living and working standards.

Section (e) of Article 3 of the Treaty already makes it incumbent upon the institutions of the Community, within their respective powers, to "promote the improvement of living and working conditions of the labour force in each of the industries under its jurisdiction so as to harmonise those conditions in an upward direction". The Committee of 21 believed that a statement should be inserted in Article 68 to the effect that nothing in it should be interpreted as putting obstacles in the way of the implementation of Article 3 (e). Furthermore, a paragraph should be included in the Article, pledging the governments to harmonise their social security systems in an upward direction.

The final item in the Treaty's social provisions, to which the Committee of 21 suggested amendment, is the free circulation of labour in the Community. The trade unions are strong advocates of free movement, and the present provisions of Article 69 seem, to them, to fall short of the desirable. In the Article, the member states bind themselves to renouncing restrictions based on nationality, on the employment of workers of recognised qualifications in the coal and steel industries. They also guarantee there will be no discrimination in pay or conditions as between national and foreign workers, and pledge themselves to work out administration procedures which will bring supply and demand requirements for employment in the Community together.

The Committee of 21 proposed that the "free circulation of workers" provision be extended to those who are not nationals of a member state, but who had two or three years residential qualification in one of the Community countries. It is pointed out that there has been no substantial movement of labour since free migration was introduced.

The Committee was also of the opinion that a Community Employment Bureau ought to be created, and should be provided for in Article 69. The Christian Trade Union Federation makes a similar suggestion, and has proposed almost identical Treaty amendments as the Committee of 21 concerning the free circulation of non-nationals and the harmonisation of social security systems.

The Christian Federation makes the interesting suggestion that the High Authority should be competent to hear appeals or disputes arising out of the application of free migration and European Labour Card provisions, agreed in 1957. It also proposes that the High Authority should promote safety measures at work, attempt to standardise safety regulations, and publish statistics on safety. It should promote negotiations between employers and workers with a view to balanced progress being made in the Community concerning living and working conditions, and should, itself, mediate between employers and workers, in certain circumstances, where coal and steel supplies are threatened by an industrial conflict. The High Authority should also hold regular consultations with employers and workers in the Community's transport industry. The Christians suggest that all these proposals should be incorporated in appropriate Treaty Articles.

The general picture is that the international trade union organisations in Luxembourg agree, to a great extent, on the shortcomings of the Treaty in the field of social provisions. The main criticism is that the High Authority has not enough powers on social questions. Both organisations feel that the balance of its economic and social powers is maladjusted, and is weighted rather towards the former. This situation, it is felt, should be redressed, but the proposals made to achieve this balance are more in the nature of an extension of established principles in the Community than an exploration of new territories–an indication that the trade unions are generally pleased with the record of the Coal and Steel Community. This contrasts with their attitude to subsequent integration projects and Treaties, such as the Common Market, which are considered to fall far short of standards set by the ECSC in social matters.

Institutional Provisions

The trade unions in Luxembourg have never been convinced that the High Authority's Consultative Committee, on which one third of the members are trade unionists, has been as useful as it might have been, or has paid sufficient attention to the claims of the organised workers of the Community.

The Committee of 21's proposals for Treaty Revision put forward a solution for the shortcomings, as seen by them. They would have had Articles 18 and 19 amended to give the trade unions some representation in the consumers and dealers group of the Consultative Committee. It is alleged that the present situation is unsatisfactory because a good number of the members of this group are trade consumers who are also employers, and they can combine with the employers group, and always form a majority against the workers. Trade Unionists, it is argued are final consumers, and should be represented in the consumers' group.

Secondly, the provision making it possible for a meeting of the Consultative Committee to be called, at the request of a majority of its members, to discuss a specific question, should be amended to allow such a meeting at the request of a unanimous group of the Committee, or one third of its members.

Another of the Committee of 21's proposals was that the Assembly should be able to consult the Consultative Committee directly, or, failing that, through the medium of the High Authority. It feels such a provision to be necessary in order that the members of the Assembly, many of whom are not experts on the Community's economic and social questions, should have an opportunity of hearing some technical advice from the Consultative Committee before making policy decisions.

The proposals of the Christian trade unions for the Consulative Committee are far more radical. They would have the Committee become independent of the High Authority, with the power to meet, and discuss all problems of the Community in its own right, and tender advice, which should be published, on its own initiative. They would like to see the Committee considerably enlarged from its present membership of 51. The new Committee could accommodate all representative workers' organisations in the Community, thus enabling the special observer status, held by some trade unionists in lieu of seats on the Committee, to be abolished. The Committee should also seat employers and workers representatives from the coal and steel-using industries. It would be necessary to examine how independent experts, and representatives of consumers organisations should be seated in the larger Committee.

Because of the effect it may have on the employment situation, the Christians would make it an obligation for the High Authority to consult the Consultative Committee before exercising any of its rights concerning agreements and concentrations among enterprises.

One matter on which the Committee of 21 and the Community's Christian Trade Union Federation disagree is whether the present powers of the High Authority and the Council of Ministers, relative to each other, are correctly balanced. The Christians believe that Treaty provisions concerning the composition of the High Authority should remain unaltered, and that, having regard to the provisions of the European Economic Community on similar matters, it is not desirable to amend the relations between High Authority and Council of Ministers at the present time. The Committee of 21 states, quite categorically, that the independence of the High Authority relative to the Council of Ministers should be increased. All the Treaty Articles which require the intervention of the Council should be re-examined with a view to deciding whether this intervention should be maintained or abolished; and, where maintained, whether those provisions now requiring unanimous decisions by the Ministers should need only a qualified majority, and whether those now requiring a qualified majority need only a simple majority.

The ICFTU-affiliated unions have always been mistrustful of the Council of Ministers' powers, and are even more doubtful about the enhanced powers of the Councils for the European Economic Community and Euratom. The main reason for this doubt is that they feel the Council of Ministers does not have the same attachment to the supranational ideal as do the full time executive bodies, or the Assemblies of the Communities. The trade unions are firmly wedded to a demand for more supranational powers in Western Europe, as can be observed in their proposals for modifying the Treaty provisions for the Assembly.

The Christian Federation has expressed the view that this question is best examined in the context of the Economic Community and Euratom agreements, as the ECSC now shares an Assembly with the new Communities. It has therefore refrained from making any proposals for its modification. But the Committee of 21 drafted its proposals much earlier, when the replacement of the old Common Assembly was not imminent. Consequently its proposals relate to that Assembly, but may still be regarded as laying down the general lines of its thinking relative to the new Assembly.

The Committee of 21 would have liked to have seen a development of the powers of the Assembly, and believed that it would be better and more democratic when it could be directly elected by universal suffrage in the Community, instead of being chosen by national parliaments. Provision is made for events to move in this direction by Article 2 of the Convention relating to common institutions in the European Communities. This redrafts Article 21 of the ECSC Treaty, to make provision for the Common Assembly being replaced by the European Assembly, and includes the statement "The Assembly shall draw up proposals for elections by direct universal suffrage in accordance with a uniform procedure in all Member States". In the meantime, the new Assembly is composed in the same way as the old one – by appointment of delegates from national Parliaments.

The main extensions of power which the Committee of 21 would give to the Assembly are "the right of initiative", the power to ratify texts agreed by the Council of Ministers to obviate recourse to national parliaments, the power of political control over the Council of Ministers as well as the High Authority, the right to decide questions on which the High Authority and the Council are in disagreement, the power to dismiss individual members of the Authority in certain circumstances, and greater powers than at present in budgetary matters.

If all these proposals were put into effect, a very large step towards a European Political Community would have been achieved. The Assembly would have what amounted to complete parliamentary powers in Western Europe over the three Communities. In most important respects they would be akin to national parliamentary powers, though in a somewhat more restricted field. There could be no more explicit testimony to the fervour with which the ICFTU-affiliated unions of the six countries advocate full-blooded integration, than these proposals to increase the Assembly's powers.

As far as the Court of Justice is concerned (now a common Court for all three Communities) both the Committee of 21 and the Christian Trade Union Federation are of the opinion that trade union organisations in the Community should be allowed the same right of recourse to the Court as are the Governments, enterprises and associations of enterprises, as defined in the Treaty. The Committee of 21 does not accept the argument that as the trade unions are not subject to the High Authority's jurisdiction, in the way that governments and industries are, they have no grounds for appeals to the Court. It maintains that the workers are the people who feel the consequences of High Authority decisions, finally, and they should therefore have the right of Court appeal.

Economic Provisions

The proposed Treaty amendments examined so far have been largely concerned with social and institutional matters, which affect the organised workers of the Community in a very direct way. Proposals have also been made for the amendment of certain economic provisions of the Treaty. These provisions have a less direct effect on the workers than the others, but are considered important by the trade unions because they impinge on the social provisions, and because they play a large part in setting the tone and direction of the Community's policies— a topic on which the unions feel qualified to express their views, as representative of a large section of public opinion.

The proposals of the Committee of 21 favour an extension of the purposes for which the Community levy can be used. They would have added to Article 50, which enumerates these purposes, powers to contribute to the financing of coal stocks and to the financing of the social investments, already mentioned. In connection with Article 54, which sets out the powers of the High Authority, in regard to investment programmes and financial assistance to enterprises, it is proposed to make these less restricted. Where the High Authority now needs the unanimous approval of the Council of Ministers before it can give financial assistance to enterprises which contribute to increasing production, lowering costs or facilitating marketing; the amended Article would make a simple majority in the Council sufficient. The High Authority should be free to decide on investment programmes which are completely self-financed.

The Committee of 21 was not satisfied with the provisions in the Treaty for keeping down the prices of coal and steel. It suggested that something might be done with Article 61 to improve the position, but no specific proposals were put forward. This Article gives the High Authority power to fix maximum or minimum prices for ECSC products in certain circumstances. The Committee insisted that an improvement in the living conditions of miners was essential, but thought that methods of financing this, other than by high coal prices, could be found. The Committee seems to have indulged in a little wishful thinking here, as it had no concrete proposal, and did not indicate how prices could be kept down merely by clauses in a Treaty.

This attitude on prices is made to look rather strange by comparison with their comment on another aspect of the question. Article 63 of the Treaty gives the High Authority certain powers to prevent discrimination by buyers, and to enforce adherence to the rules of the Community by buyers and agents. The Common Assembly's Market Commission recommended that the High Authority should take direct control of the trade regulating domestic coal supplies, which would possibly mean the amending of Article 63. Surprisingly, the Committee of 21 declared against this on the grounds that it would not be practicable for the High Authority to control the retail trade. It suggested, instead, that the wholesalers should be required to control the retailers, and that the High Authority should persuade the governments to regulate the prices of coal to the final consumer.

The present provisions of the Treaty contained in Articles 65 and 66 come under criticism from the Committee of 21. These Articles deal at length with the High Authority's powers to prevent restrictive agreements, which would be against the public interest, between organisations and concentrations in the coal or steel industries. It was pointed out by the Committee of 21 that new concentrations could not operate in the Community without prior authorisation from the High Authority, but that it has been possible for those formed before the Treaty was established to maintain their existence. It is argued that as the Authority has power to prevent new concentrations coming into existence, it should, logically, be able to liquidate old ones. It is suggested that the present powers, conferred under Article 66, Paragraph 7, to proceed against concentrations, when abuses can be proved, are insufficient, though useful.

A further point that has been made by the Committee on this subject is that the formula devised by the High Authority, under the powers conferred on it in Paragraph 1, of Article 66, for defining the sort of transaction constituting a concentration, is not good enough. The High Authority has decreed that all agreements to form concentrations controlling more than a given percentage of the market must have their prior authorisation. The Committee pointed out that certain concentrations controlling smaller percentages of the market than specified can be more dangerous than the larger ones if, for instance, they operate in one region only, or turn out a product of exceptional quality. Accordingly, it is proposed that the criteria be defined more certainly, and that they be written into the Treaty.

The Committee stated its belief that free competition in the Community's coal industry is incompatible with its best interests, and that there should be some form of organised competition. This should not be achieved through cartels, however, and a compromise between the extremes is suggested. Special organisations should be set up by the High Authority, and under its control, which would ensure a sound system of coal distribution in the public interest. An additional clause permitting this could be written into Article 66.

If the Christian Federation in the ECSC has not been as critical of the economic provisions of the Treaty, it is not because it is diffident about intervening in this general policy field. The reason is that it believes a more satisfactory economic policy could be achieved in the Community by a broader interpretation of the appropriate Articles, as they exist.

The Christians have set out, for the general guidance of the High Authority, what they think should be included in its economic policy. The High Authority should examine how retail prices of coal and steel can be reduced, should publish data relating to cost prices of coal and steel, should make use of levies for the financing of stocks, and should control wholesale and retail prices and conditions of sale. This last point shows a difference of view from the Committee of 21, which believed it impracticable for the High Authority to control the retail trade. But the other three points are generally in accordance with the views of the ICFTU unions of the six countries.

Conclusions

While neither the trade unions affiliated to the Committee of 21, nor the Christian Trade Union Federation in the ECSC, wish to alter the basic principles of the Treaty, both urge modifications in a number of important provisions. The two trade union organisations have spoken with similar voices on many of the suggested modifications.

The Committee of 21 proposals were adopted on 29th May, 1957, and those of the Christian Federation on the 24th January 1958. Although there has been no official co-operation between the two organisations on these proposals, the similarities in them are so close, especially in relation to social provisions, that, bearing in mind the later publication date of the Christian Federation's proposals, it must be assumed that they were inspired by the Committee of 21's document.

It is significant that the main trends of the trade union arguments about the Treaty are towards a more vigorous pursuit of the basic aims and principles in it, rather than for a change in direction. This indicates that the first Western European integration project has been fairly successful, at least as far as satisfying the trade union viewpoint concerning its general intentions. Doubts which were expressed when the scheme was first mooted, especially among German trade unionists, seem to have been largely dispelled in the meantime.

The unions of the six countries have inevitably made comparisons between the ECSC and the more recent Treaties of the European Economic Community and Euratom. In most respects the two latter Treaties have come off badly in the light of the comparison, as far as trade union aspirations are concerned, but there are one or two exceptions. These comparisons are developed in Part 3 of the study. The trade unions are anxious that the ECSC Treaty should not be brought into line with the EEC and Euratom Treaties in those respects where the latter are considered to be inferior.

An examination of the full proposals for the revision of the ECSC Treaty by the two trade union organisations shows that there are four main heads under which their policies can be listed.

(1) An extension of social powers in the Community. This should lead to more money being used for social investment, and a raising of workers' standards in connection with readaptation, housing, health and safety. Wages, conditions and social security benefits should be harmonised in an upward direction, but without prejudice to the present right of trade unions to bargain freely with employers. The ICFTU unions would agree to common policies on wages and conditions if governments gave the High Authority powers to pursue a common economic and employment policy.

(2) Extended trade union rights in the Community. These would

include a higher proportion of trade unionists on the High Authority's Consultative Committee and the establishment of the right of trade union organisations to appeal to the Court.

(3) Greater supranational powers for the Community. These would include greater powers for the High Authority to take independent action on readaptation schemes and on uses of Community finance, particularly for social purposes. They should also, according to the Committee of 21, have greater powers *vis-à-vis* the Council of Ministers. The Assembly's powers should also be increased, and it should become a form of international parliament.

(4) Increased economic powers in certain fields. These, if used properly, would enable prices to be kept down, possible abuses by large private economic empires to be eliminated, and the regulation of competition and distribution to avoid malpractices.

If the trade unions feel, as they do, that the European Coal and Steel Community is less than perfect in these respects, it is not surprising that they feel the Treaties of the European Economic Community and Euratom are somewhat less satisfactory. A study of the provisions of these latter Treaties shows that, generally speaking, there is a partial retreat from just those policies and powers which the trade unions wished to see extended in the ECSC.

PART THREE

THE WIDER INTEGRATION PROJECTS

CHAPTER X

THE ROME TREATIES

Much of the experience gained by the trade unions in their work in the European Coal and Steel Community has gone into determining their attitude to subsequent integration projects in Western Europe, and into the erection of new structures for trade unionism, which will enable unions to act with efficiency and assurance on whatever problems arise.

Before studying trade union aspects of the new integration projects, it is necessary to review, briefly, just what the connecting links are between the latter and earlier projects, to sketch in the general background to the Treaties and to give an indication of their chief provisions. Because of the rapidity with which events moved in the latter 1950's, concerning Western European integration, and because of the multiplicity of names and initials which have consequently found their way into political and economic vocabularies, a good deal of misunderstanding has resulted. This is particularly so in European countries which are not among the six of "Little Europe". In Britain, especially, distinctions between the various projects of the "Six", and the more widely discussed Free Trade Area and Free Trade Association, are hazy to many people, trade unionists included.

It had been intended that the European Coal and Steel Community, set up in 1952, should be followed by projects to integrate the Western European defence and political systems, through the European Defence Community (EDC) and the European Political Community, for both of which Treaties were drafted. But plans failed to materialise when the French Parliament rejected EDC in August, 1954. The next major move was not made until the Foreign Ministers of the "Six" met in Messina in June, 1955. This meeting paved the way for the European Economic Community (EEC) and the European Atomic Energy Community, or Euratom.

At this Messina meeting, proposals to set up two such Communities were submitted by the Benelux countries, and it was decided to set up a special committee under Paul Henri Spaak, the Belgian Foreign Minister, to go into the question. Since this meeting, the six countries have frequently been called the Messina Powers.

The report of the Spaak Committee, which dealt thoroughly with the mechanics and techicalities of setting up the Communities, was discussed by a further meeting of the Foreign Ministers in Venice, in May, 1956, and was adopted as a sound basis for negotiating the necessary Treaties. Much of the final work was done by a treaty-drafting conference, also under M. Spaak; and after outstanding points of difference had been settled, the Treaties were signed in Rome on 25 March 1957, and the necessary ratifications in the Parliaments of the "Six" countries were completed by December the same year. They became known as the Rome Treaties, and came into force on 1 January 1958, with major action reserved until a year later.

The European Economic Community

The technical name for an association of countries operating a common market is a customs union – a term laid down by the General Agreement on Tariffs and Trade (GATT). However, the agreement of the "Six" has become widely known as the Common Market, a rather more expressive name. When the Treaty was signed, it was decided to give it another new name – the European Economic Community – a title more suited to an agreement that goes well beyond the field of commerce in its provisions. But because the name is more widely known, it will subsequently be referred to as the Common Market on most occasions, in this study.

One of the vital provisions of the Common Market Treaty is to bring a customs union into existence – that is, to erect a common tariff barrier around the six countries, rather than have each maintain its own separate tariffs at differing levels, in respect of the same goods. The three Benelux countries, which are now in the larger Community, have had their own customs union since 1948; and Belgium and Luxembourg had their own customs union as far back as 1922. The new Treaty provides for a common tariff against imports from outside countries, which will be an average of tariffs in force in the six countries as at 1 January 1957. By the end of the transitional period of the Common Market (12 to 15 years), the new common tariff will have been introduced – in most cases by stages, at four-yearly intervals.

The new market consists of about 165 million people, and allows for greater specialisation and efficiency, leading, it is expected, to higher productivity and standards of living. Internal import duties on goods moving between member states will be reduced, in stages over the transitional period, by fixed percentages, and will be abolished altogether after 12 to 15 years. When the first reduction of 10% was made in 1959, the "Six" decided, however, to extend it to all member countries of

GATT. The stages are intended to be four-yearly periods but may be extended if the necessary progress has not been made. But the total transitional period must not exceed fifteen years, and, at the time of writing, the "Six" were considering shortening this.

During the same time, import quotas must be increased by percentages, at intervals, until they cease to be restrictive, and export duties and quantitative restrictions must all be be removed by the end of the first stage of the transitional period.

Tariffs on agricultural products will also be abolished, but a free market will not operate in this field. A common policy is being worked out, resulting in an organisation being set up to regulate the markets and the prices in accordance with needs and resources. For transport, also, a common policy is being worked out, which will abolish discriminatory rates and state subsidies.

Agriculture and transport are special cases requiring common policies, but the aim of the Common Market is to harmonise the general economic policies of the member states, as well. To this end, the signatories aim at a common commercial policy concerning the rest of the world, common regulations to restrict monopolies and associations working against the general interest, a suppression of state subsidies or other policies which distort competition, and common action to iron out exchange rate and balance of payments difficulties. In these respects, the Common Market may have a higher degree of international co-ordination and community feeling than the ECSC Treaty made allowance for.

Social policies are also to be co-ordinated, particularly in respect of readaptation schemes, mobility of labour, industrial insurance, conditions of employment, social security and the setting up of a European Social Fund.

Other special funds which are to be set up include one for giving aid to underdeveloped regions in Europe, controlled by a European Investment Bank, and a fund for the development of those overseas territories of member states which are to be associated with the Common Market. The overseas territories will be able to compete with Community products on equal terms, and the economic preferences which have existed between those territories and the particular countries with which they have had special arrangements, will become applicable to all member states.

All the funds mentioned, and also general finance, will be raised from the member states in equitable proportions, mainly on the basis of their capacity to pay, which has been worked out in advance. In the case of the fund for development of overseas territories, allocations for expenditure have been made in proportion to the size and need of the territories concerned. Out of a total of 581.25 million dollars to be contributed in the first five years, the territories associated with France will receive the lion's share–511.25 million dollars.

For general finance, a study is to be made of the possibility of replacing government contributions by the Community's own resources–particularly by revenue accruing from the common tariff.

The Common Market will ensure that workers, capital and services are free to move within the Community by the end of the transitional period. There will be a method of centralising information regarding the availability of jobs and labour, and provisions will be made to ensure that the minimum of hardship arises from labour movement. Capital movement will be freed, except in dangerous economic circumstances, and a plan to allow services to be offered, without distinction, is to be drawn up. Rules will be made for the common recognition of individual qualifications, and all restrictions on the freedom of establishment of enterprises are to be abolished.

The institutions of the Common Market are modelled fairly closely on those of the Coal and Steel Community. There is an Assembly, a Commission of nine members, a Council and a Court of Justice. The Commission is roughly the equivalent of the High Authority in the Coal and Steel Community, and the consultative body which assists it, instead of being called the Consultative Committee, as in the ECSC, is named the Economic and Social Committee, and has a rather different basis of composition. The Committee is a common institution for the Common Market and Euratom.

The Assembly and the Court of Justice are common institutions for the Common Market, Euratom and the Coal and Steel Community, and replace the Assembly and Court previously operating in the last-named.

The European Atomic Energy Community

Commonly known as Euratom, this integration project, which was negotiated and signed in parallel with the Common Market Treaty, has received comparatively little publicity–perhaps because it was overshadowed by the larger project. It is, nevertheless, of great importance, being an effort by the same six countries to pool their resources and their knowledge, to develop nuclear energy for peaceful purposes. They believe that this common action will make Europe capable of developments in production which cannot be achieved by independent working. Standards of living in the Community would thereby be raised, and trade with other countries increased. Britain has concluded a co-operation agreement with Euratom.

Although it shares an Assembly, a Court of Justice and an Economic and Social Committee, Euratom has a Commission of its own, containing five members, and also a Council of Ministers.

Article 2 of the Euratom Treaty sets out, concisely, the intentions of the provisions in the rest of the Treaty:

"For the attainment of its aims the Community shall, in accordance with the provisions set out in the Treaty:

(a) develop research and ensure the dissemination of technical knowledge,

(b) establish, and ensure the application of, uniform safety standards to protect the health of workers and of the general public,

(c) facilitate investment and ensure, particularly by encouraging business enterprise, the construction of the basic facilities required for the development of nuclear energy within the Community,

(d) ensure a regular and equitable supply of ores and nuclear fuels to all users in the Community,

(e) guarantee, by appropriate measures of control, that nuclear materials are not diverted for purposes other than those for which they are intended,

(f) exercise the property rights conferred upon it in respect of special fissionable materials,

(g) ensure extensive markets and access to the best technical means by the creation of a common market for specialised materials and equipment, by the free movement of capital for nuclear investment, and by freedom of employment for specialists within the Community,

(h) establish with other countries and with international organisations any contacts likely to promote progress in the peaceful uses of nuclear energy."

An interesting aspect of the Euratom Treaty is the possibility it gives of supranational powers being exercised, which would be unrivalled in any other integration project. Article 52 specifies that a commercial Agency shall be set up which shall have a right of option on all ores, raw materials and special fissile materials produced in the territory of member states, and with the exclusive right of concluding contracts for the supply of ores, raw materials and special fissile materials originating inside or outside the Community. The Agency is a corporate body, and financially independent, but is under the ultimate control of the Commission, which may veto its decisions. Another innovation is the provision that special fissile material shall be the property of the Community.

In summary, it can be said that the Rome Treaties owe a great deal to the inspiration of the ECSC, and many of their provisions follow closely on its precedents. The Rome Treaties owe their direct origin to a proposal of the Benelux countries put to a meeting of the six Foreign Ministers in Messina, in 1955, some little time after those countries had failed to set up a military integration project, the European Defence Community. The Common Market and Euratom Treaties both came into operation in January 1958.

The Common Market will eliminate, over a transitional period of 12 to 15 years, all restrictions on trade between the member countries and erect a common tariff wall around the Community. Agriculture and transport will be co-ordinated by special provisions, but the Community will also endeavour to co-ordinate economic, commercial and social policies on a fairly wide scale. Special funds will be set up for social purposes and for economic development in Europe. Another fund will help development in associated overseas territories, which form part of the Common Market. There will be freedom of movement for labour, capital and services. Both the Common Market and Euratom have a Commission, a Council of Ministers, an Assembly, a Court of Justice and an Economic and Social Committee. The Assembly and Court are shared between three Communities, including the ECSC.

Euratom is a project to co-ordinate the efforts of the "Little Europe" countries in the field of nuclear energy development, which it is believed has great potentialities for increasing living standards and trade. Work will be co-ordinated in the fields of research, security, investment and supply supervision, and the Community will own special fissile material, create a common market in materials and equipment and establish relations with outside countries and organisations. There will be an appreciable measure of supranational control.

CHAPTER XI

THE TRADE UNIONS AND THE ROME TREATIES

As in the case of the European Coal and Steel Community Treaty, the general reaction of the trade unions to the Common Market and Euratom Treaties has been that they are a start in the right direction, and therefore to be fully supported, but that they do not travel anything like far enough along the road to full economic integration. An editorial in the ICFTU's magazine "Free Labour World", for April 1957, said that the Common Market Treaty, just signed, "is the result of a compromise and is a pale shadow of the original idea".

The section of the ICFTU European Regional Organisation's special conference, which represented the trade unions of the Common Market countries, passed a resolution on the Common Market, in May 1957, which read, in part:

> "that the Free Trade Unions' objectives are aimed at replacing the existing overnationalistic tendencies which have not been eliminated from the present Treaty, by a regime in which truly community-inspired conceptions prevail."

As far as Euratom is concerned, the editorial referred to in "Free Labour World" observed that this Treaty was also a compromise, and only a beginning; and that the pooling of efforts on atomic energy questions would have to be extended if its use for peaceful purposes only were to be guaranteed. Otherwise the Treaty would not become of real importance to the man in the street.

In order to find out why the trade unions believe the Rome Treaties fall short of the desirable, it is necessary to examine the more detailed criticisms which were made of them when they were in draft. It is also necessary to compare them with the ECSC Treaty, bearing in mind the observations already made on it by the trade unions, in the light of their own experience.

The detailed criticisms of the Rome Treaties have been made, not by the Committee of 21, which dealt with the ECSC Treaty, but by the ERO, which represents most of the national trade union federations in Western Europe, and not just those of the "Six". Although there are few fundamental differences of viewpoint between these two bodies of

ICFTU unions, on integration questions, there are naturally, some differences of emphasis appearing in the comments on the Rome Treaties, and which might be mistaken for inconsistencies, when compared with ECSC Treaty comments, if prior knowledge of the different authorship were not recognised.

The same thing applies to the comments of the Christian unions. The critique on the ECSC Treaty was made by the Federation of Christian Trade Unions in the ECSC, whereas the comments on the Rome Treaties are made by the International Federation of Christian Trade Unions (CISC), from the Brussels headquarters. Their comments have been rather less detailed than those of the ERO.

The main trade union criticisms of the Rome Treaties are centred around their belief that the rate at which Western Europe is moving towards truly supranational authorities is too slow. Indeed, it has been suggested that, following on the ECSC, the Rome Treaties are a backward step in this regard.

It is true that in a number of respects there is less likelihood of supranational powers being used effectively in the Common Market Treaty, for instance, than in the ECSC Treaty. This does not necessarily mean that a deliberate decision was made to retain more national powers than under the other Treaty. It does mean that supranational provisions tend to be conditional in the Common Market. This is really an admission that practical difficulties are much greater in a project of this magnitude. There is also the factor that shifts in the economic and political circumstances in certain countries have made a modification of policies necessary since the ECSC Treaty was signed.

The ECSC Treaty negotiators assumed a supranational authority for coal and steel as a precondition for entering into discussions. The Spaak Committee, which produced the drafts of the Rome Treaties, knew that such a precondition would probably have been unacceptable to potential members. Accordingly, the documents were drafted on the basis of expert reports on the feasibility of introducing a common market. The institutional structure and powers had to be within the limits the technicalities would allow, if a practical solution to integration difficulties was to be found.

The trade unions have certainly been aware of the difficulties experienced in negotiating the Treaties, and of the complex political situations which limited the manoeuvrability of the national negotiators. While it is true to say that the unions believe that more could have been achieved, it would be unwise to assume that they are convinced that all their proposals could have been written into the draft Treaties, with any good chance of them being implemented.

What the trade unions have done is to put themselves on record as advocating the ideals at which they believe the European Communities should aim. It may be concluded that trade union disappointment over the limitations of the Treaties is exceeded by their pleasure that the Treaties are in operation, at last.

The general lines of trade union criticism of the Rome Treaties can be conveniently classified under the same heads as those which grouped the ECSC Treaty revision proposals. That is, a desire for:

(1) An extension of social powers in the Communities.
(2) Extended trade union rights in the Communities.
(3) Greater supranational powers for the Communities.
(4) Increased economic powers in certain fields.

They must be examined, one by one.

Social Powers

Both the ERO and the CISC have regretted the lack of provision in the Common Market Treaty for an active social policy to be pursued by the Community, or its institutions. Both would like to see Articles in the Treaty committing the Commission and the Council to certain definite social obligations. What references there are to general social objectives are more vague, even, than those in the ECSC Treaty. In the social field, the Commission and the Council are given permissive powers rather than specific duties.

As far as readaptation provisions are concerned, the trade union pleas that these must be written into the Treaty have been accepted, but the unions are not completely satisfied with the form which they take.

A European Social Fund is being set up under the Treaty, financed by contributions from the member states, roughly in proportion to their capacity to pay. Its task is to promote "employment facilities and the geographical and occupational mobility of workers" (Article 123).

The Fund is intended to cover 50% of expenses used for the purposes of ensuring productive re-employment of workers by means of occupational retraining, resettlement allowances and granting aids to workers where employment or remuneration would otherwise suffer owing to the conversion of their enterprise to other forms of production (Article 125). However, the request for such aid must come first from a member state, and Article 127 empowers the Council to fix the conditions under which assistance may be granted. It can only do this on the proposal of the Commission, and after the Economic and Social Committee and the Assembly have been consulted.

A further severe restriction is that assistance granted by the Fund for occupational retraining, resettlement allowances, or to maintain wage levels during changeover, are all subject to a waiting time of six months. In the case of assistance due to conversions, there is a further restriction that the plans for the conversion must previously have been submitted to, and passed by, the Commission. In any case, the Council has first to decide on the categories of enterprises where workers will be eligible for this type of assistance, and it can only do so after negotiations with the other Community institutions.

Article 126 provides that the Council, after going through the consultative procedure, may decide the future of the Fund, and the forms of assistance mentioned, from the end of the transitional period. It can decide, by a qualified majority, that all, or part, of these forms of assistance shall cease. Unanimously, it may determine new tasks for the Fund.

Notwithstanding all these restrictions, Article 124 states that the administration of the Fund is the Commission's responsibility, and that it is to be assisted in the task by a Committee presided over by a member of the Commission, and composed of representatives of Governments, trade unions and employers' associations.

The ERO has welcomed the decision to set up this committee, but on all the other provisions concerning the European Social Fund, has expressed many doubts. It dislikes the restrictions on the use of the Fund, and particularly the six month waiting period for assistance. Too much depends on the Council, and the Commission has less power to act on its own initiative than does the High Authority of the ECSC, which the unions had wished to see strengthened in this regard. There is a feeling that the procedure for granting assistance is so elaborate that it may stifle the whole scheme.

On the other hand, it is difficult to make criticisms of the Treaty Articles concerned, as specifically as was possible with the ECSC. The powers of the Commission and the Council could actually be greater than in the ECSC, depending on how it is decided to interpret the Articles. The permissive powers are there, but the trade unions will not be able to pinpoint the faults of the Fund until some years of experience have shown how the provisions are interpreted in practice.

The trade unions are disappointed that none of the extensions of readaptation, proposed for the ECSC, have been adopted in principle in the Rome Treaties. These are that the Community should not have to wait for a government request before taking action and giving assistance, that local organisations should be given some power of initiative in approach for assistance, and that the Community should be able to finance more than 50% of the scheme if the occasion demanded.

It is possible, however, that the new Treaty Articles, if generously interpreted, could give power to act when unemployment arose through causes rather more diverse than those provided for in the ECSC. If so, the unions would have gained a point.

As the Rome Treaties were negotiated before the Committee of 21 proposals on the ECSC were published, those proposals, as such, could not have influenced the Treaty negotiations. But the trade union movements had made their general views on readaptation and other questions known well before the Rome Treaties were drafted, so that it is quite relevant to make comparisons based on ECSC revision proposals.

There are a number of social provisions in the Treaty which the trade union movements have found pleasing. One of them is contained in Article 119, and provides that during the first stage of the transitional period of the Common Market, member states will introduce or maintain a system of equal pay for equal work as between men and women, whether working on time rates or piece rates, and will include all emoluments in the principle, as well as basic rates of pay. The unions have no complaints about this provision.

They are also pleased about the provisions concerning the payment of overtime, contained in a special protocol dealing with matters of concern to France. In the protocol the opinion is expressed that by the end of the first stage, overtime rates in member countries' industries will correspond to those existing in France. If they do not, France will be authorised to take protective measures for the industries affected, under the supervision of the Commission. The proviso for this action by France is that, in the meantime, the average increase in the wages level in other countries has not exceeded, by a specified percentage, that occurring in France.

There should be two main effects of this arrangement. Firstly, that French employers will not find themselves at a competitive disadvantage in maintaining their present high rate for overtime payments, either because other countries will level up to them, or because the base rate on which they are calculated in those other countires will increase more rapidly than France's, during the first stage. This latter process would tend to eliminate the extra burden of French labour costs. The second effect may well be spontaneous efforts by industrial interests in other member countries to harmonise their overtime rates with France, to avoid sudden safeguard measures against them which would jeopardise their competitive positions after the first stage. Failing these alternatives, co-ordination by the governments is a possibility. In any case the trade unions will feel that a real gain has been made by their members.

The third example of the Treaty dealing directly with conditions of employment is Article 120, which states simply: "Member States shall endeavour to maintain the existing equivalence of paid holiday schemes." Until it is seen how this is interpreted, the Article can be satisfactory to nobody, as the phrase "existing equivalence" could mean many things, or nothing.

Treaty Article 48, which is satisfactory to the trade unions, deals with the free movement of workers. It is quite categorical, and more far-reaching than the comparable ECSC provision, when it says: "The free movement of workers shall be ensured within the Community not later than at the date of the expiry of the transitional period". There is no limiting reference to "workers of recognised qualifications", as in the ECSC Treaty. The only limitation in the Common Market will be on employees in public administration. All others may move freely, and employment, remuneration and working conditions in their new country must be the same as that given to the nationals of that country.

The Commission and Council, in consultation with the Economic and Social Committee, are given the task of inaugurating some form of machinery "for connecting offers of employment and requests for employment, with a view to equilibrating them in such a way as to avoid serious threats to the standard of living and employment in the various regions and industries." (Article 49.)

Further encouragement to mobility is given in Article 50, which provides for a common programme to encourage the exchange of young workers, and in Article 51, which provides for a system to be worked out whereby social security benefits will carry over without loss, on the basis of qualifying periods, to a worker who moves to another Community country. This latter provision, when implemented, will meet a long-standing trade union demand.

Another trade union demand has been for the upward harmonisation of social benefits in an integrated Europe, for reasons outlined in Chapter Three. The Common Market Treaty does not give any specific guarantee that this will take place, but there are provisions whereby such a policy could be implemented, depending on Treaty interpretation. It is useful to consider the full texts of Treaty Articles 117 and 118, in this connection.

"Article 117

Member States hereby agree upon the necessity to promote improvement of the living and working conditions of labour so as to permit the equalisation of such conditions in an upward direction.
They consider that such a development will result not only from the

functioning of the Common Market which will favour the harmonisation of social systems, but also from the procedures provided for
under this Treaty and from the approximation of legislative and
administrative provisions.

Article 118

Without prejudice to the other provisions of this Treaty and in conformity with its general objectives, it shall be the aim of the Commission to promote close collaboration between Member States in the
social field, particularly in matters relating to: employment, labour
legislation and working conditions, occupational and continuation
training, social security, protection against occupational accidents and
diseases, industrial hygiene, the law as to trade unions, and collective
bargaining between employers and workers.

For this purpose, the Commission shall act in close contact with
Member States by means of studies, the issuing of opinions, and the
organising of consultations both on problems arising at the national
level and on those of concern to international organisations.

Before issuing the opinions provided for under this Article, the Commission shall consult the Economic and Social Committee."

The Articles are loosely worded, and do not lay down a social policy.
But they do pave the way for a very progressive policy, if the Commission and the member states follow through on the lines indicated.

As far as social security systems are concerned, Articles 100 and 101
open up further possibilities of them being harmonised upwards. They
provide for the approximation of legislative and administrative provisions of member states in certain circumstances, where they have a
direct effect on the establishment or functioning of the Common Market,
and particularly where disparities in these provisions distort the conditions of competition.

Both trade unions and employers in Common Market countries have
held that differing levels of charges in the social security systems do
distort the conditions of competition; but evidence from other sources
has called this in question, on the grounds that social security cannot be
considered in isolation from other economic influences. A report by a
group of ILO experts[1] has concluded that as taxes levied for social
security purposes, in whatever form, are only one element affecting
conditions of production and employment in a country's economic

---

1. "Social Aspects of European Economic Co-operation: Report by a Group of
Experts", *Studies and Reports*, New Series, No. 46. ILO, Geneva, 1956, paras.
172 and 173.

policy, it is doubtful whether harmonisation in this field, alone, would be desirable.

It is argued that if harmonisation is to be considered, it should be considered, at the same time, for other aspects of economic policy which may, themselves, have distorting effects on trade. Furthermore, even if a fairly wide range of economic and social policies were harmonised, it would not necessarily mean that a less distorted structure of production and trade would result. They conclude that such harmonisation should be attempted only if the inequalities in the pattern of production and trade are substantial, and if the systems in operation in one or more countries give rise to considerable, uncompensated, inequalities in the burdens as between the various industries within the same countries.

The ERO has concurred in as far as it has stated that a harmonisation of general social conditions in the Community would necessitate the harmonisation of monetary policies first. But as far as social security benefits are concerned, in isolation from other factors, the trade unions would still like to see these harmonised upwards, if only because they have the welfare of their members in mind, international economic policies apart.

To revert to Article 118 of the Common Market Treaty, this also made provision for the Commission to promote the collaboration of member states on a number of questions, including industrial safety and hygiene. The proposals must be a disappointment to the unions, because of their limitations. Both the Committee of 21 and the Christian Trade Union Federation, in Luxembourg, have urged that the ECSC High Authority should have wider powers in this field, including the financing of studies and the publication of results. It appears that the Commission does not have wider powers than the High Authority in this regard.

In the case of the Euratom Treaty, the provisions for industrial health and safety are more rigorous, as becomes the nature of the dangerous materials with which it is concerned. The trade unions had demanded that the Treaty should be used in connection with the peaceful aspects of atomic energy, only, and this plea has been heeded. The ERO had laid stress on the need for adequate health and safety precautions for workers and general public, alike, and this has also become one of the Treaty's main intentions.

Articles 30 to 39 deal with health protection, and should be farreaching in their effect. The Commission is endowed with the task of working out basic standards, in conjunction with experts, for the protection of health of workers and public, in order to determine the maximum degree of radiation permissible for individuals, and the means of medical supervision for workers. These must be confirmed by the Council and the Assembly, after consultations between the Commission and the Economic and Social Committee. Member states must then introduce legislation in accordance with these standards. For particularly dangerous experiments, member states must consult the Commission and adopt extraordinary health precautions.

Control facilities for the level of radioactivity in atmosphere, water and soil must be set up, to which the Commission will have access. It must be kept informed by member states of their levels of radioactivity. It will make recommendations concerning this level, and will have power to enforce compliance with basic standards, if necessary, through the Court. The Commission must be consulted on the disposal of radio-active waste, and it must set up a Section for documentation on, and study of, health protection within the Joint Nuclear Research Centre, to be established.

Supranational responsibilities in the field of health and safety in nuclear industry are wide, and appear to satisfy the trade unions, in most respects.

On the question of research in the Communities, there is provision for technical study programmes and research in the Euratom Treaty, but little on social research, such as the ECSC trade unions proposed, in either of the Rome Treaties. While there is nothing specific, Articles 118 and 122 of the Common Market Treaty appear to open the possibility of some such research being undertaken if the Commission wish to do so. The first of these provides that the Commission shall act in close contact with member states in order to promote close collaboration on a wide range of social topics by means of studies, and other methods. The second makes it incumbent on the Commission to include a chapter on the development of the social situation in its annual report to the Assembly. The Assembly may invite the Commission to draw up reports on special problems concerning the social situation.

Such powers, if widely interpreted, could undoubtedly put in hand enough social research to satisfy the trade unions, but the provisions, as they stand, do nothing to satisfy the desire for specific obligations in these matters. The unions will have to rest content until they see, over a period, how the Articles are interpreted by the Commission.

The trade unions in the ECSC have asked for the High Authority to be given more powers to use Community finance for programmes of social investment, including research, health and safety measures; and most important of all, workers' housing. There is no specific provision in the Common Market Treaty for this, and there is no mention of housing. But, again, a particular Treaty Article may cover it, if so interpreted. It is Article 130, defining the functions of the European Investment Bank.

The Bank, it states, cannot subsidise schemes, but only grant loans and guarantees on a non-profit-making basis, for financing projects for developing less developed regions. Loans could also be granted for projects of interest to one or more member states, particularly for modernising or converting enterprises or creating new activities which are too large to be financed by the available means in member states. However, it is specifically stated that such projects may be in all sectors of the economy. It seems possible, therefore, that this could cover social projects, including housing; but if read in conjunction with Article 20 of the special protocol on the Bank, it would appear to need a rather specialised interpretation to make it do so. This Article makes it a condition of granting loans, or providing guarantees for projects, that "the execution of the project contributes to the increase of economic productivity in general and promotes the development of the Common Market".

In the overseas territories of the member states the prospects for social investment are somewhat brighter. The special Development Fund, into which members will pay, during the first five years, a total of 581.25 million dollars, for use in the overseas territories, may be used for social as well as economic purposes.

The Commission, which administers the Fund, is obliged to draw up general programmes, annually, for the allocation of finance to different projects. Article 3 of the special Implementing Convention relating to the association of Overseas Territories, states that these general programmes shall include schemes to finance: "certain social institutions, in particular, hospitals, teaching or technical research establishments and institutions for vocational training and for the promotion of professional activities among the populations". These are in addition to "economic investments of general interest"; and the whole programmes are intended to ensure that technical development projects do not outstrip the pace of social and general development.

The ERO has welcomed the idea of the association of the overseas territories of member states with the Common Market, and in a statement issued shortly before the signing of the Rome Treaties, said that it had always favoured a maximum joint effort aimed at the economic and social development of these territories. But such association must not be carried through in any way which would hamper the political evolutions of the territories, or the human aspirations of their populations.

The ERO also expressed the belief that: "any measures intended to associate overseas territories with the Common Market shall be undertaken only with the consent and the co-operation of the peoples of the territories concerned. Regardless of the degree of self-government which these people have reached, they must be given the right through appropriate channels, to express their views on all questions of concern to them".[2] The CISC made a similar comment, about the same time, and added that consultations with representative trade union organisations of the territories should be held to discuss the social objectives of the association.

Although their advice was not taken, the trade union movements have continued to support the association, in the belief that it will open new opportunities for the territories and peoples concerned.

Of social powers in general, it may be said that few specific ones are provided for in either of the Rome Treaties, as the trade unions would have wished. But if the Commissions and the Councils feel so inclined, in either case, they can interpret the wording of the Treaties so as to give themselves ample scope to carry out far-reaching social policies in the Communities.

Trade Union Rights and Influence

Both the ERO and the CISC are disappointed at the comparatively small responsibilities which trade unions and trade unionists are allotted under the Rome Treaties, and with regard to the allocation of seats on Community institutions. The reason for this must be examined.

The Economic and Social Committee is the rough equivalent of the ECSC High Authority's Consultative Committee, and operates for both the Common Market and Euratom, with appropriate specialised sections for Euratom, and for agriculture and transport in the Common Market. It may have sub-committees working in specific fields, or on specific problems.

Whereas the ECSC Consultative Committee had 51 members, the Economic and Social Committee has 101, made up of 24 each from Germany, France and Italy, 12 each from Belgium and the Netherlands, and 5 from Luxembourg. The Christian trade unions in the ECSC had wanted an enlargement of their Consultative Committee, to bring in wider interests, but had had in mind maintaining the parity between employers and workers. They are certainly uneasy, as is the ERO, about an enlargement of the kind laid down in the Rome Treaties.

The specific ECSC formula of one third of the seats each to groups representing producers, workers, and consumers and dealers, is gone. Instead, Article 193 of the Common Market Treaty lays it down that:

2. *Free Labour World*, February 1957, p. 48.

"The Committee shall be composed of representatives of the various categories of economic and social life, in particular, representatives of producers, agriculturists, transport operators, workers, merchants, artisans, the liberal professions and of the general interest."

Trade unionists have been given 35 seats on the Committee, or approximately one third of the membership. The unions have protested, as they did in the ECSC, that this is insufficient, and makes it likely that their votes will be swamped by employers. The reason is that certain people nominally called to service on the Committee as representatives of some interest group other than producers, are also, as it happens, employers. Together with the producers' group they outnumber trade unionists. The trade unions claims that there are 45 members of the Economic and Social Committee who are actually employers.

In the case of the Consultative Committee, the representative organisations nominated by the Council submitted their own lists from which individuals were appointed. Under the Rome Treaties, the lists are submitted by the member states, for the Council to choose from. This is not a particularly good omen for the trade unions. In the ECSC, members were appointed for two years; under the Rome Treaties, the mandate is for four years. In all three Communities the members are appointed in their personal capacities, and must not be mandated by outside organisations or interests.

There is no provision in the Rome Treaties for the Economic and Social Committee to be convened by its President, on the request of a majority of its members, as there was for the ECSC's Committee. The President may only convene it at the request of the Council or the Commission. This will be regarded by the unions as a backward step, as the Committee of 21 had been pressing for the ECSC Consultative Committee's President to have the power to call it together at the unanimous request of one of its Groups, or one third of its members.

Whereas in the ECSC Treaty, it was only the High Authority which had the specific duty to consult its Committee where prescribed, in the Rome Treaties this is obligatory on both the Commission and the Council, where prescribed, and the prescription appears quite frequently in Treaty Articles. In any other cases, the Commission and the Council may consult their Committee whenever deemed appropriate, as could the High Authority. In the new Treaties, therefore, it is quite possible that the Committee will have more to do, and have more influence than its ECSC counterpart, although it is not possible to tell, as yet, whether the trade union members will have as much influence.

There is no provision in the Rome Treaties whereby the Assembly may consult the Economic and Social Committee, as the Committee of 21 proposed there should be in the ECSC, for its Consultative Committee. Neither is there any concession to the ECSC Christian Trade Union point of view, that the Committee should have greater independence, with the right to meet on its own initiative, discuss what it wished, and submit advice to the Community institutions (unsolicited if necessary), and publish it. There is a marked determination in the Rome Treaty provisions to keep the Committee in its place as a body with purely consultative status.

It will be remembered that there were a number of other channels through which trade union influence operated in the ECSC institutions, apart from the Consultative Committee. One of the important ones was through the trade union members on the High Authority. The ERO has constantly stressed that trade unionists should be represented, similarly, on the Commissions of the Common Market and Euratom; and, indeed, on as many other Community institutions as possible, if the integration projects are going to be realistic in outlook, and bear the concerns of ordinary people in mind.

In spite of trade unions having a third of the High Authority membership for a good period, not a single trade unionist has been appointed to the Commissions of the Common Market or of Euratom, which is a great disappointment, keenly felt by the unions. The Common Market Commission has nine members, and the Euratom Commission five. Their terms of office are for four years, and they are appointed by the governments of member states, acting in common agreement.

For Euratom, the members must each be of different nationality, and in fact, one person from each member country, except Luxembourg, has been appointed, including a French President. This was Louis Armand, in the first instance, but on his resignation he was replaced by fellow-countryman Etienne Hirsch, in January 1959. The Common Market Commission may not contain more than two members of the same nationality. Those actually appointed are two Germans, including Walter Hallstein, the President, two Frenchmen, two Italians, one Dutchman, one Belgian and one member from Luxembourg.

Once decided among the member states how many seats are to go to each of them, the individual governments, naturally, have the main voice in determining to whom the seats of their own nationals shall go. As far as is known, only the Italian Government offered a seat to a trade unionist for the Common Market Commission, and when this individual was unable to accept, the trade unions were left without any representation.

The Italian trade unionist concerned was Giulio Pastore, then General

Secretary of the CISL, the larger of the two national trade union centres in that country affiliated to the ICFTU. Pastore is a member of the Italian Parliament, and after the death of Di Vittorio, the former General Secretary of the WFTU-affiliated CGIL, was, perhaps, the best known trade union leader in the country. This was probably the reason that he declined the offer at the time, perhaps against his personal inclination. It is widely thought that the initiative of the non-communist trade union movements in Italy may have fallen behind that of their communist rival, if Pastore had left at so critical a time, and that this is why the offer of the seat was declined. Since then, however, he has been replaced as CISL General Secretary, after being appointed a Government Minister.

The trade unions have been pleased to note the provision of Article 124 of the Common Market Treaty, concerned with the functioning of the European Social Fund. This states that in administering the Fund the Commission shall be assisted by a Committee composed of representatives of Governments, trade unions and employers' associations.

In the case of the European Investment Bank the Board of Directors are appointed by the Board of Governors (composed of Ministers of member states) on the nomination of member states and the Commission. There are twelve directors and twelve alternates, and they are the main controlling body of the Bank, working within the general objectives laid down by the Board of Governors. The trade unions have one representative, Roger Boyer, who sits as an alternate on the Board of Directors.

The trade unions expressed the hope that there would be at least one person with trade union experience designated as one of the seven judges of the Court of Justice, as there was when the ECSC Court was set up. The hope has not been borne out. The one trade unionist from the Christian Movement who was on the original ECSC Court, no longer has a seat on the new Court which replaces it, and acts for the three Communities.

One extension of trade union rights that had been hoped for, and advocated in ECSC revision proposals, was that the unions should have the right of appeal to the Court on matters of Treaty interpretation. No provision is made for this in the new Court. The right of appeal is given to member states, the Council and the Commission, on grounds of incompetence, errors of substantial form, infringement of the Treaty or of any legal provision relating to its application, or of abuse of power.

The right of appeal also applies to "any natural or legal person", under the same conditions. But this appears to exclude trade unions because it applies only in the cases of appeals against decisions addressed to that person, or if it is of direct and specific concern to him. The

Commission or the Council have, of course, no powers to address decisions to trade union organisations. The unions are disappointed that they should have no right of appeal on matters of Treaty interpretation, particularly when these can be of direct concern to them.

Supranational Powers

Both the ERO and the CISC have a preference for strong supranational powers and institutions to control Western European integration projects. It will be recalled that the two international trade union organisations in the Coal and Steel Community have made critical comments on the insufficiency of supranationalism in the ECSC Treaty.

The Common Market Treaty, and, to a lesser extent, the Euratom Treaty, have been a considerable disappointment to the unions in this respect. The European unions are great believers in setting down, in writing, the specific powers and obligations of institutions, so that they know where they stand; even, perhaps, at the expense of flexibility of policies and institutions. Their complaint is that the Common Market Treaty, particularly, does not, in most cases, specifically state the supranational powers and obligations of the Community's institutions, and that where it does so, they are insufficient.

On the other hand, some international civil servants who have been closely associated with the drafting of the Treaty maintain that such criticisms are unjustified, and that provisions for supranational powers are ample, should they be needed. At the same time, it is stressed that the essential philosophy behind the Treaty is not to institute economic planning where it is anticipated that the Community's economy will function satisfactorily without much supranational direction.

Where action is necessary, it is pointed out, Articles 100, 101 and 103 give very wide powers. These Articles provide, firstly, that directives may be issued "for the approximation of such legislative and administrative provisions of the Member States as have a direct incidence on the establishment or functioning of the Common Market" (Article 100); secondly, that where disparities between such provisions distort the conditions of competition, directives may be issued, after consultation with interested Member States, to eliminate these distortions (Article 101); and, thirdly, that measures may be decided upon, and directives issued for their application, concerning policy on economic trends which are regarded as being of common interest (Article 103).

These powers appear to be very wide, but, in fact, in each case, they may be taken only by the Council acting by means of a unanimous, or qualified majority vote, (according to circumstances)[3] on a proposal of the Commission. Under these conditions it is clear that measures intended for the betterment of the Community as a whole could be frustrated by the negative vote of one member state which happened to be less favourably affected, in cases where Council unanimity was required.

This formula for arriving at decisions of importance occurs frequently, throughout the Treaty. Another one, occurring in a number of Articles, requires decisions to be reached or implemented by the Council on a proposal of the Commission and after the Economic and Social Committee and the Assembly have been consulted. In such circumstances, the fatality rate of any original proposals or initiatives may well be high, and the progress of the remainder, from idea to implementation, will necessarily be slow.

It is the proliferation of this sort of clause in the Common Market Treaty which caused the ERO to state of the draft Treaty, that it consisted of half-measures hedged round by so many reservations as to virtually exclude the possibility of any effective action, and that the Common Market would be managed completely by the Council, rather than the Commission.

There can be no doubting that under the Common Market Treaty, far more of the real policy decisions will be taken by the Council of Ministers than is the case in the ECSC, where the High Authority is the real moving body. However, many of the decisions which the Council is empowered to take will be on the initiative of the Commission. The crux of the issue, as far as the unions are concerned, is whether Ministers, being direct Government representatives, will tend to act as such, rather than in a more aloof and altruistic Community spirit. It is feared they will.

Although the Christian trade unionists were not very concerned about it, it will be recalled that the Committee of 21, representing the majority of trade unionists in coal and steel, was strongly in favour of the powers of the High Authority of the ECSC being increased *vis à vis* the Council, although they are already a good deal stronger than those of the Commission *vis à vis* the Council in the Common Market. There was also the suggestion that the ECSC Treaty clauses may be re-examined with a view to substituting qualified majorities for unanimous decisions,

3. Article 148 states: "Where conclusions of the Council require a qualified majority, the votes of its members shall be weighted as follows: Belgium 2, Germany 4, France 4, Italy 4, Luxembourg 1, Netherlands 2. Majorities shall be required for the adoption of any conclusions as follows:—twelve votes in cases where this Treaty requires a previous proposal of the Commission . . ."

and simple majorities for qualified ones, as far as the Council's provisions for voting procedures for certain questions were concerned. There are no concessions to this union viewpoint in the new Treaties.

The CISC has commented that, in the Common Market, if the Commission is not going to have many real powers, at least it ought to have the power to co-ordinate economic and social policies. It believes that the Treaty provisions in this regard are quite insufficient.

The Committee of 21 was in favour of increasing the powers of the Assembly in the ECSC, which institution is now common to the three Communities, and their view still holds good for the wider projects. The trade unions are pleased about the provision for the new Assembly which obliges it to draw up proposals for its own election by direct universal suffrage from all member states. This would eventually replace the present system whereby delegates are nominated from national legislatures. It is conceivable that when this comes about, the Assembly's powers may be extended to meet the trade union proposal that it should have power to ratify texts of the Council, instead of these reverting to national Parliaments.

But on all other counts, the ICFTU unions are disappointed. None of their proposed reforms is to become manifest. The Assembly will have no right of initiative, it will have no political control over the Council, nor will it adjudicate on questions of difference between Council and Commission. It will not be able to dismiss the Commission by a simple majority vote; the figure remains at two-thirds majority, as in the ECSC. Individual members of the Commission will not be subject to dismissal by the Assembly.

The ERO believes that the Euratom Treaty does not go far enough in providing for international ownership and control of nuclear materials. It would have liked to have seen the provision for the Community ownership of special fissile materials extended to all fissionable materials and their by-products. It also wanted wider powers than those given, for supranational institutions to be set up, so that Euratom could effectively control, rather than merely co-ordinate, the whole atomic energy industry.

The general picture, then, is that the ICFTU unions, particularly, wished to see the two Commissions and the Assembly all have greater international powers of control over member states and over enterprises, than had their ECSC counterparts. In particular, they wished to see the Common Market Commission strengthened relative to the Council of Ministers. In fact, the opposite has taken place, and the Common Market Council is more powerful than in the ECSC. The Assembly has not radically changed its functions or powers, but the

CISC would rather have seen the old Assembly adapted to the new functions, than a complete new body created.

Economic Powers

In a number of respects, the ECSC Treaty is more comparable with the Euratom Treaty than with the Common Market Treaty; the main reason being that the last-mentioned does not, and cannot, deal specifically with individual industries; agriculture and transport excepted. The ECSC deals with two industries which are basic to the whole of the economy of Western Europe, and were therefore very liable to attract political interest, which would ensure that they behaved themselves. Atomic energy is rather in the same category.

The Common Market Treaty is necessarily an "umbrella" Treaty, and could not, even if that were desirable, make provisions that could bring about any degree of direct control over the scores of industries, large and small, which comprise the Community's economy. Nor would there be any great support for so doing. It is felt by governments that all that can be done, and is necessary to do, is to regulate general economic policy, by agreement, so as to provide the best available climate for the individual industries to operate in, and make the most of the chances of economic expansion. The governments do not see the job of the Community institutions as being to organise this process rigidly, but to encourage it to work within an ordered social and economic system, appropriate to the mid-twentieth century.

For these reasons, it is not very relevant, in this section, to study the general trade union proposals for the revision of the economic aspects of the ECSC Treaty, in relation to the Common Market Treaty. There can be no intention of attempting to regulate industries, in general, by the sort of provisions applicable to particular, and basic, industries. There are two possible exceptions, concerned with the means and uses of Community finance, and the control of monopolies.

The Committee of 21 proposed that the levy on the production of coal and steel, which is the ECSC's revenue raiser, should be eligible for wider usage than at present provided for. New uses should include the extended financing of social development, and extended investment programmes.

As has been seen, provisions for social or economic investment in the Common Market would derive from special funds, and not from the general revenue. Nevertheless, there are a number of projects of a social nature, mainly research, which it is expected will be carried out by the Secretariat of the new Community, and would be financed through normal Community income. The unions are keen for these projects to be as comprehensive as possible, and are therefore much concerned with sources of finance.

The ERO much prefers the novel form of ECSC finance to the Common Market reliance on government contributions, which have to be incorporated in national budgets. It has therefore suggested some form of special tax, or direct levy, to replace the present provision in Article 200 of the Common Market Treaty, which fixes the proportions of the financial contributions from member states. In this connection, Article 201 will be of some comfort to them, because it obliges the Commission to study how the provisions of Article 200 could be replaced by other resources, particularly by revenue accruing from the common customs tariff. Any proposals would go to the Council, which could then recommend member states to adopt provisions.

The Committee of 21, in Luxembourg, made several penetrating criticisms of the Articles in the ECSC Treaty concerning monopolies and restrictive agreements. The criticisms were designed to show that the High Authority's powers of control were insufficient. The fact that the ERO has remained silent on the equivalent provisions in the Common Market Treaty is a testimony to their more far-reaching implications, which seem to meet the trade union point of view, in this connection.

Article 85 is more categorical than was the ECSC Treaty. It says:

"The following shall be deemed to be incompatible with the Common Market and shall hereby be prohibited: any agreements between enterprises, any decisions by associations of enterprises and any concerted practices which are likely to affect trade between the Member States and which have as their object or result the prevention, restriction or distortion of competition within the Common Market."

The Article mentions a number of practices which are particularly banned, including price fixing; restriction of production, markets, technical development or investment; market sharing or supply sharing; supply discrimination and conditional sales.

Exceptions to these bans are provided for where such practices "contribute to the improvement of the production or distribution of goods or to the promotion of technical or economic progress while reserving to users an equitable share in the profit resulting therefrom", provided certain other conditions are fulfilled. The Council, acting on a proposal of the Commission, and after the Assembly has been consulted, is to draw up the necessary regulations and directives to implement the provisions of Article 85, including fines, and other penalties for non-observance.

Article 86 prohibits one or more enterprises from taking "improper advantage of a dominant position within the Common Market or within a substantial part of it," by methods similar to those disallowed by the preceding Article, if such action would affect trade between Member States.

There is no doubt that the necessary powers to satisfy the trade unions are written into this part of the Treaty. This will not necessarily end the constant struggle that the trade union movement has waged for many years against monopolies and restrictive agreements. It may only be the beginning of a long battle, which the unions will follow with close interest, to see whether the new institutions of Western Europe have the resolution and the strength to impose their will on the most powerful of all forms of economic rule.

One major criticism that the ERO has made of the economic provisions in the Common Market Treaty, is in respect of the European Investment Bank. It claims that the capital of 1,000 million dollars will be insufficient. It says that insofar as this may mean recourse to private investment, it would delay basic development in underdeveloped areas. It has also severely criticised the restrictions imposed on the Bank by the Treaty, and the attached Protocol. It considers that these will give the Bank the basic character of any other bank, and will tend to divert it from directing investments to the greatest benefit of the Community. The main benefits would be gained, instead, by private capitalists.

Two major basic industries will not be provided for under the Common Market Treaty, by the general provisions applicable to others. Agriculture and transport have special needs, and special provisions for them have been laid down, and have come under the critical survey of the trade union movements.

In agriculture, common policies are to be evolved during the transitional period, and a common organisation for agricultural markets will be set up. In the meantime, minimum prices may be applied to agricultural products by member states, within certain defined limits. This provision, in Article 44, is sharply attacked by the ERO, which claims that such minimum prices, combined with a common external tariff, would raise agricultural prices and the cost of living in some member countries, contrary to the Treaty's objectives. In any case, the fixing of such minima should not be left to individual countries.

In this instance, the ERO seems to be showing an exaggerated concern for the consumer, even at the expense of the standards of the agricultural population. Article 44 specifically states that the minimum prices should not be at a level which would impede the volume of normal trade in those products between member states, and that they should be applied only "to the extent that the progressive abolition of customs duties and quantitative restrictions between Member States may result in prices likely to jeopardise the achievement of the objectives set out in Article 39". These objectives include ensuring fair living standards for the agricultural population, increasing their individual earnings and stabilising markets.

From this it would appear that the ERO is mistaken in believing that such minima would raise agricultural prices in some countries. As far as can be seen it would only prevent them sinking to a level which would depress the agricultural living standards in certain countries which cannot compete with major agricultural countries in the Community. As it has been generally recognised that nearly all countries have to protect their agricultural industries, it seems unlikely that these minimum price provisions, which are only a temporary continuation of protection, will have any very harmful effects, before the time when they will be replaced by a fully co-ordinated Community policy.

The ERO makes the further points that agricultural prices should not be determined by the least efficient producer, and that out-of-date methods should be eliminated. This viewpoint is met in the Treaty by two of the other objectives of the common agricultural policy as stated in Article 39. The first is "to increase agricultural productivity by developing technical progress and by ensuring the rational development of agricultural production and the optimum utilisation of the factors of production, particularly labour", and the other is "to ensure reasonable prices in supplies to consumers".

The special section of the Common Market Treaty on transport does not go as far in its provisions as the trade unions had wished. Both the ERO and the International Transport Workers' Federation (ITF), affiliated to the ICFTU, have stated that a European Transport Authority, empowered to create and control a common European transport market, should be set up. The ITF wanted it to work within the European Commission. The ERO wanted transport to be co-ordinated so as to establish a European network of canals, roads and electrified railways, which would operate with standardised equipment.

The Treaty does not, specifically, go as far as this. The European Commission will be the controlling body for a common transport policy and rules, and it will be assisted by a special committee with consultative status; composed of experts appointed by the governments of member states, as well as by the Economic and Social Committee, which has transport operators included in its membership. But there is nothing which would prevent the network proposed by the ERO being established, and the equipment being standardised within the framework of the common policy, if the member states so agreed. ITF proposals for better social conditions and the improvement and co-ordination of safety measures could also be met.

It will, again, be a case of waiting to see how the provisions of the Treaty are interpreted, before knowing whether trade union demands will be met. The unions, meanwhile, will be suspicious that the loose wording of the Treaty, in this section, as in others, may be used as a convenient excuse for little being done. This is the reason why they insist that obligations should be written into treaties, wherever possible, even at the expense of making them less flexible.

Conclusions

Although the trade unions have made a number of criticisms of the Rome Treaties, in principle, it is not possible for them to tell to what extent they are likely to work along the lines preferred, until they have been in operation for some years. The reason is that the wording of the Treaties is loose, and will allow a great deal of room for differing interpretations by the Commissions and the Councils of the two projects, according to the political and economic circumstances of the Community countries at any given time.

The unions are pleased that the Treaties are in operation at last, notwithstanding their deficiencies, and since their signing have put most of their energies into making them work, rather than grumbling about them. But the criticisms the ERO made of the draft Treaties, just before signing, bear a fairly close resemblance to those made by the Committee of 21 on the ECSC Treaty, where the two are comparable. Christian trade union criticisms are much briefer and have been generally less outspoken on the Treaties' faults.

As with the ECSC criticisms, the comments on the Common Market and Euratom Treaties fall broadly into four categories: proposals for extended social powers, extended trade union rights, extended supranational powers and certain increased economic powers in the Communities. In all these, perhaps the two dominating issues are whether the institutions of the Communities should have strong supranational authority, and whether the trade unions have the representation on the various institutions and sub-bodies to which they believe they are entitled. The unions feel strongly that serious deficiencies in either of these respects could prove a grave danger to the smooth functioning of the new projects.

Ultimately, any deficiencies in the Treaties which become obvious after some working experience has been gained, can be remedied by Treaty amendment, provided for in both the Common Market and Euratom. Proposals for revision have to be submitted to the Council by the Commission or a member state. After consulting the Assembly and the Commission, the Council may declare itself in favour of a conference of member states for this purpose. Any amendments decided on by common agreement at such a conference would have to be ratified, nationally, by the "Six". The unions would therefore have some hefty procedural obstacles to overcome if it were decided, eventually, to press for amendments. But such action is unlikely for some years.

CHAPTER XII

TRADE UNION STRUCTURE IN "LITTLE EUROPE"

When the Rome Treaties were signed in March 1957, they posed to the trade union organisations in Europe the problem of deciding what was the most appropriate way of organising themselves at the level of the new Communities. There would undoubtedly be heavy commitments requiring their attentions in this new field. Should they treat the three European integration projects separately, or organise themselves, umbrella-fashion, to cover all three? Should the individual unions, the national centres or the International Trade Secretariats be left to deal with specific industrial problems in the ICFTU's sphere of influence? Or should it be some combination of all three? Should the machinery of the European Regional Organisation, or that of the Committee of 21, be adapted to meet new needs, or should an entirely new structure be set up? Should all affiliated European trade union organisations be represented in any new structure, or should it be confined to unions from the six Community countries?

All these questions, and many others, had to be answered soon, and action had to be taken quickly, if the unions were not to miss opportunities to increase their influence by adaptation. The ICFTU-affiliated organisations solved their difficulties at a series of conferences at which the considerable differences of viewpoint on all these problems were thrashed out, culminating in Dusseldorf, on 16 and 17 January 1958, when the basic principles of organisational structure were agreed, and a provisional Executive Committee was set up. A number of details concerning actual representation were not finally decided, however.

The eventual formula followed, closely, the organisational lines which had been advocated by Harm Buiter, the General Secretary of the Committee of 21, in an article which appeared in the Report to the Eighteenth International Metalworkers' Congress, in September 1957. On page 114, he said:

> "A 'Board of Administration', composed of representatives of these organisations (i.e. national trade union federations plus the most important industrial unions, previously referred to) should be set over a secretariat, in order to carry out the duties with which it is entrusted. The secretariat might be made up of full time secretaries.

Below this Board of Administration the establishment of the 'basic committees' could be envisaged. These committees might appropriately be set up first and foremost in conjunction with the three European institutions to start operating shortly. Accordingly, we would have a Committee for the Coal and Steel Community, a Euratom Committee and a Committee for the Common Market in General. For each of these committees the competent trade unions should designate their representatives. In the case of the Committee for the Coal and Steel Community, it would be the miners' and metalworkers' unions which would nominate such representatives, with the International Trade Secretariats appointing observers. The idea could be entertained of establishing committees for transport and agricultural questions, for instance, side by side with, or subordinate to, the Committee for the Common Market in General."

The fact that the actual structure bears close resemblance to this outline is an indication of two things. Firstly that the trade unions of the Community countries consider that the structure of the Committee of 21 has proved adequate, and secondly that they do not feel that trade union organisations outside the "Six" should be associated with them in Community affairs.

The General Secretary of the ERO, Walter Schevenels, had wanted his organisation to be closely associated with any new trade union structure for the Community, or even to be the official co-ordinating agency. Some of the ERO delegates from countries outside the Community had also hoped it would have a major hand in affairs. In fact, the ERO has no higher status than any other participant in the new Executive Committee of the "Six", or in its Sub-Committees which deal with the Common Market and Euratom, respectively. The unions of the "Six" want the ERO representative to be merely the liaison link between them and the other members of ERO.

Before the decisions on the new structure were taken, some measure of rivalry had grown up between the ERO and the Committee of 21, which was not entirely divorced from their associated personalities. It concerned the claims of each for filling the organisational vacuum in "Little Europe". The basis of representation in the new structure is similar to that used in the Committee of 21, and indicates that the trade unions of the "Six" eventually got their way.

Harm Buiter has been appointed General Secretary of the new Co-ordinating Committee, and he must now be counted a trade unionist of the highest rank in Europe.

The new structure provides for a General Assembly, which will meet as required, probably at least annually. The Committee of 21 found it desirable to hold conferences periodically, but, unlike the new Assembly, these were not provided for by constitution. The Assembly is composed of eighty delegates: sixteen each from Germany, France and Italy; eight each from Belgium and the Netherlands; four from Luxembourg and three each from the ERO and the Committees for ECSC, the Common Market and Euratom. It is expected that the national centres will normally compose their delegations so as to represent a wide variety of interests.

The Trade Union Executive Committee is actually the executive body of the Assembly, and consists of thirteen members: two each from the national centres of Germany, France and Italy; and one each from Belgium, the Netherlands, Luxembourg, the ERO, and each of the three Community Committees. Robert Bothereau of the French *Force Ouvrière*, who did a good deal of the preliminary work on the draft structures, was appointed President. Willi Richter of the German Trade Union Federation, and Antoine Krier of the Luxembourg Trade Union Federation, were appointed Vice-Presidents.

The more specialised interests are catered for by more specialised committees. There is a major Sub-Committee for each of the integration projects. National centres, and some individual national unions, are represented on these Sub-Committees. The Euratom Sub-Committee, particularly, is chosen from among trade unionists with specialist experience. Observers from Britain, Scandinavia, Austria and Switzerland are invited to meetings of the Common Market and Euratom Sub-Committees, in line with the normal invitation to the ECSC Committee.

Finally, a number of Industrial Committees for dealing with particular interests and industries is provided for, mostly in connection with Common Market problems, and they are composed largely of representatives of individual national trade unions which operate in the industries concerned.

The ERO has representation on the Sub-Committees for the Common Market and Euratom, as well as on the Executive Committee, but does not have representation on the ECSC Sub-Committee, which replaces the Committee of 21, or on the Industrial Committees.

The International Trade Secretariats generally send observers to the different Sub-Committees, but their status varies from one to another, and a good deal of their activity, up to 1958, had been in the Sub-Committees for transport, chemicals and agriculture. It seems strange that the trade union organisations which have the most international experience in specific industrial matters should not be invited to play (or themselves demand to play) a more prominent part in the Common Market structure, particularly. A duplication of effort is a likely consequence, for reasons which are expounded in Chapter Four, where a system of developing European Sections of the ITSs was suggested.

The seat of the Executive Committee is established in Brussels, the headquarters of the Common Market and Euratom, but the ECSC Sub-Committee, and its Secretariat, remain in Luxembourg. The Brussels Secretariat is financed by national trade union centres, but specific costs, for industrial sectors, are charged to those sectors.

It is hoped by the ERO that close liaison with the Executive Committee of the "Six" can be achieved. The ERO Executive expressed the fear, in March 1958, that the work of their organisation would be disrupted if this liaison did not take place, and also indicated disappointment at the lack of ERO representation in the sub-bodies of the six countries' trade union structure.

If the liaison is to be a two-way process, then the ERO should encourage the Executive Committee of the "Six" to have representation on the ERO's own Executive, and at the Biennial Conference, even though the "Six" are not enthusiastic about it, yet. Observer status is hardly satisfactory, but full representation could only be achieved, in the long term, by amendment of ERO statutes. In the short term, the possiblilities of co-option might be explored.

The Executive Committee, in due course, is likely to perform very much the same sort of functions as did the Committee of 21; that is, to be a medium through which the trade unions of the various Community countries can draw directly on each others' experience, and to act as the main body through which representations to the European Commissions, Councils, and other institutions can be made. The Executive Committee and its main Sub-Committees will also be valuable as permanent liaison bureaux for exchanges of views and information between unions and Community institutions.

As far as actual negotiations are concerned, the new Committees are in very much the same position as was the Committee of 21 – they are not competent to carry them out. Basic matters, such as pay and conditions of employment, will still be decided, in the main, within the framework of national negotiations between unions and employers. The Commissions or the Councils are not employers, as the High Authority was not in the ECSC, and they will not normally enter into negotiations on these matters.

There are certain social questions to be considered, on the fringe of working conditions, in which the Commissions will be the prime movers. They will probably wish to consult the unions in such matters, even outside the framework of the Economic and Social Committee meetings, and a little bargaining may possibly take place in such circumstances. But that is as far as it is likely to go in the near future.

The trade unions of the six countries do not envisage the pay and conditions of their members being governed by international collective bargaining in the near future, and if they did, it is by no means certain they would agree that the Executive Committee, or its Sub-Committees, would be the appropriate bodies through which this should come about.

Some of the trade unionists most closely associated with European integration developments confess that their idealism leads them ultimately to favour international collective bargaining, but even they see no immediate prospect for the idea. Observance of the functioning of the European Coal and Steel Community leads them to believe, however, that there will be a tendency in the new Communities for pay and conditions to move towards the levels of the countries in which they are highest.

On 27 May 1958, the International Federation of Christian Trade Unions (CISC) officially established a European Organisation within its structure. In fact the Organisation had already been working in an unofficial capacity for some months previously. It is competent to deal with the problems of the Common Market, and is also taking over the CISC's liaison functions in Strasbourg and Paris–with the Council of Europe and the OEEC, respectively. It is possible that it will also become the appropriate Christian trade union authority for dealing with problems which may arise if any wider association of OEEC countries is negotiated for Europe. Owing to lack of membership in the Free Trade Association countries, it is unlikely to have any functions in that direction.

The European Organisation is not taking over the functions of the Federation of Christian Trade Unions in the ECSC, which remains intact. Contact between the Christian trade unions in the two Communities is unlikely, therefore, to be as close as in the case of the ICFTU unions, with their general Executive Committee.

The CISC European Organisation is managed by a Committee of 24, which elects a small Executive from amongst its members. A European Conference of Christian Trade Unions will be held, periodically, to supervise the whole. The Organisation is likely to have its own permanent Secretariat, headed by a young and able secretary, J. Kulakowski, of the CISC's general Secretariat.

At a meeting in Paris, on 2 and 3 September 1958, called by the French CGT and Italian CGIL, it was decided to set up a Trade Union Co-ordination and Action Committee of the Common Market countries, for the benefit of WFTU-affiliated unions. Apart from the French and Italian unions, there were representatives present from the Netherlands, Luxembourg and some of the associated French Overseas territories. Agostino Novella, General Secretary of the CGIL, was elected President.

The position is rather strange, because while the CGT is uncompromisingly opposed to the Common Market, in line with WFTU policy, the CGIL is not, although it is a strong critic of many of the Treaty's provisions. However, the Committee's official statements cloak this fundamental difference, and declare that its task will be to:

"... face up to the consequences of the implementation of the Treaties by co-ordinating the action of the trade union organisations taking part, and by working for united action by workers and trade union organisations of all affiliations. With this in view the committee will examine the many problems of economic and social policy common to the workers in the countries concerned, in preparation for any action that it might be necessary to take against either the employers or the Common Market Authorities."[1]

Some of the problems for priority treatment, in the Committee's view, in respect of the above, are the fight against unemployment and the defence of immigrant workers; shorter working hours; higher wages; guaranteed wages and differentials problems; social security questions; workers' rights and trade union liberties, and the respecting of agreements and contracts of employment.

The campaign to persuade unions of other international affiliations to work in with them, on Common Market problems, was soon got under way. Its success seems in great doubt.

Whether the unions in this new Committee will have any form of direct contact with the institutions of the Common Market remains to be seen. The requests of the CGT and CGIL, to their respective governments, for a share of the trade union seats on the Economic and Social Committee, were turned down flat. If contact were desired with the Community authorities, it would have to be attempted directly. It is conceivable that the new Committee may decide that at least it should have some sort of office near the Community headquarters, for liaison purposes. If it does not do so, it may be difficult for the unions to act as effectively on behalf of their members, as do their rivals.

The High Authority of the Coal and Steel Community has pursued a policy of recognising trade union organisations which were recognised by the Community's member Governments. As it happens, because of

1. Text of official statement printed in the WFTU journal *World Trade Union Movement*, November 1958.

WFTU aloofness, they were never faced with the decision of whether to recognise organisations affiliated to it. But if the new Committee should attempt to form a liaison Bureau with the new Communities, the Commissions would undoubtedly be placed in a very difficult position, over recognition.

No WFTU-affiliated organisation in Western Europe is recognised by its government for the purposes of nominating individuals onto official trade union panels, from which representatives to international bodies are chosen. But as the CGT and the CGIL, and their national affiliates, represent the largest groups of trade unionists in their respective countries, it is debatable whether the Commissions could legitimately refuse to receive their opinions, or their representatives, merely on the grounds that the Community's member governments do not like communists. The answer to this will possibly remain unknown, as neither the CGT nor the CGIL may wish to force the issue.

Whatever the Trade Union Co-ordination and Action Committee may decide to do, the ICFTU and the CISC-affiliated unions and national centres will do their utmost to strengthen their international structures in Europe. Whether the trend is towards international collective bargaining, or more towards the fulfilment of their policies by using stronger internal influences in the Community organs, the trade unions will find it essential to work through strong central organisations.

CHAPTER XIII

THE FREE TRADE AREA PLAN

Since the establishment of the Organisation for European Economic Co-operation (OEEC) in 1948, there has been one guiding principle among its member countries in their trading relations with each other – that is, non-discrimination. When six of those member countries decided to form an Economic Community among themselves, this meant that although trade barriers between the "Six" would be gradually removed, they would maintain an outside tariff which would discriminate, for the first time, against the other eleven members of OEEC,[1] if some plan to avert the danger were not evolved.

The OEEC was in favour of the Common Market plan, but decided that a way would have to be found to avoid discrimination against the other members, which would be a blow at all the organisation stood for – co-operation based on equality of treatment. A Free Trade Area for Western Europe was suggested as a possible answer, and in July 1956, an OEEC Working Party was established to "study the possible forms and methods of association, on a multilateral basis, between the proposed Customs Union and Member countries not taking part therein".

The Working Party concentrated on the study of the possibilities of a Free Trade Area, and in January, 1957, published its report,[2] which concluded that a Free Trade Area could be satisfactorily operated, but that there were many open questions as to its exact nature.

A month later, the British Government, whose own trading problems may be radically affected by the Common Market of the "Six", published a "White Paper", in the form of a memorandum to the OEEC. This set out its views on the establishment of a European Free Trade Area – or, as it should have been more precisely called, an Industrial Free Trade Area, because the British proposals would have excluded agricultural products from its provisions.

For a year, or more, after that, most of the international discussions

1. Member countries of the OEEC are: Austria, Belgium, Denmark, France, Germany, Greece, Iceland, Ireland, Italy, Luxembourg, the Netherlands, Norway, Portugal, Sweden, Switzerland, Turkey and the United Kingdom; and from 1959, Spain.

2. *Report on the Possibility of Creating a Free Trade Area in Europe*, published by OEEC, Paris.

and negotiations, conducted within the OEEC, took the British proposals as a starting point, and it was only later on, that a way out of an impasse was attempted by negotiating, instead, on the basis of the Economic Community provisions, to find out to what extent they were applicable to a Free Trade Area. Neither process was successful.

The technical characteristics of a Free Trade Area are specific, and generally recognised, and the principal ones were included in the British plan. The viewpoints of the British TUC and the ICFTU European Regional Organisation on a Free Trade Area were mainly based on the theoretical concept, such as that taken in the OEEC's study of the possibilities, and not on the British proposals.

Before examining trade union attitudes, it is helpful to study the original British plan, in order to obtain a clear picture of the course of events, and further possibilities.

The British Plan, and Subsequent Proposals

The British Government welcomed the negotiations to establish the Common Market of the "Six", officially, but said that the UK could not become a member because of her Commonwealth commitments. The Government could not contemplate entering an agreement which would make it impossible for the UK to treat Commonwealth imports as favourably as those from Europe. And such would be the case if the UK had to erect the Common Market external customs barrier.

It was therefore proposed that a Free Trade Area (FTA) be created, open to the OEEC countries, including the Common Market countries, whose membership would be essential. All customs barriers between FTA members would be dismantled, and so would all other restrictive regulations on trade. The "Six" would maintain their external customs barrier against the rest of the world, but the other FTA members would be free to keep their own separate and distinct external tariffs.

An important condition in the proposals was that agricultural produce should be excluded from the scope of the FTA to enable Commonwealth preference and home protection to be continued.

It was stated that a high and stable level of employment would be essential for the effective working of a FTA. The British Government believed that the plan would strengthen the Western European economy by raising industrial efficiency and by increasing specialisation, large-scale production and technical development. The FTA would put Western European nations in a stronger position to liberalise their outside trading relations, and it would not, in any case, mean the creation of new trade barriers against anyone. It would be in full conformity with the provisions of the General Agreement on Tariffs and Trade (GATT).

The British Government did not envisage as desirable the sort of institutional framework proposed for the Common Market. It believed that the far-reaching integration of policies intended for "Little Europe" would not be appropriate to a FTA, which would be primarily concerned with the removal of trade restrictions. Institutions could not be decided on in advance, but the FTA should be established within OEEC. Close co-ordination between Common Market and FTA institutions would be necessary.

The British Government did not accept the view that disparities between social regulations in different countries necessitated the harmonisation of them in a FTA. It took very much the same viewpoint as the economic experts of the ILO, whose views on this question were outlined in Chapter XI. Namely, that social regulations are only one of the factors potentially affecting the pattern of international trade, and cannot usefully be considered outside the full economic picture.

The White Paper stated that it was highly desirable that the method of reduction of tariffs during a FTA transitional period should be as nearly as possible identical with that adopted in the Common Market, and that the rules governing the reductions should be clear, unambiguous, and should contain a large element of certainty and automatic procedures. This would enable industry to plan in advance.

The FTA and the Common Market should adopt the same rules for the removal of quantitative restrictions, but the FTA would have to have an escape clause procedure in case of acute balance of payments difficulties facing any country .Another reservation was that the member countries of a FTA should maintain the right to levy duties for revenue purposes.

The British Government was of the view that certain provisions of GATT would have to be applied, and, perhaps, strengthened, in the proposed plan, against practices which were liable to frustrate the objectives of a FTA, such as the use of subsidies, artificial aids to exports, export controls, certain types of state trading and freight rate discrimination. There were also certain private monopolies, and restrictive commercial practices, which might thwart FTA purposes; and ways of dealing with these would have to be thought out.

The British Government publicised the proposals well in their own country, and they had the backing of the Parliamentary Opposition for their broad principles. The TUC, and the great majority of industrialists, supported the proposals, and a good deal of public and private planning, research and enquiry started on the basis of them, and the effect a FTA would have in the country.

The fact that there were serious divergences of opinion concerning the British proposals, within the OEEC, was not hinted at by the Government for a long time. The rather disconcerting position in Britain was that trade unions and industries found themselves caught unawares by the belated news that the original British proposals had no chance of acceptance in the OEEC, and that France, particularly, was opposed to them. The careful plans and studied attitudes on both sides of industry were consequently knocked awry, and a long period of uncertainty ensued.

It should have been obvious from the outset that Britain could hardly hope to maintain her position whereby agricultural products would be excluded from consideration, altogether, in the Treaty. Those potential FTA countries with a strong agricultural sector in their economies, such as France, the Netherlands and Denmark would obviously not allow unlimited entry of British industrial products without duties if they were not, in return, going to be allowed to export agricultural produce to Britain, on a freer basis. Neither British nor continental viewpoints would ever accept, or expect, complete free trade in agriculture. But the continental countries would expect a system of regulation of agricultural trade, combined with co-ordinated policies, as provided for in the Common Market Treaty. Later on, Britain inevitably conceded that she would be willing to discuss her agricultural policies with the other countries of the OEEC.

Some of the other objections to the British proposals, mainly from the French, have been, firstly, that it would be extremely difficult to operate a system of definitions of origin of goods, needed to prevent deflections of trade which would take place because of the differing tariff barriers against the outside world, as between the six Community countries and the other FTA countries. Secondly, that the maintenance of British Commonwealth preferences might, for instance, attract American capital to Britain under an FTA. American-owned enterprises could then buy raw materials from the Commonwealth at preferential rates, export them to Community countries, and thus avoid the tariff barrier against outside countries. Thirdly, the FTA countries could have an unfair competitive advantage over Common Market countries by virtue of the fact that they would be enjoying all the privileges of Common Market membership without shouldering any of the burdens which the "Six" have to carry under their Treaty, such as heavy social investment and the upward adjustment of certain conditions of employment.

It seems quite possible that if Britain had been less dilatory in making concessions to the continental viewpoint in the Free Trade Area negotiations, a breakdown might have been avoided. But too little was conceded, too late; and the advent of the Fifth Republic in France caused a hardening of opinion against making concessions to the British viewpoint, and a general tapering off of enthusiasm for integration projects, in French official circles. Hopes that some form of agreement might be concluded to associate the OEEC and the Common Market countries before the first Common Market tariff cuts were made on 1 January 1959, came to nothing, and the search had to be continued on the basis that a somewhat different form of association might be negotiated under a new title. One name suggested was a European Economic Association. The proposals for the smaller grouping of the "Outer Seven" did not become public until the end of May 1959, and had not even been officially hinted at until a month previously.

An alternative to the former British proposals was made by Signor Carli, the chief Italian representative in the original negotiations. His plan sought to achieve some proximity between the customs barriers that the FTA countries would have imposed against the outside world. There would have been no compulsion to approximate them, but those countries continuing to apply tariffs very different from the average level would have been liable to have their exports to other FTA countries subjected to appropriate compensatory charges.

Whatever the eventual and final form of agreements to liberalise European trade generally, including a possible form of association between the "Six" and the "Seven", there seems little doubt that the trade unions will support it in principle. That is assuming, as seems justified, that the governments concerned do not turn their backs on the necessity for maintaining full employment and enlightened social and economic policies. The possibility of the governments risking trade union alienation, by refusing reasonable safeguards to the workers, does not seem likely.

The Trade Union Movements and the Free Trade Area

The most important statement made on behalf of the international trade union movement, concerning the original FTA, was that issued by a special conference of the ERO, in May 1957, which was mentioned in broad outline in Chapter III. It was reinforced at the 1958 Conference, by a general resolution. The Christian International, the CISC, made no detailed statement on the FTA, but it is known to have generally supported the principle of setting it up. The World Federation of Trade Unions, the WFTU, was also reticent on the project, but it was known to oppose it in principle, along with other Western European integration, or co-ordination, schemes.

Some fairly detailed points of policy emerged in the ERO's statement.

They give several indications of the sort of association of all OEEC countries, with the Common Market countries, which would find favour in trade union eyes.

The ERO's stated views are probably not firm on exact details, and may be subject to some modification, according to changing circumstances. Flexibility in the ERO's viewpoint may grow, as the strength and cohesion of the new Trade Union Executive Committee of the "Six" grows. It is likely that the trade unions of the "Six" will exert an increasingly centralised influence in the Councils of the ERO, especially concerning the form of association considered best for the existing Communities.

It may be recalled that the special ERO conference was convened at the request of the British TUC, which had earlier issued its own policy statement on its attitude to association with the Common Market countries, some three months before the British Government's proposals were issued. These proposals incorporated a number of items which coincided with the policy of the TUC. The ERO statement was made some three months after the British Government's proposals, but it still owed a great deal of its inspiration, and even authorship, to the TUC's document. It did not appear as if the statement was intended to be a comment on the British Government's proposals, but only a theoretical definition of the trade union position.

The conclusion of the statement sets out, concisely, the ERO's attitude:

"The establishment of a Free Trade Area holds out to Europe an opportunity of increasing productivity and living standards. Full use should be made of this opportunity, whilst the Free Trade Area must rest on the solid foundation of a fully employed expanding European economy, and the Treaty must recognise this as the primary aim of national and international economic and social policy. In such a framework the co-operation of the trade unionists of Western Europe in the establishment of a Free Trade Area will be possible and will be forthcoming. It is, moreover, imperative that, at every stage of the negotiations and (assuming that the negotiations are satisfactorily completed) of the implementation of the Treaty, Governments should be prepared to consult with the representatives of the free trade union movement and to take full account of the legitimate aspirations of the working people of Europe."[3]

The general lines of the above are similar to statements made during

3. *Free Labour World*, June 1957, p. 44.

negotiations for the Common Market Treaty, and a further examination of the detailed paragraphs reveals a similar result.

The ERO wanted a FTA based on the same four major principles as it asked for in the Common Market–full employment, higher living standards through fair distribution of the scheme's economic benefits, upward harmonisation of social conditions and adequate trade union representation, at all stages, in all institutions.

On the question of full employment the ERO wanted a FTA Treaty to go further than the Common Market Treaty. Not only should the aim have been stated, and the individual provisions framed towards this objective, but the Treaty should have included a "general statement on the methods which the member countries will, individually and collectively, adopt in furtherance of this aim." The ERO stressed, in particular, that full employment must not be jeopardised by a low level of economic activity, through member states following such a policy in an attempt to surmount balance of payments difficulties. Taking jobs to the workers in the interests of full employment would be of primary importance in the Area, and governments' powers to control the distribution of their industries must therefore remain.

In the case of disruptions in industry owing to the implementation of a FTA, governments should be ready with plans to assist displaced workpeople. These should include adequate unemployment pay and provisions, similar to the readaptation provisions in the ECSC and the Common Market–that is, retraining facilities, support during retraining, and assistance, where necessary, for workers and families to move to new areas.

The paragraph supporting the upward harmonisation of social conditions is tactfully worded. The ERO had wanted not only the upward harmonisation of conditions, but also of social regulations (i.e. in connection with social insurance and statutory regulations) in the Common Market Treaty, and had been partly successful. However, the TUC did not want international interference with social regulations, so the ERO statement on the FTA showed deference to this viewpoint by asking only for the harmonisation of social conditions–a process which could be undertaken without international authority.

The resolution passed by the 1958 ERO Conference, on social harmonisation, was ambiguous in that it stated its conviction "that the integration of Europe must be accompanied by a harmonisation of the social conditions between the countries concerned", without any indication as to whether the succeeding proposals for social minimum standards should apply to any wider association, as well as to the Common Market. The ambiguity ensures that the trade unions of uncommitted countries do not have their hands tied.

Two other matters in which the ERO differed in its attitude to the FTA, and the Common Market, were the free movement of labour, and strong supranational institutions. It had wanted both these for the Common Market, but the TUC thought them inappropriate to the FTA, and respect was shown to this view in the FTA statement. The circumstances are described in Chapter III.

The ERO statement was non-committal on agriculture, while recognising the difficult problems it would raise in a FTA. It could not accept the TUC's point of view that agriculture should be excluded. Exclusion, of course was what the British Government had proposed. The National Union of Agricultural Workers, which has a strong voice in the TUC, also wanted its exclusion. The British Labour Party's view was similar. The TUC would therefore have had strong influences pressing it to put the case for the exclusion of agriculture.

There was a widespread misconception at one time, especially in Britain, that the inclusion of agriculture in the Common Market meant free trade in its products, and the end of home protection. It was felt that this would be an impossible situation for Britain, if these imagined provisions applied to a FTA Treaty, also. The ERO made it clear in its statement that the Common Market Treaty provided for a regulated agricultural marketing system, and, by implication, hinted that some such solution may be found for the FTA.

The ERO statement did not commit itself on the question of whether overseas territories associated with member countries of a FTA should have a special arrangement with the Area, as was the case with the overseas territories of countries in the Common Market. But it did insist that if a decision to associate such overseas territories was taken, it must give full weight to the views of the peoples of those territories, and must be based on the principle of freely accepted co-operation.

The statement also made a number of policy points on the economic aspects of a FTA. Rules of competition, which would prevent restrictive trade practices by cartels and monopolies, including price-fixing, export subsidies, preferential raw material prices for domestic industries and protectionist transport tariffs, should be included in a Treaty.

The statement seemed uncertain whether it considered free capital movement desirable or not, and here again TUC influence was noticeable, as there was no ERO objection to capital movement in the Common Market. The FTA statement said that there may be a clash between "the full ideal of the free movement of capital and the practical requirements of national administration", and that, in the last instance, governments should have control over private capital movements.

The ERO did not envisage great difficulties arising out of the necessary transitional provisions for a FTA, which it assumed would spread over 12 to 15 years, in line with the Common Market. However, there should be some flexibility in the method of tariff reduction, in case radical adjustments were necessary. The European Payments Union (EPU) ought to have been retained, mainly because the tariff reduction programme might possibly have demanded special credit or payments arrangements, for which its machinery would have been useful.

It was thought that for escape clauses, the period over which they might have been applied in case of special difficulties, should have been taken beyond the end of the transitional period. Where these were necessary, it agreed with the OEEC Working Party that the most appropriate form of assistance would be the temporary introduction of quantitative trade restrictions.

The ERO had a well-reasoned paragraph on the necessity that may arise to impose quantitative restrictions, or quotas, on certain goods, in case of balance of payments difficulties. So that the permission to impose quotas for balance of payments difficulties should not be abused, countries adversely affected by these quotas should have the right to take compensatory action. The imposition of quotas must also be subject to the approval of the competent international authority, but the ERO would not be in favour of a right to refuse such approval on the grounds that an alternative solution of deflationary measures could be taken by the country concerned. Neither should it be possible to oblige a country to impose overall trade restrictions rather than selective ones, against inessential commodities, in granting permission for it to use escape clauses. The paragraph concludes with the suggestion that there should be provision for co-operation by member countries to promote balance of payments equilibrium, and the responsibility for taking action to correct disequilibrium should be placed on creditor, as well as on debtor countries.

On the whole, this statement of the ERO's on FTA problems bears the hallmark of the TUC's approach and has less of the idealism which was the keynote of its previous statements, on the Common Market.

In particular, the stolid and pragmatic approach to the project indicates TUC influence. The wealth of detailed economic analysis on a scheme only in its theoretical stages, suggested strongly, the cautious British concern with consequences, possibly at the cost, even, of losing sight of an ultimate objective. To use an analogy, it may be said that the British would look upon a Free Trade Area, associated with the Common Market, more as a marriage of convenience than a fertile union of devoted partners.

The cautious approach was not unwelcome to the other potential FTA members, apart from the "Six". The Scandinavian countries were, perhaps, more engrossed with the problems of bringing their own proposed Common Market into being, and tended to regard the FTA as a useful expedient for associating their project with the larger Common Market of the "Six", without becoming enmeshed too closely with German economic might. Austria and Switzerland saw the FTA as a very useful method of associating themselves with the larger European markets without risking the loss of neutrality that they believe full Common Market membership may bring.

The ERO's General Secretary, Walter Schevenels, has plenty of work to do keeping a sense of unity within the organisation in which a great variety of views have to be thrashed out by the unions. He has to try and ensure that the organisation's policy is acceptable to both the "Six" and to other countries–hence the tempered statement on the FTA. This is a skilful job for a man who has his own strong personal opinions and ideals, where integration questions are concerned.

Whatever decision is finally arrived at by OEEC member governments, attempting to secure a wider association, it is likely that support, in principle, will be forthcoming from the ERO, after the various trade union national centres have composed their differences. But a statement of policy in the ERO concerning any wider European project, such as a combination of the "Six" and the "Seven", will contain a hidden threat to trade union unity if it does no more than gloss over basic differences of viewpoint, by a special form of words. Compromise in idea should replace compromise in words.

Another danger is that a growing competitiveness between the ERO and the Trade Union Executive Committee of the "Six" may reach the stage of rivalry if great discretion and tolerance are not exercised. It is a truism that all organisations wish to increase their field of influence, and neither the ERO nor the Executive Committee of the "Six" are exceptions to this rule.

The chief personalities in both bodies have an eye on the prospects for an extension of their organisation's influence. This could be achieved by becoming the international trade union body for co-ordinating the policies and activities of the unions participating in a wider European association, The ERO, as the pioneer of European integration, and the Executive Committee of the "Six", as the experienced organisation in the field, both feel they have strong claims to the exercise of these functions. However, the more recent creation of the "Outer Seven" group is likely to mean that any co-ordinating body set over the unions of those countries (even, possibly, the ERO itself) will have a substantial negotiating influence if a combination of the "Six" and the "Seven" becomes a reality.

The ERO and the Executive Committee of the "Six" would do well to consider, as soon as possible, an association between themselves which is very much closer than at present. Strangely, the ERO's status on the Executive Committee has been kept down, by a small representation, and the representation of the Executive Committee at ERO level is non-existent, although its Secretary, Buiter, is a co-opted member of the ERO Economic Committee. Surprisingly, the Executive Committee is not asking for fuller representation, at the moment, because of a belief that developments in the first few years of existence will not warrant it. A lack of co-ordination and joint activity will tend to drive the two organisations apart, if a full working agreement is not reached. As further governmental negotiations proceed, co-ordination might even recede, as far as these two organisations are concerned, unless differences are settled on a compromise basis.

The WFTU, as such, has no special organisation to deal with Common Market questions, but its French and Italian affiliates have formed a Trade Union Co-ordination and Action Committee for this purpose. As it has no affiliated strength to speak of in Western European countries outside the "Six", there is little possibility of its forming any special organisation to watch over the "Outer Seven" or a wider association.

The CISC has set up its own European Organisation, as outlined in Chapter XII, in order to deal with Common Market problems and trade union co-ordination. It is anticipated that this organisation would also be competent for any wider association, but it is doubtful if it will have many functions in respect of the "Outer Seven", alone, as it has virtually no membership in the member countries, other than Switzerland.

To sum up, the original proposition for a Free Trade Area arose from a desire in the OEEC not to break the tradition of non-discrimination against members, which a Common Market of the "Six", by itself would do. The initiative, in concrete terms, came mainly from the British Government, which proposed a plan excluding agriculture from consideration, and was based on a desire for increased co-operation and co-ordination of European commerce, and not for economic integration. Britain would not agree to any form of association which jeopardised her trading relations with the Commonwealth.

The proposals proved unacceptable to a number of the other potential partners, particularly France, and the British Government had to modify its position. If a formula for a wider association ultimately emerges, perhaps for linking the "Six" and the "Seven", it is likely to differ very considerably from the original proposals.

The only trade union International which has responded actively, and given detailed consideration, publicly, to the scheme, is the ICFTU, or more exactly, its European Regional Organisation. The statements it has issued coincide in many respects with the TUC statement, but on some important matters, where there was a strong opposition viewpoint from continental countries, rather non-committal clauses were inserted.

The settlement of policy differences between the trade unions of the "Six" and those of other OEEC countries should not be insoluble if the governments find a satisfactory solution on a wider form of European association. But the position will have to be watched carefully by the trade unions if they are to avoid a disruption over the question of whether the ERO or a widened Trade Union Executive Committee is to be responsible for co-ordination in any new and wider scheme which may draw the "Six", the "Seven" and possibly the other OEEC countries together.

CHAPTER XIV

THE EUROPEAN FREE TRADE ASSOCIATION

The increased effort made by the British Government, in the latter half of 1958, to find a way out of the impasse on the original Free Trade Area negotiations was of no avail. The British tried hard to obtain some agreement so that an initial tariff reduction in any wider association could be made at the same time as the "Six" made their first reduction – on 1 January 1959. The Government made certain concessions which some people thought would bring success, at last, to the long-drawn-out negotiations.

But the hopes were dashed. The French Government had further objections, and did not seem prepared to enter into any association which it was thought may have even small adverse effects on the French economy. The other members of the "Six" were not as hostile to the British proposals as France was, but they were unable or unwilling to coax their partner to the point where she would make sufficient counter-concessions to the British to conclude the negotiations successfully. It is widely felt that, even at that time, the Six countries had sufficient Community feeling to put a united viewpoint in negotiations with other OEEC members.

France's partners were prepared to act together in the negotiations, even if this meant backing her in a stand which they themselves would have been prepared to modify. Once they found France to be determined in her viewpoint they were prepared to close their ranks. It was inevitable that the reaction to this feeling of closer affinity between the "Six" should have been closer affinity between those countries trying to negotiate an agreement with them. Thus the idea of the "Outer Seven" was born – a popular title coined to distinguish the proposed new grouping quickly from the "Inner Six".

The official title of the new grouping is the European Free Trade Association, or EFTA. It is quite possible that its initial membership of seven may increase shortly after this is written, but the basic reason for its creation was a feeling of urgency on the part of seven countries – Britain, Norway, Sweden, Denmark, Austria, Switzerland and Portugal – that failing an agreement with the "Six", they must devise some means which would enable them to expand their own overseas markets, as a counter-weight to the trade which they would probably lose in the Community countries when the "Six" started to dismantle their internal trading restrictions.

It was felt that as trade restrictions within the Community were removed, so it would put industries within that grouping in a much more favourable competitive position for selling inside it than the industries of Britain, Scandinavia, or other OEEC countries which would have to overcome the external tariff barrier of the Community to do so. But if these other OEEC countries were also to dismantle trade barriers between themselves, this would enable them to expand their own trade with each other, and to give each other's exports a competitive advantage over Common Market exports to them, which would still have external tariff barriers to overcome.

In fact, the main reason for the creation of the new grouping was that such a combination would put the participating countries in a better position ,so they believed, for negotiating, eventually, a wider association with the Common Market; in view of the fact that negotiations in the OEEC had broken down, and a series of bilateral negotiations would have been an unworkable alternative. It looked at first as if there was an unwillingness on the part of the Common Market countries to reopen negotiations, but at the time of writing it seems possible that American interest and initiatives in attempting to link Western Europe, economically, with themselves on an Altantic basis may turn out to be a unifying factor in Western Europe itself. However these events move with great rapidity and may only be the preliminary rounds of a general "rethinking" concerning international or regional economic and trading policies.

There is little danger that the countries of the European Free Trade Association could come to regard their own grouping as anything other than a second best to a wider association which included the Common Market countries; at least as far as trading advantages are concerned, which seem to be their main concern. They are therefore likely to continue to try and use their new grouping in a united endeavour to achieve a link-up. The basic facts about the European economy indicate the reason for this.

Out of their total imports for 1958, the seven EFTA countries together obtained 16.1% of them from other EFTA countries, as compared with 27.6% from Common Market countries. And their exports to other EFTA countries amounted to only 17.7% of the total compared with 22.4% to Common Market countries. Thus, taken together, the trade of EFTA countries with each other has, in the past, been less important to them than their trade with the Common Market countries taken together.

Although this pattern would almost certainly alter so that the seven countries conducted a greater proportion of their trade with each other if there was no link-up with the Common Market, the fact is that trade potentialities with Common Market countries for the EFTA countries, together, are greater than internal potentialities. The basic reason is that while the population of the Association countries is nearly 90 millions, that of the Common Market countries is about 165 millions. And foreign trade plays a greater part in the EFTA group than in the Common Market.

The official descriptive pamphlet "European Free Trade Association – the Stockholm Convention and Freer World Trade", published by the seven governments, gives the significant facts in brief summary on page 19:

"Whereas the population of the EFTA group is little more than half that of the EEC, its combined national income is about two-thirds, and its combined imports and exports three-quarters. Switzerland and Austria have particularly strong trading ties with their continental neighbours, drawing more than half their imports from EEC countries. All the EFTA group look in varying degree to the industrial centres of the EEC for some of their manufactured imports: in fact, some 45 per cent of their supplies under this head come from the Six. Portugal, Norway, Sweden, Denmark and Switzerland buy more from the EEC countries as a whole than they sell to them. Federal Germany has a particular dependence on markets among the Seven, where she sells more of her manufactures (27 per cent of the total in 1957) than she does among her EEC partners (24 per cent)."

It is fairly clear from this that there are bound to be strong interests in most of the EFTA countries which will press hard for a wider association giving easier access to the markets of the "Six" in addition to those in their own grouping. And the purely trading interests of certain Common Market countries would undoubtedly make a link-up highly desirable to them also. In Germany and the Netherlands, for instance, there are strong interests which would benefit from a wider association and wider tariff-free markets.

It was inevitable that there should be a good deal of speculation about the action the non-Common Market countries of the OEEC would take after the breakdown of negotiations on the original Free Trade Area plan. But it was not for several months that the newspapers picked up the story that a "Little Free Trade Area" was a probability, when the comings and goings between British and Scandinavian government officials had been observed. Shortly after newspaper stories, it was announced, officially, on May 26th 1959, that the governments of OEEC countries who were not members of the "Six" were considering a free marketing arrangement between themselves which would be consistent with the provisions of GATT and developments of world-wide multilateral trade.

By mid-July a draft plan for a European Free Trade Association[1] had been worked out by officials and was considered by Ministers from the seven countries at a two day meeting near Stockholm. The Ministers agreed to recommend the plan to their Governments, to have it published, and to instruct officials to draw up a Convention based on it which should be submitted to them before the end of October. This Convention was duly prepared and submitted to a further meeting of Ministers in Stockholm, where it was initialled on November 20th 1959, and the intention was stated of having it ratified not later than March 31st 1960.[2]

Before the Convention was initialled several bilateral and multilateral arrangements had been made between participating countries in respect of industries which were to be excluded from the main provisions of the Convention, particularly agriculture. Britain, for instance, made arrangements with Denmark over dairy produce and with Norway over fish, which would allow the Scandinavian countries to expand exports beyond the previous level, but without damaging British interests severely. The purpose of these arrangements was to smooth the way for the Free Trade Association by ensuring that all countries had a fair chance of gaining from it.

Finland has expressed interest in the new grouping, and would like to become associated with it if suitable circumstances prevail. This arises from the common interests she has with the other Scandinavian countries, and from the fact that she was previously associated with moves to bring a Scandinavian or Nordic Common Market into operation—a project which had been discussed for some years. It now appears as if this scheme will be shelved in view of the Free Trade Association agreement; but Finland does not want to feel completely excluded from any scheme affecting the other Scandinavian countries. Hence her interest in the EFTA.

However, Finland is not a completely free agent in this matter—she has to consider the views of her powerful neighbour, the Soviet Union. The USSR has strongly opposed the European Common Market, so Finland could not join the "Seven" if it was thought that the group's

1. *Stockholm Draft Plan for A European Free Trade Association*, HMSO Cmnd. 823, July 1959, London.
2. *European Free Trade Association: Text of Convention and other Documents*, HMSO Cmnd. 906, November 1959, London.

only purpose was to link up with the "Six" at the earliest opportunity. But if she could be conditionally associated with the "Seven" without having any potential obligation in this regard, then it would be to her economic advantage to do so, and the move should not have any serious political repercussions with the Soviet Union. Remarks which have been made in Russia about Finland's possible membership of the Free Trade Association appear to have warned only against Finland doing anything which would tie her to the Common Market. It seems quite possible that the Soviet Union is not opposed to the Free Trade Association, as it stands, because it regards it as more likely to divide Western Europe than to unite it.

The Convention

The objectives of the Free Trade Association are set out in Article 2 of the Convention. They are:

"(a) to promote in the Area of the Association and in each Member State a sustained expansion of economic activity, full employment, increased productivity and the rational use of resources, financial stability and continuous improvement in living standards,

(b) to secure that trade between Member States takes place in conditions of fair competition,

(c) to avoid significant disparity between Member States in the conditions of supply of raw materials produced within the Area of the Association, and

(d) to contribute to the harmonious development and expansion of world trade and to the progressive removal of barriers to it."

Article 3 makes provision for the gradual elimination of tariffs between member states starting with a 20% cut in July 1960 and further reductions of 10% in each successive year so that no tariffs at all operate from 1st January 1970. In the case of some Portuguese duties the dates will be later than for other member countries. In other words the reductions, generally, are in step with those operating in the Common Market. Provision is made, however, for reducing tariffs at a faster rate if need be. This latter provision was drafted with a view to member states being able to keep pace with the Common Market countries who are, at the time of writing, considering whether to shorten the transitional period of their own Community.

In addition to tariffs, all other restrictions on the internal flow of EFTA trade are to be removed, although each country is free to keep or re-arrange its tariffs in respect of the rest of the world. There must be no discriminatory revenue duties imposed on imports so as to put them at a disadvantage with domestic products; export duties are prohibited; quantitative import restrictions (with certain exceptions) have to be reduced to nil over the transitional period and quantitative export restrictions must go by the end of 1961. Member states shall not put any new restrictions on the establishment of economic enterprises in their countries by nationals of other member states, or regard such establishment any less favourably than domestic establishment. One instance when action may be taken against other members is to prevent dumping or the subsidisation of imports.

Many of these provisions are surrounded by important qualifying clauses which seem virtually to eliminate the possibility that genuinely supra-national decisions could be arrived at. On some fundamental matters the Council of Ministers would appear to be almost powerless to do anything effective if one of the members should flout the spirit or the letter of the Convention. The basis of the Association is intergovernmental and not supranational, and on major issues the voting of the only institution directly provided for–the Council of Ministers–has often to be unanimous in order to be effective. The Council is not equipped with powers for enforcing decisions or recommendations on any member state.

The successful operation of the Association will clearly depend upon the goodwill of the member states in the attitude they adopt when faced with difficulties. The terms of the Convention Articles in most cases are fairly elastic and it appears as if any member state could seriously endanger the Free Trade project if it chose to be obstinate. For instance, a main criterion is contained in a very elastic phrase which occurs in several of the Articles, to the effect that practices which "frustrate the benefits expected" from the main provisions of the Convention are incompatible with it. It seems likely that "the benefits expected" would be almost impossible to define in any test case.

The Convention itself appears to provide several measures which could tend to frustrate the benefits which may be expected by several member states. The first paragraph of Article 19, for example, states:

"Notwithstanding the provisions of Article 10, (i.e. the Article providing for the elimination of quantitative import restrictions) any Member State may, consistently with its other international obligations, introduce quantitative restrictions on imports for the purpose of safeguarding its balance of payments."

Certain qualifications follow this, it is true, but they are not severe qualifications.

Again, in Article 20, there is provision for member states to take special safeguarding action in certain circumstances where the application of the rules for freeing trade leads to serious difficulties. This Article may be invoked when there is an appreciable rise in unemployment in a particular sector of industry, or in a region, as a result of a substantial decrease in the internal demand for the product of a domestic industry and where this decrease in demand results from an increase in imports from other member states as a consequence of the EFTA. The approved means of the safeguarding action is, again, by quantitative restriction, for a period not exceeding 18 months, unless the Council authorises its extension by majority vote. The Council may also authorise measures other than quantitative restrictions, if asked to do so.

The provisions of Article 19 and 20 are undoubtedly there partly to satisfy the trade unions that the dangers of unemployment arising due to the operation of the EFTA would be limited. Indeed, it seems that they are the type of provisions that the TUC, for example, had asked for, except that they do not go far enough. But this is the point where fundamental differences arise between British and Scandinavian unions on the one hand, and continental unions on the other. The continentals argue strongly (and it is not confined to the unions) that it is rather pointless trying to achieve closer regional unity if there is no intention to follow through in spite of difficulties. They undoubtedly have serious doubts whether an association having such wide escape clauses as the EFTA can function properly. And they believe that if countires operating such a system were associated with the "Six" it may harm the Common Market's chances of success.

The continental approach does not ignore the dangers of unemployment. Opinion in the six countries is that a close harmonisation of economic policies, free movement of labour, controlled international investment funds, readaptation schemes and upward social harmonisation can prevent serious unemployment occurring as a result of the Common Market's operation. And none of these remedies, they would point out, interfere with the fundamental objective of removing all trade barriers.

As EFTA countries' tariffs to the rest of the world will continue to be fixed individually, and will vary, it was necessary to incorporate rules which would establish the source of all imports. These are known as origin rules, and, broadly, they seek to prevent goods from the rest of the world "leaking" into those countries of the EFTA which have higher tariff levels, through those having lower levels, thus avoiding their full duty, and putting domestic industries at a competitive disadvantage. Many observers regard these rules as the crucial testing point of whether a free trade area can, in fact, function satisfactorily, and a good deal of interest will be taken as to whether the origin rules will provide an efficient and a sufficient check in identifying the products of outside countries to which the tariff reductions will not apply.

There are also provisions designed to prevent deflections of trade arising from member states with low external tariffs, exporting to, and having a competitive advantage in, the domestic markets of other member states with high external tariffs. This would arise because of the lower cost to the exporting countries of raw materials etc., imported from outside, which are incorporated in the value of their manufactured exports.

The Convention includes provisions to ensure that the benefits to be expected from the removal of tariffs and quotas are not nullified by the introduction of other measures, such as subsidies, restrictive business practices and discriminatory restrictions against nationals of member states wishing to establish businesses anywhere in the area.

Agricultural goods are excluded from the general provisions of the Convention, except for those seeking to discourage dumping. However, member states are encouraged to pay due regard to the interests of each other in their agricultural policies, bearing in mind traditional channels of trade. The objective is to expand agricultural trade and provide "reasonable reciprocity to Member States whose economies depend to a great extent on exports of agricultural goods". (Article 22.) The policies of member states set out in this same Article are designed:

"(a) to promote increased productivity and the rational and economic development of production,

(b) to provide a reasonable degree of market stability and adequate supplies to consumers at reasonable prices, and

(c) to ensure an adequate standard of living to persons engaged in agriculture."

It is noteworthy that these aims are almost the same as those set out in the agricultural section of the Common Market Treaty, in Article 39, although not as precisely worded. The last one (c) should particularly appeal to the trade unions. It appears that the protests of the British, particularly, at the time of the earlier negotiations designed to achieve a wider free trade area associated with the Common Market, could not have been as fundamental as their sponsors claimed. They had said that the agricultural undertakings the "Six" had made in their Treaty were quite unsuitable for the potential Free Trade Area countries. It now turns out that the EFTA countries, nevertheless, have the same ends in view as the "Six" in this field.

Although the detailed aims, (a), (b) and (c) of the agricultural section are not incorporated in the Articles on fish, in other respects fish and marine products are subject to similar provisions. In particular, these products are also excluded from the general provisions of the Convention but the same objective concerning "reasonable reciprocity" is written in, as with agriculture.

The Convention makes direct provision for only one institution of importance, the Council. This can meet either at Ministerial or Official level, and each member state is represented and has one vote. Decisions and recommendations are by unanimous vote, with exceptions provided for in the Convention, notably in dealing with complaints by member states, which is done by majority vote. The Council is charged with general oversight of the application of the Convention, and it has to consider any further action that should be taken to promote its objectives and to facilitate close association with other countries or economic groupings. It is empowered to establish relationships with other international organisations, particularly the OEEC.

The Council may set up subordinate bodies to assist it. It may make decisions or recommendations, and the former are binding on all member states. The Council is empowered to adopt its own procedure rules, set up the necessary Secretariat services and make financial and budgetary arrangements. It is planned to establish the Secretariat in Paris, outside EFTA territory, presumably to facilitate close contact with Common Market countries and the OEEC.[3]

The Council is little more than an intergovernmental committee, in effect, and its supranational powers are minimal. Article 30 provides that member states should pursue their economic and financial policies "in a manner which serves to promote the objectives of the Association", and shall have periodic exchanges of views; and the Council is empowered to make recommendations to member states in this regard. It is also empowered to examine complaints of member states and make recommendations concerning their rectification, under Article 31. Under these same provisions it can also authorise member states to suspend Convention obligations towards any other member which does not comply with such recommendation. It may also authorise interim safeguarding action by member states which are adversely affected.

A member state is entitled to complain to the Council under this Article if it considers that "any benefit conferred upon it by this Convention or any objective of the Association is being or may be frustrated and if no satisfactory settlement is reached between the Member States

3. The French Government told the EFTA countries, in early 1960, that it was unable to agree to the Secretariat being established in Paris.

concerned". The Council can set up examining committees, on such terms and conditions as it shall decide, to look into any such matter. They are to be composed of independent persons "selected for their competence and integrity". (Article 33.)

These powers of recommendation and authorisation can be taken by majority vote, and are therefore the only real examples of supranational decisions. Other decisions provided for in Article 32, which may be binding on all member states, are by unanimous vote only, so cannot really be regarded as supranational. The only coercive power these decisions could have would be to prevent a member state changing its mind once it had voted.

The Convention enters into force when all ratifications have been deposited, (Article 40) and any other state may accede to the Convention with the approval of the Council (Article 41). The Council is also empowered, in this latter Article, subject to ratification by member states, to negotiate an agreement with "any other State, union of States or international organisation, creating an association embodying such reciprocal rights and obligations, common actions and special procedures as may be appropriate". This Article was specially drafted to permit the concluding of a wider agreement between the Association and the Common Market–a basic aim which was pointedly expressed in a resolution adopted by the seven Ministers at the time the Convention was agreed in November 1959.

Article 42 provides for the withdrawal of any member state on twelve months notice. Amendments to the Convention of the Association can enter into force if approved unanimously by the Council and accepted by all member states. (Article 44.)

Article 43 provides that the European territories of member states are included in the Association and the territories of the Faeroe Islands, Greenland, Gibraltar and Malta may also be included if the member states responsible for their international relations so desire. (Under a separate protocol, the Principality of Liechtenstein, which forms a customs union with Switzerland, also comes under the provisions of the Convention.) The Convention recognises that at a later stage member states may wish to propose the extension of it to cover non-European territories for which they are responsible, and the Council may make provision for this by unanimous decision. This could allow for the eventual membership of some British Commonwealth countries and the associated overseas territories of other member states, if so desired.

Trade Union Views

On 18 August 1959, there was a long, special, meeting in the TUC's

London headquarters between trade union leaders of the ICFTU-affiliated national trade union centres of Britain, Norway, Sweden, Denmark, Austria and Switzerland. That is, all the EFTA countries excluding Portugal, which is considered by the other unions not to have any free and representative trade union movement of its own. The meeting studied the draft plan for the European Free Trade Association (the actual Convention had not then been drawn up) and issued an agreed statement on the attitude of the member countries' unions. A representative of the ICFTU's European Regional Organisation (ERO) was also present.

It is interesting that an *ad hoc* conference of unions from the countries concerned was called, and that the machinery of the ERO was not used. Furthermore, the unions agreed to maintain contact and have further consultations, if necessary, in the light of developments, and so as to be able to make further joint representations to their Governments. This could be the nucleus of a new international grouping on similar, though less elaborate lines, to that of the Executive Committee for the unions of the six Common Market countries.

The agreed statement of the Free Trade Association unions concentrated, as was to be expected, on the full employment question, and bore a heavy similarity in text to previous statements of the TUC's on the original Free Trade Area proposals. Indeed, the statement began by reaffirming the basic approach that had been made by the ERO unions to the wider scheme, an approach which had also fairly clearly borne the stamp of TUC authorship. The unions regretted the breakdown of the previous negotiations and hoped that the proposed new Association would lead to a bridge for forming a wider economic association in Europe.

The references in the plan to full employment were welcomed, as were those to increased productivity, the rational use of resources and the need for sustained expansion of economic activity. Governments should be required to define their full employment aims, and progress on this, and connected matters, should be reported at least annually to the Council, and should be published. There should be joint consultation of member governments where any measures by one country were "liable to affect substantially the general level of employment in the others", or wherever employment difficulties of any sort arose. Whether employment difficulties in particular sectors arose through causes internal or external to the Association, the Convention ought to provide for collective action to be taken to solve them.

The unions felt that the Convention should not "impede the operation of state enterprises as public utilities", but neither should such enterprises be used for the purpose of protection or trade discrimination.

There was full agreement that the trade union movements concerned should have a permanent and adequate place in appropriate institutions which may be established in the EFTA. To quote the statement:

"The trade unions should be represented on an equal footing with employers; the bodies in which they participate should meet regularly; they should have the right to place whatever items they desire on the agenda of such meetings; they should have access to the Council of Ministers, the governing body and the Secretariat; and they should have the right of representation in a consultative capacity on sub-committees dealing with matters directly relevant to the interests of labour."

The unions believed that as regards agriculture and fish, a system of "confrontation and subsequent agreement" would probably be the most satisfactory, but that this might require further consideration when more details were available.

The statement emphasised that the Contracting Parties should recognise the contribution the free unions had made, and would make, to the promotion and maintenance of full employment and the improvement of living and working conditions. It urged that the Convention should "guarantee to workpeople freedom of association and should recognise without reservation the right of the trade unions to enter into collective agreements with employers". There can be little doubt that this particular paragraph was aimed at Portugal, a country which the trade unions of the ICFTU have always believed does not allow the same liberties in the industrial and trade union spheres as do most other countries of Western Europe.

The statement concluded by pledging the representatives of the Conference to draw the attention of their own governments and negotiators to their conclusions, and to maintain contact between themselves with a view to further consultations.

The unions' statement made no reference to the fact that there were to be no equivalents in the Free Trade Association of the Commission, Assembly or Court of the European Common Market. As it has turned out, neither is there an Investment Bank, an Overseas Development Fund, a Social Fund or an Economic and Social Committee provided for, and these facts also escaped union comment. Although these missing features would doubtless be regretted by the unions of the Common Market countries, this is not necessarily so in the case of the unions directly concerned. The British and Scandinavian unions are probably just as anxious to keep far-reaching supranational powers out of the EFTA as are their respective governments. Austria and

Switzerland, for more practical reasons of political neutrality, tend towards the same viewpoint. The unions appear to favour the nature of the Association being limited to the minimal functions of a free trading agreement, provided full employment is aimed at and attained, and that they are consulted on appropriate matters.

There are other significant differences between the policy outlined in this statement of the Free Trade Association unions, and the policies consistently pursued by the Common Market unions. There were no references in the statement to a comprehensive social policy, or to upward harmonisation of social provisions, as provided for in the Common Market Treaty and eagerly supported by the unions concerned. There is no specific mention of whether the EFTA unions would desire free movement of labour to operate, as it will in the Common Market, with full union support. Indeed, certain parts of the statement, on the employment question, seem to imply that the unions are rather frightened that increased mobility might upset full employment in certain countries. The joint statement made no reference to the question of the control of private economic power or cartels – a subject on which the unions of the Common Market countries had been very voluble. It would appear that the EFTA unions would prefer the question of such control to remain a matter for individual governments, and not the Association.

All these factors show that there is a fairly wide divergence of viewpoint not only between the Governments of the "Inner Six" and the "Outer Seven", but also between their trade union movements. It is centred mainly on the question of the extent to which there should be supranational authority in the groupings, and whether the groupings are mainly for the purpose of easing trade, or for promoting complete economic integration in Western Europe, leading, later, to political unity.

The statement issued after the London Conference of the unions was, of course, drawn up before the text of the Convention of the Free Trade Association was known; and union views will be more specific in the light of Convention Articles. It is known, for instance, that the TUC is dissatisfied with the provisions for full employment as they stand, and believes they should be strengthened considerably. It is also of the view that less attention should be paid to the purely trade aspects of the Association if it is to go forward to the all-important task of reconciliation with the Common Market Six.

The Trade Union Executive Committee of the Common Market countries, and the ICFTU, itself, have both issued statements defining their attitude to the EFTA. The Secretary of the Executive Committee of the "Six" presented a report to his Annual Conference in Luxembourg in November 1959, which regretted that the Common Market had only six members, and did not include Britain or the other members of the EFTA. While it was important not to underestimate the willingness of other European countries to reduce trade barriers, this was not the same thing as willingness to move in the direction of a political union. It was hoped that an early solution to the problem of relations between the "Six" and the "Seven" would be found, and their Executive Committee would give all possible help to this end. In the meantime, they would seek common solutions to common problems with non-Community countries.

The Sixth World Congress of the ICFTU, meeting in Brussels in December, 1959, passed a resolution on regional economic integration. Such integration was welcomed wherever it occurred. The resolution included specific references to developments in Europe, and the problems raised by the division there. The appropriate section of the resolution said that the Congress:–

"Welcomes the creation of the European Economic Community and of the European Free Trade Association;

Regrets, however, the division that exists between these two groups of European countries;

Declares that it is in the interest of both groups that there should be immediate negotiations with a view to arriving at a close association between them;

Recognises that the action of the countries of the European Economic Community in extending to the other countries their first tariff reductions is an indication of their readiness to pay attention to the interests of other countries generally;

Hopes that the countries of the European Free Trade Association will reciprocate . . ."

The resolution went on to stress that the need is not only for more countries to be brought into regional integration schemes, but that such economic groupings must be outward-looking, so that international trade, generally, can be liberalised and expanded, and underdeveloped countries can be helped.

Walter Schevenels, secretary of the ICFTU's European Regional Organisation was, himself, optimistic about the prospects of a reconciliation between the "Six" and the "Seven". In an article he wrote in the November, 1959, issue of "Free Labour World" he expressed the view that the will to find a compromise would be very strong at the first signs of serious difficulties arising, and the two sides would be likely to come to terms.

Conclusion

It is apparent that all sections of the trade union movement with ICFTU connections take a broad view of the economic situation in Europe. None of them is so concerned with promoting the success of one project or another that it fails to put the unity of the differing groups as the first priority. This is an encouraging sign of a truly international outlook. Judging from previous attitudes, it is also likely that ICFTU organisations will not be opposed to the idea of the United States and Canada helping to overcome European differences of approach by broadening their scope and adopting an Atlantic basis for a wider association, as seems possible at the time of writing. The ICFTU has taken the view, previously, that the more comprehensive the dismantling of barriers to international trade, the better for all.

It is not very clear what part the ERO is likely to play in co-ordinating union activities, in view of developments. It seems possible that it may, again, be left without a major role in co-ordinating a limited group of European unions, or national centres. If the EFTA should run any length of time outside any wider arrangement with the Common Market, the unions of the "Seven" would probably create their own co-ordinating organ, as did the Common Market "Six". The ERO could play a substantial role, however, in attempting to bring the two together, and if it succeeded, in continuing to perform general co-ordinating work. If the two groupings should link up the great majority of the ERO's affiliates would be involved, especially if the suggested association of Greece and Turkey with the Common Market should come about.

As the trade union national centres of Western Europe are very concerned that the division which has appeared in the region should be closed with all haste, it is appropriate to consider what direct action they can take to help to achieve this, other than urging governments to continue negotiations. There appears to be one issue of particular significance in which the unions have a vital interest—the question of social provisions. The approach to this issue divides the views of the "Six" and the "Seven". The former have incorporated a number of social provisions in their Treaty, the latter have not. The "Six", and particularly France, believe that while this difference remains, a link-up would put Common Market trading prospects at a disadvantage *vis à vis* the EFTA.

A main reason why the "Seven" have no social provisions is because their unions have not pressed their governments for them to be incorporated. The British TUC, for instance, likes industrial conditions to be settled by collective bargaining, and is afraid that greater labour mobility, such as the Common Market is to have, may threaten the full employment position. It also fears that upward social harmonisation may be undesirable because it would bring state legislation into the industrial field.

Scandinavian unions tend to take a similar approach. A possible way out of these difficulties is suggested in more detail in the Conclusion to this study. However, it can be said, here, that it seems a little over-cautious on the part of British and Scandinavian national trade union centres to be shy of agreeing to social improvements because they would come from an unusual source: legislation based on international pro-visions. If they could adjust their policies, in this respect, it is quite possible that they could also persuade their governments to adopt an international policy, for instance, of counteracting any unemployment by readaption schemes and of putting some of France's fears at rest by agreeing to upward social harmonisation for any wider association.

If, by a move of this sort, the EFTA countries could persuade the Common Market countries that they were prepared to consider a link-up that was something more than a pure trading arrangement, then the pattern may well be set for counter-concessions which could bridge the remaining differences between them, and lead to a unity of Europe in the fullest sense.

PART FOUR

THE NATIONAL TRADE UNION MOVEMENTS

INTRODUCTION

No study of trade union viewpoints on, and participation in, Western European integration trends can be complete without an examination of the viewpoints and the role of the trade union federations, or national centres, in the countries most directly affected. In the case of the ICFTU, and its European Regional Organisation, attitudes have been very much influenced by the most powerful of their national affiliates; and their published statements, in some respects, are only the highest common factors of those national viewpoints. This may not be as true of the WFTU and the CISC, which have a higher degree of central authority; but in all cases the views of the national centres are of real importance, even where they are not the ultimate determining factors of the attitudes adopted by their Internationals.

A second important reason for examining trade union viewpoints at national level is because of the influence—in some cases considerable—that these have on more general attitudes in those particular countries, relative to integration questions. Although it is seldom possible to pinpoint specific instances where Governments of countries have taken a stand on particular issues as a consequence of trade union pressure, or influence, it is safe to say, nevertheless, that such pressures and influences have had considerable effect in the whole process.

In order that the viewpoints of national trade union centres may be seen in their correct context, it is necessary in each of the Chapters dealing with a country having a divided trade union movement, to begin with a brief outline of the organisational position, so that an assessment can be made of the relative influence of each of the national centres in that country. Only the largest of these centres, with potentialities for applying significant pressure, have been included.

Part Four is mainly concerned with attitudes to the newer integration projects of the Common Market and Euratom, and with the possibilities of a wider European association. Individual national centres in the Community countries, generally, are not greatly concerned about the "Outer Seven" agreement, as such, except insofar as it poses the question of what form of wider association, if any, may be negotiated between the "Six" and the "Seven". Information on national attitudes and experience in the Coal and Steel Community has been studied elsewhere, such as in the book "The Uniting of Europe", by Ernst B. Haas. Although the international trade union viewpoints and experience in the ECSC, as examined in Part 2, are very significant for this study, the national approaches are not of such great importance, because they are necessarily concerned more with specific national problems relating to the industrial sectors of coal and steel, rather than with attitudes to integration in the more general context, which are the subject of this study.

Special importance is attached to the attitudes of national centres to the original Free Trade Area proposals, and, by implication, to any eventual form of wider association which would include all, or most, of the OEEC countries. These attitudes will, no doubt, be taken into consideration by the individual Governments, when deciding what form of wider association would be acceptable. The position of Britain, as the main supporter of a wider association, and the most powerful of the Western European economies outside the Common Market, is of special importance; particularly because its TUC is, perhaps, the most influential trade union centre in Western Europe. A special Chapter has therefore been devoted to Britain.

Although proposals for a wider association in Europe were intended by their sponsors to be open to all members of OEEC, the advent of the European Free Trade Association appears to have made those seven member countries more likely to be participants in any general linking-up than those outside both the "Six" and "Seven" groupings. Iceland and Ireland have shown least signs of interest; Greece and Turkey are possible associates of the Common Market, but their trade unions are hardly destined to play an important part in the near future. Portugal, although a member of the "Seven" has no significant trade union movement in the accepted Western European sense. This leaves, in addition to Britain with a chapter to herself; Sweden, Norway, Denmark, Austria and Switzerland; and a brief survey of the positions of their trade unions is useful. This survey is largely concerned with the original Free Trade Area proposals, as their joint views on the EFTA are outlined in Chapter Fourteen. The approaches indicated give a general idea of their attitudes to a wider association.

Sweden

The main Swedish trade union organisation, the LO, favours a Free Trade Area type of wider association, rather than joining the European Common Market, because this would allow all the Scandinavian countries to keep their own, comparatively low, tariff barriers against the outside world, instead of levelling up to a higher common tariff, and running the risk of having trade restricted. A Free Trade Area would have been a good complement to their own proposed customs union in the Scandinavian countries, which the unions support. The LO believes that, owing to her high wage level, Sweden would need to concentrate on developing industries using a high ratio of capital to labour, in order to remain competitive without cutting wages, or jeopardising high employment levels. Greater specialisation would therefore be necessary. Investment planning and labour market planning would be essential for obtaining Swedish trade union support for joining a wider association. The Swedish unions are not as keen on the idea of social harmonisation being written into any wider treaty, as are the unions of France, and some of the other "Six". They tend to share the British view that this may not be natural to the system that has evolved in their countries, and believe that a complaints procedure, as envisaged by the British Government, would be sufficient provision against hardship arising.

Norway

The main trade union centre in Norway takes a similar view to its Swedish counterpart, on most matters. It states that a FTA, or wider European association, would be not worthwhile if it did not have as its primary objects the achievement of a more rapid growth in production and living standards, and of greater economic strength for its participants. There is some apprehension about transitional problems, and the effect of European competition on domestic markets, but the unions have stated that any unemployment arising from these difficulties ought to be absorbed in food production. There must be a comprehensive scheme for workers who would need to adapt themselves to new jobs; and although not opposed to freer labour mobility, internationally, in a wider association, the Norwegian unions would demand guarantees against immigrant labour being allowed to depress wage and other standards, arrived at by collective bargaining. Particular importance is attached to the rationalisation of international capital movement, in view of the effect it can have on employment levels. An Investment Bank is favoured, similar to that in the Common Market. There are some dissentient voices inside the organisation; but the majority wish for a wider association, linked with the Common Market of the "Six", and with any Nordic customs union which may operate eventually; provided the above policy points are incorporated and the unions are consulted during negotiations.

Denmark

Denmark is, perhaps, in the most difficult position among the Scandinavian countries. Although she has strong ties with Norway and Sweden, she sends the bulk of her agricultural exports to Britain and the countries of the "Six", and these are fundamental to her economy. If she joined the Common Market of the "Six" she would compete well with the Dutch, but tend to lose her privileges in Britain, as she would have to impose the higher Common Market tariff against British manufactured goods. If she did not join, she might lose to the Duch in exporting agricultural products to Germany, and other Community countries, although holding British markets. If she joined both the Common Market of the "Six" and the Free Trade Area, or some similar wider association, the Dutch would be able to claim similar privileges in the British markets. And all this is complicated by the British desire to exclude agriculture from a wider European free trade arrangement. This unenviable economic situation inevitably conditions Danish trade union thinking, as the national centre, the DSF, has a high proportion of agricultural workers in its membership. The DSF definitely prefers a development of the existing Nordic co-operation, perhaps in the form of a customs union, to any thought of joining the Community of the "Six", which it is believed may restrict Danish sovereignty too much, and is of a political character which is not favourable. There is also a fear that it would be a threat to the country's high wage levels. The DSF does not favour joining Euratom because it is closely linked with the Common Market. It prefers increased co-operation for the peaceful uses of atomic energy through OEEC, and through Nordic co-operation arrangements. It favours a wider free trade arrangement for Western Europe, provided agricultural products are included and the scheme is as comprehensive as possible, covering all commodity groups; and is given very liberal origin rules. The abolition of import restrictions should take place more slowly for low tariff countries, like Denmark, than for high tariff countries; and there should be adequate escape clauses so that a country would not be forced into deflationary policies if balance of payments difficulties arose.

Austria

The thinking of the central Austrian Trade Union Federation, the ÖGB, on European integration questions, is, as in the case of the DSF, conditioned by the country's economic and political situation. In many respects, therefore, ÖGB attitudes are synonymous with a mainly united "national" viewpoint. Considerations of Austrian neutrality have set the country against thoughts of joining the Common Market, because Russia tends to regard the Community as a hostile anti-Soviet bloc. At the time when preparations for signing the Common Market Treaty were being made, Austria, because of her special relations with Hungary during the uprising, had to be particularly careful in her relations with Russia. In any case, Austrian borders, for a large part, are contiguous with communist countries. But Austria then sent about half her exports to Community countries, and three quarters of all her exports to OEEC countries. She was therefore very interested in joining the proposed Free Trade Area, which she anticipated would not incur the same hostility from Russia. The ÖGB therefore welcomed the prospect of an FTA, and Austria's membership of it, but with some reservations. It wanted a social fund, and clauses to prevent restrictive practices of a monopolistic nature; as well as full employment policies, and an institution to deal with investment. Although the principle of labour mobility was favoured, stress should have been placed more on bringing work to localities where labour was available. The inclusion of agriculture would have been welcomed, though with special provisions; and trade unions should have been represented in any executive or legislative institutions set up for a FTA, in the opinion of the ÖGB.

Switzerland

The trade union movement in Switzerland is not as united as that in Austria or the Scandinavian countries. As well as the large federation, the USS, there is a Christian (Roman Catholic) national centre, a smaller Protestant centre, and several independent centres. Nevertheless, the USS is by far the most influential, catering for about five-eighths of all organised workers. It has considerable influence on Government thinking, and is influential, also, in the referendums which are taken from time to time. Like their Austrian colleagues, Swiss trade unionists are conditioned by the need to maintain political neutrality in international affairs, and this influences them against their country joining the Common Market. Swiss tariffs are below the level of the Common Market tariff, and also below those of most other countries, which is another reason for not joining. If she did join, she would have to raise her tariffs against the outside world, which already takes rather more of her exports than do the Common Market countries. The USS felt, nevertheless, that Swiss industries would benefit from freer trade, and it was favourably inclined towards joining a Free Trade Area, along the lines proposed by the British, so that Switzerland would not be excluded from integration trends. It welcomed the Common Market as long as Switzerland did not have to join it. But it thought that the method of tariff reduction laid down for the Community would not have been suitable in a FTA, as far as Switzerland was concerned. Because of her lower tariff barriers, she should be excluded from the first few reductions, if she joined any wider scheme, until such time as the tariffs of other countries were brought down to some comparable level.

Although few trade union organisations, in any country, have given much indication of what type of wider association in Europe would be acceptable to them as an alternative to the FTA, it may be helpful to have on record these views expressed by the various national centres, concerning the Common Market, Euratom and the original Free Trade Area Plan. These views may not all be applicable to any other arrangement that is reached for OEEC countries to establish closer co-ordination of economies and economic policies, but at least they lay down the main conditions of trade union support for that type of scheme. Any scheme which ignored the wishes of such a large section of European opinion would seriously prejudice its own chances of successful operation. As far as the Common Market and Euratom are concerned, it has been shown in Part 3 of the study that the character of the Communities will depend, to a large extent, on how the Treaty Articles are interpreted by Community institutions. The prospects for smooth running will be enhanced if trade union views are given due weight. The most important of these views are set out in the subsequent Chapters.

CHAPTER XV

GERMANY

If the Hitler regime in Germany, and the world war it precipitated, did nothing else, they ensured that the building of a united trade union movement became possible in the aftermath. This is true in the Federal Republic of Germany, at least, and it is the Federal Republic only which is referred to in this chapter, as Eastern Germany is not connected in any way with Western European integration. Neither is the Eastern German trade union movement connected in any way with the movement in West Germany. In fact, each movement is condemned by the other.

In West Germany, the building up of a new democratic trade union movement was one of the tasks of the occupation authorities immediately after the end of the war. At first, this was done separately by the British, the Americans and the French in their three occupation zones, but in October 1949 the three movements effected a merger, and set up the *Deutscher Gewerkschaftsbund* (DGB), or German Trade Union Federation, for the whole of the Federal Republic.

Since that time the DGB has continued to grow numerically, starting with about 5,000,000 members, and having reached a figure of 6,125,000 in 1957, according to the ICFTU Fifth World Congress Report. It represented then, as it does to-day, the vast majority of all trade unionists in Western Germany, and it is the DGB's views on integration, therefore, which are examined as being representative of Western German trade unionism.

The other national centres in the Federal Republic are the DAG, the white-collar workers' union; the DBB, or Civil Service Federation; and the CGD, the national Christian Trade Union Movement. The first two of these have memberships in the region of 400,000, most of whom incline to independence of the DGB, either because of professional status, or because they feel they have a stronger loyalty to occupation than to industry, which the DGB's policy of industrial trade unionism (that is, all workers in one industry being in the same union) does not allow them.

The CGD membership was claimed at 40,000 and estimated at 20,000, in 1958. This was in respect of the Federal Republic, and did not include membership in the Saar. Although there has been some active campaigning for Christian trade unions in Western Germany, the fact that the

CGD exists at all is almost entirely due to the efforts of the International Federation of Christian Trade Unions in promoting a breakaway from the DGB; an operation which has proved to be a relative failure, and has caused widespread resentment in the country, which was not confined to DGB circles.

Prior to the wrecking of the German trade union movement in the early 1930s, there had been a strong contingent of Christian trade unionists organised separately, and affiliated to the Christian International. In fact, the International had relied on Germany as one of its pillars of strength, which was undoubtedly the reason it tried to make a comeback in 1955. The reason for its failure is interesting. It is obviously not due to a decline in Christian support, as the popularity of the Christian Democratic Union, the Government political party, shows.

Of the CGD's total strength, only about thirty per cent was previously in DGB membership—according to DGB estimates. Of those workers who would normally ally themselves with the Christians, politically, the vast majority will not do so in the trade unions, and they remain loyal to the DGB which has, in fact, a considerable portion of its membership with Christian allegiances. The most likely explanation of the very small response to the Christian trade union call in Germany is that there is no longer a tradition of anti-clericalism in the DGB that was present in large sections of the old German trade unions, many of which had a strong Marxist outlook. If there is no anti-clericalism, then this removes the *raison d'être* of separate Christian trade union organisations.

Workers in Germany, to-day, apparently do not see what being a Christian has to do with being a trade unionist.

The DGB, then, is the massive workers' organisation, and its opinions carry a good deal of influence in the country, although, perhaps, not as much as its size would indicate. By comparison with most continental national trade union centres it is an example of what most governments would call moderate and responsible unionism. There is a coincidence of economic interest in what is good for the nation and what is good for trade unions, in DGB eyes. The DGB would not sponsor any action calculated to weaken Germany's postwar recovery. Its insistence on partnership in industry, by means of the co-determination principle—that is, equal representation on the management or supervisory boards in industrial undertakings—is the best indication of its determination to work for improvements from the inside, on those matters not determined by national collective bargaining.

DGB influence in Germany was rather greater a few years ago, when the dynamic Hans Böckler was at the head, than it is now. It was

Böckler who persuaded Konrad Adenauer, the Federal Chancellor, to pilot the Co-determination Bill through the German Parliament, in 1951, when the Government party and the American occupation authorities were reluctant to accept it.

It appears that the death of Böckler, and a subsequent decline in militancy in the DGB, may have been largely responsible for the declining influence of the organisation's viewpoint with the Government in recent years, and also for the decline in its rate of growth, in spite of large increases in the working population. To take the latter point first, from 1950 to the end of 1957, the labour force in the Federal Republic rose by 5.5 millions–due in large part to immigration from East Germany, which reached a peak annual figure of about 300,000. In spite of this, trade union membership rose by only 200,000 over the same seven year period. The proportion of the total registered labour force in trade union membership declined form 37.6% to 30.2% from 1950 to 1957.

That the DGB has not as much influence with the Government as it believes its size warrants is clear from the fact that the Government did not take the DGB into its confidence concerning progress made, or solicit its viewpoint on detailed matters, when the Common Market and Euratom Treaties were being negotiated. The DGB, in March 1957, condemned the Government for its secrecy, but it may have done so partly with its tongue in its cheek, and in order to help the Social Democratic Party in the elections to be held later in the year.

The DGB and the Social Democratic Party have fairly close affinity and sympathies, but no organic connection in the way that the TUC and the Labour Party have in Britain. Although nearly all the DGB leaders are Social Democrats–some of them Deputies in Parliament–and the majority of the trade union membership has a similar political inclination, the DGB cannot tie itself too closely to the Party. If it did so, it would run the grave risk of estranging the large minority of its members who have Christian Democratic leanings.

Nevertheless, DGB pronouncements on political matters are not usually far from the Social Democratic Party's policies.

The DGB Approach to Integration

Even if the strength of the DGB in its own country is not all that it might be, it is still a great power in the ICFTU, and its European Regional Organisation, and, more particularly, in the Trade Union Executive Committee of the "Six". In the Coal and Steel Community's trade union structure, especially, the DGB carries great weight, and the incorporation of the Saar Trade Union Federation into the DGB has increased this influence.

The DGB's opinions on European integration questions, therefore, are of more than academic interest. A decision in any of the international trade union councils, regarding Western Europe, which was flatly opposed to the DGB's viewpoint, would be unthinkable, and probably unworkable.

In most Western European countries the opinions of the trade union national centres have reflected fairly closely the approach of their respective Governments to integration. Apart from the WFTU-affiliated unions in France and Italy, there have not been many instances of a trade union viewpoint differing greatly from the "general" viewpoint taken in any particular country. Nowhere is this more so than in Germany. The DGB's desire for partnership in industry, and the close identification of itself with Germany's postwar recovery, is sufficient to ensure a harmony of views on the merits of economic integration.

To most observers, there still appears to be a strong desire among many Germans, though not all, to atone for their country's record during the war period. There is a strong desire to be accepted one hundred per cent into the community of nations, and to show that German initiative and democracy is second to none. Many Germans have learnt the lessons of the Hitler period, and there is a reaction from excessive nationalism and political centralism. This feeling is strong in the DGB, and on the political left, generally. European integration seems, to them, to be a very important factor in checking a possible regrowth of such tendencies.

Other European countries have pointed out that Germany, of all nations, stands to gain a tremendous amount from the introduction of the Common Market, because of her great economic powers and competitive strength. In considering this undoubted truth, the strong political desire in Germany for European unification, which is important for the reasons outlined, is sometimes lost sight of, or disregarded. It is probably not an exaggeration to say that the major considerations which determine most German attitudes, and especially DGB attitudes to integration, are political rather than economic. If this were not so, it seems doubtful if Germany would have conceded to France, so easily, the special social and economic clauses in the Common Market Treaty, designed to safeguard the French economy from over-vigorous competition.

A central theme of the DGB's has been that only by banding together, economically, can the nations of Western Europe ensure their continued independence of other states and power blocs. It does not believe that the individual European countries can prevent themselves becoming, to some extent, economic satellites of other powers, if they try to keep all their national sovereignty. Without integration, future living standards will be jeopardised, and the Community Treaties must therefore be used as a basis for working towards higher standards through a genuine relationship between the two sides of industry.

This is a point already made by the ICFTU's European Regional Organisation (ERO), and the DGB has specifically stated that it accepts this international policy. Consequently, there is little basic difference in the DGB's policy, although the emphasis varies here and there. One of the points on which it has elaborated more than the ERO, is the question of trade union representation in the Communities, and the adequacy, or otherwise, of the Economic and Social Committee.

It believes, of course, that the trade unions should have a large say in the working of the new Communities and their institutions, and that trade unionists ought to sit either on all institutional bodies, or be frequently consulted by those which have excluded them from membership. If this is not done, the Common Market may be put in danger of failure by too much stress being laid on tariff reductions and other technicalities, to the exclusion of far-reaching social policies and planning. One interesting point made in an official DGB pubication[1] was that as the composition of the Assembly and Council of Ministers does not include trade union representation in its own right, the Council should take the initiative and follow the Coal and Steel Community precedent by a unanimous decision to increase the numbers making up the European Commission. This would enable trade unionists to be seated on it by co-option.

The author had a number of criticisms to make of the Economic and Social Committee, set up by the Common Market and Euratom Treaties. He claimed that the full name of the Committee is not justified as it has virtually no economic functions to perform. It has no jurisdiction over investment policy, the Investment Bank or the limits of competition, and there is no Treaty provision, even, for consultation on these matters.

Moreover, the Committee's representation should have been on a tripartite basis, following the ILO principle, and it should have been given executive powers in many spheres. Its present composition, said the author, was unlikely to result in coherent opinions being formulated, and it must inevitably rely heavily on the goodwill of the Commission and the Assembly. It would have been an improvement if other Common Market organs had set a time limit within which they must discuss any proposals of the Committee.

1. Article entitled "Der Wirtschafts und Sozialausschuss im Gemeinsamen Markt", by ERICH GOETTLICHER in October, 1957, issue of *Gewerkschaftliche Monatshefte*.

DGB spokesmen have expressed some doubts and misgivings on certain other aspects of the Common Market Treaty. The need for mobility of labour within and between Community countries is recognised, and it has been suggested that multilateral social security regulations, and the close co-operation of the various national Ministries of Labour could help to ease obstructions to free movement. As things are in the Treaty, rather too much is left to the forces of free play, and there may be some structural unemployment when competition causes shifts in the location of industry, and workers are unable to follow, because of lack of social funds, and of housing.

Nevertheless, the DGB Executive Board has felt that there is some danger of excess immigration into Germany from countries where there is not only considerable unemployment, but lower wage levels. If this were allowed to occur, the German wage structure might be threatened. It appears that the DGB would like to see some sort of planning attached to the free movement of labour, to avoid social repercussions.

As far as international improvements and harmonisation in welfare benefits are concerned, the view has been put in DGB circles that an essential prerequisite is to establish realistic currency exchange rates in the Community. This should be achieved by halting inflation in some countries, particularly France, allowing those countries to establish themselves in better competitive positions.

The DGB is distinctly uneasy about the association of overseas territories with the Common Market, and believes it could lead to a draining away of investments needed for creating new jobs and developing Germany's own economy. There is also a feeling, in some quarters, that certain of those territories where there is much civil and military strife, such as Algeria, may be a great strain on the finances and the political goodwill of Community nations which are not otherwise implicated.

There has been some DGB criticism, also, of the European Investment Bank, on the grounds that it is too much like any other bank, and its terms of reference place insufficient stress on the question of providing capital for special development.

The Social Fund must be regarded as only a beginning, in the field of readaptation in which it is intended to operate, and more far-reaching proposals ought to be forthcoming.

The DGB is a keen supporter of Euratom, and believes the scheme to be the only solution to Europe's energy problems. International co-operation on all peaceful aspects of atomic energy is regarded as vital. Having said that, it is not completely satisfied with the Treaty in its present form, and would have liked to have seen a special section of the

Euratom Commission being given responsibility for social, and particularly health and safety questions. This section could have had an advisory committee composed equally of employers and trade unionists. Two commissions, in which trade unionists would have been represented, along with employers and specialist professional people, have also been suggested. They would deal with security and with economic research and industrial training.

In spite of the close alignment of the policies of the DGB and the Social Democratic Party, the two have not always been as much in harmony on European integration questions as they are at present. At the outset of the integration process–when the Coal and Steel Community was formed–the DGB supported it, for industrial reasons, but the Social Democrats did not, for political reasons.

The politicians were strongly committed, as they still are, to work towards reunification of East and West Germany. It was feared that the inception of the common market in coal and steel would, perhaps, be an obstacle to reunification, because it would involve West Germany in what the Soviet Union would regard as a hostile political alliance.

Both DGB and Social Democratic personalities now believe that the possibility of reunifying the country, without a major change in general East-West relationships, is not to be highly rated. Indeed, politicians of all political shades have probably come to realise this unwelcome fact, and while German reunification is still regarded as an indispensable propaganda item for their policies, it is often little more than that.

Consequently, neither the DGB nor the Social Democrats have put much stress on the theoretical obstruction to reunification, which the creation of the Common Market and Euratom imply. They have been inclined to gloss over unpalatable facts about their lost lands, and to work for unification westward, rather than eastward.

A further indication of German enthusiasm for a more closely unified Europe was evident from the DGB's attitude to the original Free Trade Area plan (FTA). Knowing that Britain would be the senior partner of the non-Community countries in a FTA agreement, it may have been supposed that Germans would have been rather wary of the intensified competition which this would bring for their country.

This has not been the case. DGB leaders believed that Germany could match Britain's competition and that her industries would not be set back. But it was stressed that this was not their main concern. They wanted a FTA because it would have checked any tendency of the "Six" to become absorbed in themselves to a degree which would have cut them off too much from the outside world. They wanted a FTA because they believed in a united Europe. They would have preferred that other countries of Western Europe joined the Common Market itself, but disappointment at their failure to do so did not prevent the DGB from attempting to achieve the widest possible FTA as a second best.

It is essential, however, in DGB eyes, that as time goes on, any wider association should become more and more closely associated with the Common Market, so that European economic unification can come about gradually, and harmoniously. It has kept both projects in mind because it believes that the one does not exclude the other, but is complementary to it. The integration of the two projects cannot be achieved by one master plan, but only, perhaps, by taking an evolutionary view of the later one, and conducting policies flexibly.

Although the DGB is probably keener on having a wider association than many other national trade union centres in the six countries, this is not wholly for ideological or political reasons. It firmly believes that the close harmonisation of a Common Market and a wider scheme can be a powerful instrument for bringing about higher employment levels, higher living standards and higher social security benefits. It can also help improve conditions in the less developed countries.

The DGB is the most powerful national trade union force working in the movement for Western European integration. Its numerical strength is second only in the region to that of the Britith TUC, and it works with typical German efficiency and earnestness. The DGB faces the prospect of a unified Europe with eagerness and confidence, concerning the major role it will play in it.

CHAPTER XVI

FRANCE

The French trade union scene is one of diversity, disunity and complexity; brought about by a long history of warring groups within the trade union movement. The last major upheaval of the movement took place in December 1947, when the powerful *Confédération Générale du Travail* (CGT) was split asunder by a group of trade unionists who opposed the allegedly unnecessary strike policy which its leadership was pursuing. Previous splits had taken place in 1921 and 1939, and all through the same basic cause–intense rivalry and disagreement between the communists and the non-communists.

It may be because of this that a high proportion of French workers are not organised in any union, and those who are organised include many who fail to pay their contributions regularly. Trade unionism is often regarded by the workers with the same mixture of apathy and cynicism as was marked in the French attitude to the politicians and governments of the Fourth Republic. It is likely, also, that the trade unions have forfeited some of the membership they may otherwise have claimed, by spending too much time preaching trade union unity as an ideal, though not as a practical possibility, except in CGT eyes. Efforts could better have been expended on building up the existing organisations, which cater for diverse viewpoints, thus increasing total strength through separate sections.

The group which broke away from the CGT in 1947 was led, in the main, by the older trade unionists who had seen the bitter struggles and schisms of the past. The decision, therefore, was not taken lightly, because they knew very well the weakness it would bring to the movement, and the great difficulties that would have to be faced in setting up a new organisation. They had neither funds nor buildings of their own, but they used the Journal *Force Ouvrière*, with which they had been closely associated, as a rallying point for those who could no longer accept the policies of the CGT's communist leadership.

The initials "CGT" were well known and respected by French trade unionists, because of the organisation's long, if chequered, history. When the *Force Ouvrière* group decided to set up their organisation, they joined the two names, and called themselves the *Confédération*

Générale du Travail–Force Ouvrière (CGT–FO). However, it has commonly become known just as *Force Ouvrière*.

Large numbers of trade unionists left the CGT without transferring to the *Force Ouvrière*, and were therefore lost to the trade union movement. Many others who were not communists, and did not particularly approve of their leaders' political policies, nevertheless remained in the CGT. They have continued to do so, and it is still the largest national trade union centre in France. Its members stay because of historical tradition, because it is the most militant, and because it is still probably the best organised of the large national centres, although there was evidence of a decline in its influence during 1958. In trade unionism, as in politics, Frenchmen often prefer to protest by giving support to the more extreme organisations.

The *Force Ouvrière* has never properly got over the handicap of its difficult start, in spite of some help and advice from trade unions abroad, and from the ICFTU. It has suffered from what is a fairly severe handicap in France–apparent association with successive governments since 1947. The *Force Ouvrière* claims that it has no political ties, and yet it is well known that its general sympathies are with the Socialist Party, which has been a cornerstone in the formation of governments in the Fourth Republic. The *Force Ouvrière* and the Party differed widely in their attitudes to General de Gaulle's accession to power, however.

Add to their generally close allegiance, the fact that successive governments have found it convenient to patronise the *Force Ouvrière* in circumstances where it was desired to have an organisation to play off against the CGT, and it becomes fairly clear why it remains the weakest of the main national centres. Many trade unionists believe it cannot work for them as effectively as other organisations. Greater organisational efficiency and more dynamic leadership would help to inspire confidence.

It is very difficult to get a true indication of the relative membership figures in the separate trade union centres; firstly because the organisations have not sufficiently well organised contribution records to be certain of the figures themselves, and secondly because they are all prone to exaggerate their estimates. The *Force Ouvrière* answers membership queries with the reply that it is affiliated to the ICFTU on a strength of one million. But their actual membership probably lies between 400,000 and 500,000.

The CGT is generally supposed to have over a million members. The figure is probably nearer $1\frac{1}{4}$ millions than the $1\frac{1}{2}$ millions which supporters claim. The Christian centre, the *Confédération Française des Travailleurs Chrétiens* (CFTC) claims 750,000, but their estimate is probably on the generous side, as is that of the white-collar workers' federation the *Confédération Générale des Cadres* (CGC), which claims 160,000 for itself. Independent estimates are of 650,000 and 100,000 respectively.

The general picture is that French trade unions have a membership which is a much lower proportion of the working population than in most well-developed countries. The level of contributions for those workers who are trade unionists is a lower percentage of weekly wages than is common in most countries, even if a high proportion of the nominal contribution was actually paid, which is not the case. Lack of finance, lack of organisation, lack of unity and an excess of policies with purely political motives are the key factors in the weakness of French trade unionism.

Although the CGT is the largest trade union centre in France, successive French governments have made it part of their policy to try and deprive it of what influence they can, because of its association with the Communist Party, its affiliation to the pro-communist World Federation of Trade Unions, internationally, and the political nature of a number of disruptive strikes it has called. Government discrimination is notable in its refusal to nominate a CGT representative as the official workers' delegate to conferences of the International Labour Organisation (ILO). Instead, they usually nominate a *Force Ouvrière* and a CFTC delegate in alternate years.

The CGT is naturally dissatisfied with its treatment, in view of its membership. It considers itself to be the most representative organisation as far as the workers are concerned, but it can do little about the discrimination, in spite of the fact that the ILO Constitution provides in Article 3, Paragraph 5, for workers' delegates to be chosen by the governments "in agreement with the industrial organisations . . . which are most representative . . . in their respective countries".

There was a complaint, shortly after the ILO's inauguration, from a trade union centre in the Netherlands that, although it was the largest of all the centres in the country, the government had not secured its agreement in nominating a workers' delegate to the third session of the ILO Conference. The Permanent Court of International Justice was asked for an advisory opinion on the interpretation of the Article, which it gave in 1922. It found that there was no definition of what "representative" meant in referring to "the most representative organisations". Its own stated opinion was that they were those organisations which best represented the workers. It continued: "what these organisations are is a question to be decided in the particular case, having regard to the circumstances in each particular country at the time when the choice falls to be made. Numbers are not the only test of the representative

character of the organisations, but they are an important factor." It
further stated that "The Article throws upon the Government of the
State the duty of deciding, on the data at its disposal, what organisations
are, in point of fact, the most representative."

In view of this finding, the CGT is unable to demand effectively, that
it be given representation at the ILO, and the CGIL in Italy is in a
similar position.

The CGT in recent years, has found itself constrained in other ways,
and not always able to take up the position of implacable hostility to
the establishment that it would like to do. The reason may be that the
French workers have wearied of political strikes, and the shortage of
money and lack of achievement that go with them. There are still a good
number of non-communists in the organisation, some of them holding
responsible positions, especially at local levels. A too slavish devotion to
French Communist Party policies may alienate these people from the
CGT.

At national level, too, there are a few dissentients, and at least one
member of the CGT Executive Board, who claims not to be a communist, advocates his organisation declaring itself independent of the
Communist Party. The fact is that the CGT has now become rather
shy of taking action on some major matters unless it can obtain the
support of at least one of the other national centres for some sort of joint
action. In this, it is following WFTU policy of trying to bring about a
type of popular front among the trade unions.

It has had certain limited successes. The *Force Ouvrière* is uncompromisingly hostile, but the CFTC takes a more expedient view, and
will co-operate fairly closely when it considers that a refusal to do so
may weaken its position *vis à vis* the CGT. It takes the view that it is
rather ostrich-like to ignore the existence of anything as large as the
CGT. For example, the CFTC believes it regrettable that the French
Government decided not to grant the CGT's request to be awarded
consultative status in the Common Market's Economic and Social
Committee, in view of its large industrial membership. It believes that
this may put the CGT in a position of strength, at some future date, if
Common Market trends should not turn out well for trade unionists.
The CGT would then be able to blame the CFTC and the *Force Ouvrière*
for the position, and absolve itself from responsibility for it.

The *Force Ouvrière's* attitude is quite different. It is so opposed to the
CGT, and any form of recognition of it, that it has stated that even if
that organisation had been given representation in the Common Market,
the *Force Ouvrière* would have tried to avoid any contact at that level.
The *Force Ouvrière* and the CFTC are willing to co-operate with each

other on issues where their policies are similar, but the former's hostility to the CGT is still so great that it will not countenance co-operating with the CFTC on any issues where the Christians are, themselves, co-operating with the CGT.

As for the small white collar workers' federation, the CGC, its own position, with regard to the CGT, is self-defined as being mid-way between *Force Ouvrière* aloofness and CFTC forthcomingness. Relations between it and these latter two organisations are generally cordial. The CGC is not affiliated, internationally, to the ICFTU, the WFTU or the CISC. Perhaps this is for the same reason as it claims not to have any links, official or unofficial, with any of the French political parties. That is, it would not feel quite at home with any of them because its membership is composed largely of foremen, technicians and the lower grades of management. But it has some of the higher grades in membership as well. It is, in fact, as much a professional association as a trade union organisation. Perhaps because of the category of its membership, it exerts an influence in the trade union field which is more than proportionate to its size – mainly through personal contacts in elevated circles.

The CFTC, like the *Force Ouvrière*, has certain political influences, and adopts specific political policies. Like the *Force Ouvrière*, again, it does so without having any official links with any political party. The CFTC is affiliated to the Christian International, the CISC, and takes a major part in its activities. It also has informal consultations with leaders of the French Roman Catholic Party, the MRP, and its sympathies and membership are predominantly Roman Catholic. But there is a substantial minority of its membership which is on the political left, and does not believe that trade union policies should be closely linked with religious questions.

This is one of the reasons for the CFTC's official aloofness from the MRP. It has a ruling which applies throughout France, except for Alsace, that CFTC leaders must not be Deputies in the National Assembly. The political contacts of the CFTC have declined in importance with the rapid decline of MRP influence and voting strength since 1946.

However much the French trade union centres may deny subservience or allegiance to political parties, their natural sympathies make it impossible for them to be completely uninfluenced by political manoeuvres, or, indeed, not to be parties to them in many circumstances. The complexities surrounding the four main national centres, and their relationships with each other, are heightened by their three separate international affiliations and their internal party political sympathies. This makes it very difficult to give any detailed picture which is not invalidated shortly after it is drawn.

As events move on, the picture changes, and to-day's analysis may be obsolete to-morrow. This is noticeable in assessing French trade union attitudes to European integration. French Governments have proved the most difficult of the negotiating parties to satisfy, both in the preliminaries to the Common Market, and in the OEEC proceedings to work out the basis for a Free Trade Area. There seems to have been a corresponding number of doubts in the various French trade union centres, many of them based on a residue of mistrust and suspicion, rather than an objective critique of the policies of others.

Trade Union Views on Integration

The CGT follows a policy of complete opposition to all European integration projects, on principle. This is not surprising in view of its affiliation to the WFTU, which sets out this policy at the international level. Furthermore, the WFTU's General Secretary, Louis Saillant, is, himself, a CGT man. The CGT spokesmen state their position thus: they are opposed to free enterprise, and especially free enterprise between nations, which the Coal and Steel Community, the Common Market and Free Trade Areas imply. They are in favour of the state taking a tighter control in all matters affecting external trade, and this doctrine is reinforced by the necessity of state control as a means of correcting the present faults of the French economy, and guarding against a recession and heavy unemployment.

There are also fears expressed, which are not by any means exclusive to the CGT, that Germany, with her great economic strength, will dominate the Common Market to the detriment of France, and that the freeing of the movement of capital and labour, under the Treaty, will depress the country's standards. The CGT is particularly apprehensive that the freeing of capital may somehow bring foreign financial pressure to bear in a manner that may depress French wages. It fears that an influx of foreign labour may have the same effect.

It is also hostile to the Common Market Treaty proposals for the associated overseas territories of member states. It believes that heavy social investment must have priority in underdeveloped countries and that the provisions of the Treaty are not sufficient to ensure this. There is the consequent fear that much of the capital for development will come from American sources, which would be disastrous, from the CGT viewpoint.

The CGT has no good word to say for the European Coal and Steel Community (ECSC), and is not impressed with the prospect of a modified ECSC scheme of readaptation being followed in the Common Market. Although France has been the country in which most ECSC readaptation has taken place, the CGT believes that its scale has, nevertheless, been too small to judge its result properly.

There exists an international committee, which has WFTU support, whose purpose is to work out a joint approach to Common Market problems for trade unions of all affiliations. In fact, it is little more than a combination of forces between the CGT and the WFTU-affiliated CGIL in Italy, which, incidentally, is opposed to the Common Market Treaty in many details, but not in principle; a very different standpoint to that of the CGT.

If the CGT is asked why, in view of its hostility to the Common Market, it has tried to persuade the French Government to give it consultative status on the European Economic and Social Committee, the reply is that it is not in order to sabotage integration, as its opponents have suggested. It is to inform themselves, and gain the necessary knowledge about Common Market functioning to be able to protect the interests of its members. A parallel instance is quoted of the CGT working in with Joint Works Councils in France, although being opposed to them in principle.

The CGT claims that in its opposition to the original Free Trade Area (FTA) scheme, it was in harmony with all the other trade union centres. It believed that the FTA would do much harm to France, economically, on top of the mischief it predicted the Common Market would bring. The CGT says it is significant that French economic circles were more opposed to the FTA than were political circles, particularly in the *Quai d'Orsay*; and also that the economically strong countries, such as Germany and the Netherlands, favoured an FTA more than the other partners of the "Six".

CGT opposition to the FTA may be another way of indicating that it is opposed to any scheme which will unify the Western half of Europe, and prevent the possibility, however remote, of the Eastern half eventually being admitted to some of its institutions.

As far as the *Force Ouvrière* and the CFTC are concerned, their own attitudes to European integration, and the Common Market, in particular, have apparently been fairly close to Government and public opinion. One way to define it would be to call it idealistic enthusiasm, tempered by a nagging fear that there may be unpleasant consequences.

A predominant fear is that France may be giving too much away to other Community countries in that she has traditionally had protection, and is the country which depends least of the "Six" on international trade. The unions are all in favour of the new extended Community market, but are nervous of doing away with the tariff barriers, nevertheless.

The French trade unions, more than any others, (and French employers share their view) have insisted that upward harmonisation of working conditions and wages of the countries concerned is essential if free trade is to be allowed to operate. This is not only regarded as a means of obtaining general improvements, as it is also by the unions of other countries, but is considered essential to France's competitive interests. This is because, generally speaking, France has shorter normal working hours in industry, higher overtime payments, and the employers have heavier social welfare charges to pay than is the case in most other countries, adding to their total labour costs.

The *Force Ouvrière* and the CFTC each give a cautious welcome to proposals for free movement of labour and capital, but share, with the CGT, some doubts as to whether the labour market may be swamped from Italy, for example. However, they note that the Common Market is intended to be based on expanding economies, eased by readaptation, so are not too pessimistic about the prospects in this direction. The *Force Ouvrière* welcomes the potential influx of foreign capital because it would relieve some of France's burdens in respect of the overseas territories.

The two national centres have each placed great stress on the importance of having trade union representation at all levels in the European integration projects, and expressed dissatisfaction at the comparatively minor role which trade unionists have, in fact, been allotted. They would have liked to have seen representatives on the two European Commissions. The CFTC viewpoint is that the European Economic and Social Committee should not be confined to a consultative status, but should have executive functions in certain appropriate fields. The Christian Federation also made protests against the Government having given the unions insufficient part in the preparation for the Common Market Treaty.

The *Force Ouvrière*, which has fairly strong overseas sections, particularly in Algeria, is a keen supporter of the "Eurafrican" aspect of the Common Market Treaty – one of the aspects that has raised doubts in the minds of other trade union centres, inside and outside France. Nevertheless, it hopes, and believes, that the Common Market will engender greater international co-ordination of European trade union activities than hitherto.

The non-communist trade union centres are cautiously favourable to the idea of international collective bargaining in Western Europe. The CFTC, in line with international christian trade union policy, is in favour of using the International Labour Organisation as much as possible to achieve this. It believes that international collective bargaining could come about through the introduction of European Regional Conventions, passed by the ILO. If this proved impossible, perhaps suitable conventions could be brought into being through the Economic Community, itself.

The *Force Ouvrière* feels that settlements on conditions of employment could operate on an international level in respect of holidays, hours of work etc., within the foreseeable future. But the principle could not be extended to wage settlements until such time as an international currency exists. The CGC takes a rather more sceptical view of the whole concept and thinks there is small possibility of international collective bargaining coming about on a major scale, unless it be in the mining industry, under the ECSC.

CGC views on all aspects of European integration are worthy of note for more than one reason. Small though the organisation is, it wields a fair amount of influence, as already indicated. The problems of integration have been thought about deeply by André Malterre, the President, who is the determining factor in the organisation's policymaking, and is a member of the Community's Economic and Social Committee. He has a viewpoint which is somewhat unorthodox in European trade union circles – partly because the CGC's special category of membership, the white-collared workers, does not have interests or ideas by any means identical with those of manual workers.

In a lecture delivered at the National Mining College of St. Etienne, in January 1958, Malterre made it clear that his organisation approached the subject of European integration from a standpoint involving the national interest, rather than sectional interests. So much so, indeed, that he appears to elevate the importance of the national community to a level surpassing the international, or European, interest; and to regard it as an end in itself.

In parts, the standpoint seems jingoistic, as when Malterre declares that the geographical extent of the Common Market does not take France's traditional alliances into account, notably in the matter of the Atlantic Pact. He continues: ". . . one may doubt that the title 'Community', when it is not based, in reality, on any political solidarity, such as that clearly seen at the time of the Suez crisis, is anything more than an empty word."

It is realised that Britain's decision to stay out of the Common Market was entirely her own, but it is greatly regretted that, if France were going to be a partner in some scheme for integrating economies, she could not have been in partnership more traditionally, linked with Britain, and countries adjacent to the Mediterranean. France had more in common with them than with Germany, and other members of the Common Market, as at present composed.

To have a Common Market of six countries, and then to try and attach a Free Trade Area on to it, was rather putting the cart before the horse. It would have been better to have realised the prime importance of not dividing Europe in an unnatural way, and to have tried, instead, to do rather less, more comprehensively. A wider preferential tariff zone may have been the appropriate solution, although it was realised that this may have been difficult to reconcile with the provisions of GATT, the General Agreement on Tariffs and Trade.

The whole conception of the Common Market, is was felt, had sprung from political and ideological beliefs which did not pay sufficient heed to the economic risks and consequences for France. As Malterre put it in his lecture:

> "From the point of view of the general economy, it is to be regretted that the Treaty of Rome may have been ratified with such little consideration at a moment when France is suffering from a deficit in its balance of payments. But for some people the matter would seem to be a real act of faith, comparable to the outdated belief that the best way to teach a dog to swim is still to throw him into the river–it happens sometimes, however, that the dog drowns. To expose our economy to the full blast of the common market is to take just such a risk . . ."

Furthermore, the new system of preferences, which the inclusion of the overseas territories in the Common Market would bring about, was not in France's best interests. The investment in those territories from non-French sources would be inadequate compensation for France's loss of preferences, and autonomy in policy matters.

However, now that they had got a Common Market they must abide loyally by its provisions. But it would have been very much better if the provisions of Article 8, setting out the stages for tariff reductions, could have been framed in such a way that the first stage of four years could have been regarded as a probationary period for the six Community countries, so that there would have been no compulsion to continue with the whole scheme in that form if it had not been working out well. The ratification of the Treaty, in fact, ought to have been an act of betrothal, and not a marriage ceremony. The signatory countries had decided on a trial period of five years with regard to their commitments in overseas territories, and they should have done likewise for the general Treaty provisions.

Finally, the Common Market made the CGC nervous of the possibility of French industries being taken over by foreign capital, as this may bring about a form of foreign control which would tend to push out

Frenchmen in favour of foreigners, in some technical and administrative grades for which the CGC caters.

Their attitude to the original Free Trade Area proposals was strained between the desire for the maintenance of a close association with Britain, and their scepticism about whether it would bring any benefits for France. It was thought that several French industries might be adversely affected, and a FTA which did not provide the necessary social guarantees to trade unionists would be unacceptable, anyway. It would have been extremely difficult to harmonise economic policies in a European Free Trade Area, because the region, it was said, included countries in very different stages of economic development.

The CGC does not believe that Europe is a cohesive entity, or that the nationals of its countries are inclined to act as true Europeans. Supranationalism is therefore out of place, and France, potentially, has a more fruitful partnership with her overseas territories and with nations of the West. The CGC has rather the same sort of traditional veneration for the franc area and the French Union, as Britain has for the sterling area and the Commonwealth, and does not want the situation radically disturbed. Having said that, the organisation regarded the FTA proposals with less distaste than the Common Market Treaty–an opposite stand to that taken by other French national trade union centres.

If the *Force Ouvrière* and the CFTC had anything at all in common with the CGC on their approach to wider European integration questions, it was the viewpoint that although a FTA may have been desirable, politically, to prevent the "Six" countries becoming economic introverts, it was certainly undesirable in anything like the original form proposed by the British.

The viewpoint of these two larger Trade Union Federations was not very different from what was regarded as the normal, or general, viewpoint of France on the FTA. That is, that while the Common Market would bring harmonisation in Europe, and some benefits for France, the FTA would only have meant more severe competition. American capital would have been attracted into Britain, and goods from the Commonwealth would have leaked, tariff free, into Common Market countries, through the United Kingdom. The attempt by Britain to exclude agriculture from the scheme was resented. There was a general French desire for social provisions in a FTA Treaty, as well as in the Common Market, and this was particularly strongly echoed by the unions, which felt that if Britain and other countries were to gain the benefits of free trade, they must also shoulder some of the burdens. This would have meant, in their eyes, contributing to an investment bank, as well as approving adequate social provisions, in a treaty which would provide for full employment, readaptation of workers, etc.

Most important of all, perhaps, (and here the *Force Ouvrière* was particularly adamant) there should have been social harmonisation. By this, they meant a form of social accounting which would have had regard to the real standards of living in the various countries, with a view to narrowing disparities radically. It would not have meant trying to impose a given pattern of social charges or social benefits on the participating countries, but only trying to ensure that the total of the appropriately weighted factors, reckoned nationally, was not far out of line with the other countries. All these provisions would have to have been agreed, in principle, as a prerequisite for a FTA Treaty. Binding declarations would have to have replaced, or added to, the loose ideas and intentions for the FTA, which were proposed.

Neither the *Force Ouvrière* nor the CFTC, particularly the former, came out as directly as they might have done against the FTA proposals. The main reason was that the trade union internationals to which they are affiliated favoured the FTA, in principle. The *Force Ouvrière*, as a comparatively weak member of the ICFTU, and its European Regional Organisation, could not flout the agreed international policy, which the British TUC had a large share in formulating.

The general picture is that the CGT is opposed to all forms of integration, in line with international WFTU policy; the CGC disapproves of the form and scope of the Common Market, disapproved, less strongly, of the original FTA plan and believes that a preferential tariff zone would be better. The CFTC and the *Force Ouvrière* approve of the Common Market in most respects, but will restrainedly disapprove of any wider association unless it has similar written-in guarantees to the Rome Treaty.

CHAPTER XVII

ITALY

In some respects the postwar record of the trade union movement in Italy is similar to that of France. The French trade unions, of course, did not suffer the same complete discontinuity during the war period (although they had to go underground) as the Italian unions, which had to be set up anew under the aegis of the allied occupation authorities, following the fascist era of corporate and state-subservient unions. The similarity between Italy and France lies in the fact that each country started out with a large unified confederation encompassing a good proportion of all trade unionists. In France there was a christian federation in addition.

In each case the unity of the large comprehensive confederation has been shattered by communist versus non-communist rivalries. In each country the pattern has settled down into the operation of three major trade union centres, all maintaining their independence on account of their political differences. In each country the largest national centre is pro-communist, the second largest pro-christian and the third largest pro-socialist, though all of them are anxious to disclaim any organic links with political parties. As in France, the history of the postwar trade union movement in Italy has been one of disunity and political "dog-fighting" which has taken up a great deal of time and effort that might otherwise have been devoted to direct ways of improving conditions for the membership.

The one major difference between the two countries has been in the international affiliation of the christian trade union centre. The CFTC in France is affiliated to the International Federation of Christian Trade Unions (CISC), but the CISL in Italy is affiliated to the International Confederation of Free Trade Unions (ICFTU), along with its socialist rival, the UIL.

The largest trade union centre is the *Confederazione generale italiana del lavoro* (CGIL), or Italian General Confederation of Labour. It was formed in Naples in January 1945, with the approval of the Allied Military Government, and was the result of a Pact made by representatives of the three main political anti-fascist groups: the Communists, the Socialists and the Christian Democrats, who wished to have one unified trade union centre, not tied to any political group.

In spite of the declared aim of keeping the CGIL uncommitted, politically, it was not very long before the predominance of communists within the organisation, at all levels, became apparent. Generally speaking, this was because of the greater experience, worthier working-class records and higher state of organisation of local communist labour leaders at the end of the war. Their superiority in office in the new organisation was partly assured through this. The same can be said at the national level. Of the three General Secretaries of the organisation neither the socialist not christian office-holders were a match for the communist, Giuseppe Di Vittorio, who had an outstanding personality, and was an indefatigable worker in labour causes.

One of the factors that has enabled the CGIL to retain a large following, even after the breakaway of the christians and the socialists, has un-doubtedly been Di Vittorio's personality. He was an international trade union figure, and held the Presidency of the World Federation of Trade Unions (WFTU), as well as his CGIL post, until his death in November 1957. He was certainly the most respected trade union figure in the country, and the most revered in working-class circles.

By 1947, a membership of $5^1/_2$ millions was claimed for the CGIL, but there is no reliable way of testing whether this figure was an over-estimate, as seems likely. As in some other countries, such as France, there is no exact way for the trade union membership to be calculated, even by top officials. This is owing to the rather slack-set-up organisa-tional and contributory systems operating. Union finance suffers, also, as Italian union dues are very low, and a high percentage of members do not pay the full annual amount. This position now affects all three national trade union centres. The CGIL, perhaps, is less at a disadvantage than the other two centres, because it can rely on funds from the Com-munist Party to help it out. The other federations cannot rely on much support from the Christian or Socialist Parties.

The split of the CGIL actually came about in 1948. Co-operation within the Confederation had been possible while the three main political parties; Communist, Socialist and Christian Democrat; had been co-operating in the Government of the country. When the Com-munists were excluded from the Government in 1947, and assumed an opposition role, this spelt the end of any harmony within the CGIL, between the opposed political groups. The Christians were the first to feel that their position was intolerable, and they broke away, and formed the Free Italian General Confederation of Workers, the LCGIL.

Next, the right wing Socialist and Republican elements broke away, in 1949, and together formed the Italian Labour Federation, the FIL. It did not attract great support, and the following year the leaders decided to join with the larger LCGIL, which then took the new name of *Confederazione italiana sindacati lavoratori* (CISL), or Italian Confederation of Workers' Unions. This organisation has remained intact and grown in strength almost continuously.

The bulk of the FIL membership disapproved of the action of their leaders in deserting to the Christians, and in 1950 they joined forces with a further group of right-wing Socialists who had become disenchanted with the CGIL, and formed the *Unione italiana del lavoro* (UIL), the third of the trade union centres which has endured, and grown.

The great majority of the left-wing Socialists, associated with Signor Nenni, have remained within the CGIL, although there have been differences between them and the Communists. The CGIL continues to preach unity of the working classes, and to this end has even made it known that there is a strong body of opinion within it that is not in favour of working too closely with the Italian Communist Party, because such partisanship is held to prejudice unity. It is claimed that the CGIL has been left rather in the position of being closely associated with the Communists because the Christians, the right-wing Socialists and the Republicans left the organisation to form their own national centres, in alliance with their particular parties. The CGIL leaders give the impression that there was really nothing else left for them to do, in these circumstances, but associate with the remaining large political party, the Communist Party.

A tendency to diverge, at times, from the strict Communist Party policies was prevalent under Di Vittorio's leadership. He had never been regarded as a one hundred percent Moscow man. His successor, Agostino Novella, who also succeeded Di Vittorio as President of the WFTU, is regarded as a more rigid Party man, and it is thought in some circles that the CGIL may be brought back by him further into the Communist Party fold. The CGIL has been a more militant trade union organisation than its two competitors, but there is some evidence that its policy has been moderated in more recent years through the disaffection caused among its members by the calling of a number of politically inspired strikes, which achieved little, or nothing, for the workers.

There have been a good number of defections from the CGIL over a period of years, both at the top and the bottom. Those at the top have usually been of full time officials, who were moderate socialists, and had held on for some time for traditional reasons and for personal security. Some of them have gone over to the UIL, as and when that organisation has been able to employ them. Defections at workshop level of rank and file members have been both to the UIL and the CISL, in fairly large numbers. It is thought this is mainly owing to dissatisfaction with CGIL political policies and internal disunity, rather than for industrial reasons. There have been rifts between Communists and Nenni Socialists within the organisation, which have prevented it, at times, from showing a united front to membership and public.

The Nenni Socialists are firmly anti-clerical and will not join the CISL, which is closely connected with the Government. If their disinclination to join with the UIL's right-wing Socialists continues, as well, the alternative would be the formation of a fourth national trade union centre if they ever decide to break with the CGIL. This cannot be an attractive proposition to any trade unionist who has the faintest belief in the necessity of the working classes being unified.

One of the most difficult features of the Italian trade union scene is the assessment of actual or comparative strengths of the three main trade union centres. There is a great shortage of information, and that which is available is conflicting. Its two rival trade union centres, and some other sources, put the CGIL's membership at about three millions. The CGIL, itself, claims up to five millions. The CISL claims about two million members for itself, and the UIL claims over half a million. It is generally assumed that all trade union centres make exaggerated claims, and belittle their rivals' strength. An independent assessment of the strengths has been made by Professor Joseph La Palombara,[1] who believes that the CGIL membership is about $3^1/_2$ millions; the CISL membership is under, but approaching two millions and the UIL membership is 250,000 to 300,000. The total of the organised workers he estimates at not more than six millions, or 30% of the labour force.

It is often considered that a more reliable way of assessing relative strengths is to analyse the results of elections for Works Councils, which are usually carried out on the basis of lists of candidates supported by the differing trade union centres. The results are not entirely comprehensive, and the different unions interpret them to their own advantage. La Palombara, however, quotes a study made by Professor Neufeld of the 1955 election results[2] which concludes that in the 39 most important industrial provinces the CGIL polled 55.2% of the votes, the CISL 33.7% and the UIL 7.1%, with independents accounting for the remainder. In 1956 the CISL and the UIL made further gains at the expense of the CGIL, but in late 1957, for the first time, the CGIL began to reverse the trend and won back a proportion of the seats they had lost over the years. Then, up to 1959, the trend varied according to industry and locality, and it is difficult to generalise about it.

1. *The Italian Labor Movement: Problems and Prospects*, by J. LA PALOMBARA, pp. 109-110, Cornell University Press, New York 1957.
2. As in Footnote[1].

It may be that the 1957 reversal was only a pause in the move away from the CGIL, caused by a slackening up of the other two trade union centres after the big efforts of the previous years. Only time, and future elections, will decide whether there is some deeper significance.

Co-operation between the trade union centres amounts to very little. Between the two largest, the CGIL and the CISL, it is non-existent. The CGIL, claiming always to have the unity of the workers at heart in their own best interests, is not against co-operating with the CISL, but the latter organisation will have no part at all in any scheme, even on issues which are purely industrial, and have no ideological implications. In fact, its attitude is very similar to the attitude of the socialist *Force Ouvrière* in France, in refusing under all circumstances to co-operate with the CGT, the communist-dominated trade union centre in that country.

However, the UIL in Italy takes a less rigid stand. Although it disapproves strongly of the CGIL and its policies, it is not prepared to reject co-operation on those occasions when it appears that working with it can solidify a case against the employers, without compromising its own independence and political policies. In this, the UIL can be roughly compared with the christian trade union centre in France, the CFTC, which takes a similar midway position on questions of co-operation with the CGT.

Thus the rather strange position is that while the socialist trade unionists are rigidly against co-operation with communist trade unionists in France, and christian trade unionists, there, take a more flexible and expedient view; the position is exactly reversed in Italy. The reason is not far to seek. In France, the socialists have nearly always been associated with the Government, and in Italy the christians are always associated with it. Neither Government ever considers the communists to be other than their bitterest opponents, who must not be accommodated under any circumstances.

Another factor in the more co-operative approach of the Italian UIL, is that the right-wing Socialists, who largely comprise it, are not as implacably hostile to the CGIL, with its large internal group of left-wing Socialists, as they would be if it were entirely Communist in make-up. In fact, some left-wing Socialists, at top level, who have left the CGIL for ideological reasons, have been accepted into the UIL. The UIL undoubtedly has its eye on the possibility of further swings of allegiance.

As far as relationships between the two non-communist trade union federations are concerned, the position is one that often occurs when a large and a small organisation are operating in the same field, with similar

policies. The large one, the CISL, tends to resent the presence of the
small independent UIL, and would like to incorporate it in its own
structure and on its own (the CISL's) terms. The UIL, on the other
hand, maintains that there is room for a separate socialist trade union
organisation in Italy, with a distinct function.

Both the CISL and the UIL are affiliated to the International Confederation of Free Trade Unions. The International has been concerned for
some years with the strained relationships between the two, particularly
as their policies on many matters, including European integration
questions, are very similar. Pressure has been put on them to amalgamate,
but there have been two main reasons why this has not come about.
Firstly, a large part of the UIL strength is firmly anti-clerical, and does
not wish to be swallowed up in an organisation having close associations
with the Roman Church, as the CISL has. Secondly, the alignment of
the CISL with the Christian Democrats, and of the UIL with the right-
wing Socialists, has made them antipathetic.

Both the UIL and the CISL deny that they are tied in their actions to
any political party. This is true insofar as they do not appear to be tied
by any formal obligations. But the interests of the Social Democrats and
the Republicans are usually kept in mind by the UIL, and those of the
Christian Democrats by the CISL. Even so, Italo Viglianesi, the UIL's
General Secretary, claims that his organisation is freer from political
ties than either the CISL or the CGIL. If this is the case, the probable
reason is that the political allegiances of the main personalities in the UIL
are rather more diverse than those in the CISL, and less dominated by
one party than in the CGIL.

The CISL has not been in a particularly easy position with regard to
its own allegiances to the Roman Catholic Church, and to the Christian
Democrat Party. Its leaders are shrewdly aware that although many
Italian workers are churchgoers, they are not devout to the extent that
they would wish all aspects of their life to be dominated by church
thinking. They also know that they cannot look attractive to CGIL
members who may be thinking of changing over, if they appear to be
closely associated with the Government, through the Christian Democrat
Party. Italian workers are traditionally against the Government, as
being representative of the ruling classes. Many manual workers are
also opposed to religion being brought into trade union matters.

In spite of this, a number of the leading Christian Democrat figures
in the CISL are Deputies in Parliament, as are the leaders of the other
trade union centres in different parties. This makes their professed
independence of political parties difficult to substantiate. Indeed, the
CISL has undoubtedly forfeited a good deal of the support it would

otherwise have obtained, by the stands it has taken from time to time in line with Government policies, and even with employer policies, in opposition to the other two trade union centres.[3]

Giulio Pastore, the ex-General Secretary of the CISL, has been a leading Christian Democrat Deputy for some time, and in 1958 was made a member of the Government, and given responsibility for the development of economically backward sections of the country, particularly in the south. It remains to be seen whether this will gain or lose support for the CISL. Pastore, in the past, kept strictly in mind the necessity for his organisation not to be formally committed to Party and Church.

The CISL has joined, and remained affiliated to, the ICFTU. All other predominantly christian trade union centres in Europe are affiliated to the Christian International, the CISC. The affiliation to the ICFTU has been good strategy, but there are minority groups who wish to change this affiliation, which, in view of the heavy support which the CISC received from Italian trade unionists in the pre-fascist period, is not very surprising.

Pastore may have calculated that his acceptance of a Government post concerned with the underdeveloped south may bring him good personal publicity, which would reflect to the benefit of the CISL. After the death of Di Vittorio, Pastore was the best-known trade unionist in Italy, until he was succeeded as General Secretary in March, 1959 by Bruno Storti, who had previously been the CISL Assistant General Secretary. It is generally thought that Pastore's decision not to take the seat which was earlier offered to him on the European Commission of the Common Market was at the behest of his colleagues, who thought that he should not be lost from the national trade union scene at such an important time.

The general picture, then, is of three trade union federations, each committed through its leading personalities to one or two political parties, and each federation in competition with the others, mainly because of their differing political loyalties. Each of them, however, claims that the other two have closer political ties than they, themselves. Each claims that it would probably be completely independent were it not that they were forced to have some political alliance because the others were backing political rivals. While it is easy to deride this situation as Gilbertian, it is not easy, given Italian backgrounds and traditions, to see how the trade union movement could become permanently united.

3. See LA PALOMBARA's *The Italian Labor Movement: Problems and Prospects*, Chapter v.

Trade Union Views on Integration

On matters concerning European integration questions the analogy
between the French and Italian trade union movements breaks down.
In France, integration was strongly supported by the socialist and
christian trade union centres, and opposed by the communist centre. In
Italy, integration is now supported by all three national centres. This
was not always the case. A few years ago when the CGIL used to follow
Togliatti and the Italian Communist Party and World Federation of
Trade Union policies more closely, it declared itself in opposition to
Western European Integration. The dissatisfaction of the left-wing
Socialists in the CGIL with this subservience to communist viewpoints
helped to bring about a change in attitude. Di Vittorio, himself, although
a communist, was not the sort of person to obey blindly all the dogmas
and policies of his party if they were not serving the CGIL's best
interests. The change of view of the CGIL would probably not have
come about had a less powerful personality than Di Vittorio been at the
helm.

Senior CGIL spokesmen admit that the organisation's disenchantment
with communist policies in Europe was partly brought about by obser-
ving the dangers in following an international line, irrespective of
national interests. The periods of Stalinism and de-Stalinism have had
the effect of making many Italian trade unionists see the errors of associating their organisations too closely with political parties. The CGIL
claims that its association with the Italian Communist Party had put it
in a false position, originally, on European integration questions, and
that to have continued its old policy would have been to risk getting out
of step with the rank and file, and ignoring the potential advantages to
Italy, and to international workers' solidarity, of an economically
integrated and more independent Europe.

The CGIL was put in this false position, it claims, by the decisions of
other trade unionists to break away from it, and set up their own
national centres; allied with centre, and left-of-centre political parties.
The CGIL says it is against alignments of trade unions with political
parties, and its present policy aims to extricate the organisation from the
inadvertent alliance it had to adopt earlier because of the decisions of
the other national centres.

Independent observers are inclined to take the view that the operation
of the European Coal and Steel Community has had obvious advantages
to Italy and the Italian workers, and that the Common Market is likely
to have similar benefits. It is said that the CGIL realised it would be
disastrous to its prestige and strength to preach the WFTU and Com-

munist Party policy, that European integration can bring only economic
evils, when it was apparent to all that this was not the case. This experience, they say, was the reason for the assertion of independence
from the Party line.

While supporting the Common Market in principle, the CGIL is
very critical of a number of its features and supposed features. On
19 July 1957, the Executive Committee passed a long resolution[4] setting
out its attitude, which seems to be based, in part, on a misunderstanding
of, or a misinterpretation of, the provisions of the Treaty. For instance,
paragraph 2 (a) of the resolution complains that the Treaty prohibits
"state aid to productive sectors or economic regions of particular
importance for the national economy".

The facts are that Article 92, paragraph 3 (a) of the Treaty expressly
allows "aids intended to promote the economic development of regions
where the standard of living is abnormally low or where there exists
serious under-employment", and paragraph 3 (c) allows "aids intended
to facilitate the development of certain activities or of certain economic
regions, provided that such aids do not change trading conditions to
such a degree as would be contrary to the common interest".

Further on, in the same paragraph 2 (a) of its resolution, the CGIL
states that "the possibility of realising an executive policy of industrial-
isation and of land transformation in the south of Italy would be seriously
compromised by the application of the treaty". This, again, must be
considered invalid in the light of those parts of Article 92, quoted.

Briefly, the CGIL supports the Common Market because this tendency
to integrate "rests on real needs such as the necessity of guaranteeing
larger markets for the improvements in productive technique now
taking place, the necessity of co-ordinating efforts for the more rational
exploitation of all the technical resources both of power and human
labour (and) the necessity of guaranteeing a still more rapid development
of the economically backward regions." (Paragraph 1.)

Having said this, the resolution goes on to express concern at the
dangers within the Treaty because of "the political and military framework in which it has been conceived and because of the policies of its
promoters" (paragraph 2), and also because of the alleged restrictions
it will place on the state to manage certain aspects of its own economy.
Having deplored the restrictions that it believes the Treaty will impose
on national sovereignty in these respects, it next complains that there is
no guarantee of supranational control in other respects, such as would
direct investments where most needed, independently of monopoly

4. Reproduced in CGIL journal *Rassegna Sindacale*, 31 July 1957, pp. 420-1.

interests. Neither is there enough planning to produce an international labour market with maximum security and standards for all workers.

The next criticism is that the Treaty is not designed to provide a suitable base for expanding economic and commercial relations with the rest of the world – East and West; and the final comment is a condemnation of those provisions of the Treaty which have included the French overseas territories in the Common Market without having first consulted the interested peoples. The CGIL is particularly bitter about this, especially in the case of Algeria, as it considers the provisions to be an obligation on other European countries to shore up the "tottering French colonial empire", and to use scarce Italian capital for the job, into the bargain.

The resolution then indicates its own eight policy points on European economic co-operation, as under:

(a) Separation of the scheme from NATO, and other military pacts,
(b) The safeguarding of the member states' rights to reform and develop their own economies and social systems,
(c) The right of states, transitionally, to nurse their backward regions,
(d) Supranational authorities concerned with international investment to be independent of private interest pressures, and to receive public representations from national economic and social interests,
(e) Liberty of member states to develop policies and organs which will extend commercial relations outside the Community of the "Six", without discrimination,
(f) An upward harmonisation of social conditions and benefits combined with a full employment policy for Italy,
(g) The direct participation of trade union organisations at all stages and in all aspects of Community social policy, and
(h) The abolition of all discrimination in political and trade union representation in Community organs.

The resolution concludes by calling on all trade union organisations in Italy, and other Community countries, whatever their affiliations, to show unity of action on integration questions, as the employers and the governments are doing.

The CGIL does not share the opinion of some who say that Italy stands to gain more than any of the other countries of the "Six" in the Common Market. It believes that Italy's agricultural problems may be accentuated, that German industrial giants may triumph at the expense of Italy's less robust industries, and that other countries, particularly France, have received special economic concessions which would have been more appropriate for Italy. Nevertheless, it is realised that more may be gained by working inside the Community to improve matters, than by keeping aloof from it.

In spite of their difference in fundamental attitude towards the Common Market, the CGIL, and the CGT of France, work together in a joint committee, with WFTU support, in order to deal, on a common basis, with Community problems arising.

The CGIL feels that there should have been trade union representation, especially from its own ranks, not only in the Economic and Social Committee, but in the Executive organs of the Community. As it is, their organisation has not even been granted consultative status, and no trade unionist from any country has been appointed to the European Commission.

The CGIL believes that the freer movement of labour in the Common Market will be helpful to Italy's problems, but it is unhappy that the conditions of work abroad (e.g. in the Belgian mines) are not up to the standards that should be required before Italian emigrants accept jobs abroad.

At the time of the WFTU's Fourth World Congress in Leipzig in 1957, Di Vittorio, the CGIL's late General Secretary, who had swung his organisation from opposition to support for European integration, was also President of the WFTU, which was still implacably opposed to integration, and all the schemes that went with it. His position was therefore very difficult; but the Congress avoided passing any resolution on the subject, and the differences were smoothed over with as little fuss as possible.

The CGIL circulated a long letter to delegates which showed the differences of approach between it, and the WFTU, on this question. The letter stressed the CGIL's abhorrence of the association with French colonial territories, especially Algeria, but justified support for the Common Market by reference to the need for international working class unity to match that of the employers and the Governments in European matters. Counteracting the international unity of the employers is a main reason given by the CGIL for working in the joint committee with the French CGT.

The CGIL made no official statement on its attitude to the original Free Trade Area plan, but the general view of its officials is that a wider association in Europe would be less dangerous than a Common Market, because there would not be as much opportunity for an international alliance of monopoly employers. They believe that the presence of British employers in such an association might counterbalance German employer strength, and that British trade union strength would be used against monopolistic industrialists who would try to exploit the Common Market.

The CISL and the UIL support the Common Market avidly, and though not without some criticisms of its provisions, or shortcomings, have none of the heavy doubts expressed by the CGIL, of its benefits to Italy. Indeed, both organisations appear to be keener than any other European trade union centres to regard the Common Market as a first step on the way to their ultimate goal of the political integration of Europe. The CISL, particularly, would regard such full integration as a welcome sign that Europe would be more independent, politically, and less susceptible to Russian influences. Pastore looked forward to political integration in a Parliamentary speech, when he was still the CISL General Secretary.

Both organisations see economic benefits accruing to Italy through the importation of foreign capital and the increased emigration opportunities for Italian workers. Both express a hope that international collective bargaining may be established for wages and working conditions in the Community. Other European trade union centres have been more reserved on this question, and many of them doubt its practicability. However, Italian wages are generally lower than in the other Community countries, and trade union organisation is weaker. The CISL and the UIL hope that, through political integration and international collective bargaining, Italian wages and conditions, as well as trade union organisation, may be fortified by the presence of other countries.

As far back as September 1955, the CISL Executive Board issued a statement saying that it was in favour of an integrated Europe, that it wished to promote a greater understanding of a unified Europe among the working classes, that it would work for a common European standard for daily working hours, overtime payments and holiday pay, and that its policy was to obtain workers' representation in all administrative, executive and consultative bodies that might be set up.

The Executive also passed a resolution on 27 July 1957, after the Rome Treaties had been signed. It had dropped the insistence on common European standards for working conditions, but still made workers' representation at all levels, and in all institutions, a main part of its policy, especially where agriculture was concerned. It gave a mandate to its General Secretary to strengthen trade union action in the Community by instituting adequate information services, and other facilities, concerning the problems arising; and by co-operating in arrangements for common trade union action and institutions with the other Community Countries.

This resolution also placed great stress on the need for the Italian Government to make its own provisions for economic development, both agricultural and industrial, before the Treaty of the Common Market actually became fully effective. This should include a speeding up of the Vanoni Plan for economic development, so that the country would be in a position to benefit fully when markets were enlarged and when economic and agricultural policies were harmonised with those of other countries. (The UIL completely shares this view.) Reform of Italy's social security system was also regarded as an essential prerequisite to Common Market participation.

It has been made clear by the CISL that it would not, under any circumstances, approve of the CGIL being considered by the Government for inclusion in any body of workers' representatives nominated for consultative or other functions to the European Communities. Affiliation to the WFTU, which is opposed to integration, was sufficient reason to make them ineligible for such representation, in CISL eyes.

The CISL did not go into a great deal of detail when considering the shortcomings of the Common Market Treaty. But it found that the European Coal and Steel Community had worked to the benefit of Italians, and believed that the Economic Community would do likewise. Perhaps Pastore summed up his organisation's position best, when he said in Parliament, on 26 July 1957:

"The Common Market and Euratom Treaties represent an important stage of development in that experience of a mixed economy adapted to the new technological, productive and social needs which for some years have been characteristic of the free world. As to the negative consequences that the enactment of the Common Market may have on our economy, which is weaker than that of other countries, certainly they are not to be underestimated; it should be recalled, however, that the only alternative–unless we wish to consider the so-called Communist way for a 'New Europe'–is the everlasting continuation of the present condition of power deficiency and inferior productivity of the European countries."[5]

In July 1958, the CISL submitted a memorandum to its Government, setting out its views on the original Free Trade Area plan. It expressed the hope that a wider economic association in Europe would eventually lead to the accession of other countries to the full Common Market. As some countries did not feel able to take this step at present, the FTA proposals were welcomed as an alternative. But in order that a FTA did

5. As reported in *CISL News* (English Language Edition) on 30 July 1957.

not constitute any danger to the Common Market, there were three essential preliminary conditions.

First, that the Common Market countries should have an opportunity to draw up their own Community's fundamental economic and financial policies, so that they could negotiate a wider Treaty, acting as a single group. Second, that the Area should have supranational institutions, sufficiently powerful to promote balanced trade development, to guarantee employment levels, and to ensure effective policy co-ordination. Third, there should be general undertakings, concerning the defence of the level of employment, which would consist of obligations to promote national plans for the development of employment; to influence consumer demand and investment levels, to this end; to assure balanced distribution of industry, and the development of under-developed zones; and to develop and reinforce an international employment service.

The statement concluded by indicating the need for Government consultation with the CISL on all these matters, and regretted that there had been a lack of such consultation, up until that time.

In 1958, leading figures in the UIL were prepared to say that they were very favourably inclined towards the FTA scheme because they saw it as an additional factor tending towards the political unification of Europe, and they would wish Britain to be a part of any such process. Signor E. Dalla Chiesa, Secretary of the UIL's International Department, put his organisation's point of view at the European Industrial Conference in London, in February, 1958. He said:

> "In the opinion of my organisation, the UIL, the Common Market is not an end in itself but a means to an end to promote in a wider frame-work the harmonious expansion of the economy of each of the member countries. The European Economic Community must be a starting point and not an end in itself for economic integration: The Free Trade Area must be considered as an extension of the Common Market and as supplementary to it."[6]

In this speech, made in England, the economic rather than the political aspects of integration were stressed; but the UIL was not certain, in fact, as to whether the economic aspects of the original Free Trade Area plan would have been beneficial to Italy, and the Economic Community, or not. Its main reason for support was its desire for the wider concept of European integration, political and economic. Spokesmen made it clear

6. Full Report of European Industrial Conference on 19 to 21 February 1958, at Church House, London, p. 38, published by United Kingdom Council of the European Movement.

that they would have liked to have seen many provisions in a FTA Treaty similar to those in the Common Market Treaty. That is, full employment policies, social harmonisation, public investment funds and investment co-ordination, free movement of labour, the inclusion of agriculture in some form and a body such as the Common Market's Economic and Social Committee, which would allow for strong trade union representation.

The UIL makes no secret of the fact that it looks forward to the Economic Community becoming a full political union. It strongly supports the Community for similar reasons to the CISL; namely, that it will benefit Italy economically – mainly through the influx of foreign capital needed for development, and through the improved opportunities that the free labour market will offer for emigration of Italian workers. This will relieve the internal unemployment problem. It is also believed that the Common Market will bring a narrowing of the differentials between Italy and other Community countries, in respect of wages and conditions of work. Harmonisation of social benefits is hoped for. Like the CISL and the CGIL, the UIL is in favour of workers' representation, through the trade unions, on all possible Community institutions – consultative or executive.

The Common Market Treaty has several shortcomings, in the UIL view, and one of them is that the institutions do not appear to have as much supranational power as those of the Coal and Steel Community. Neither are there sufficient safeguards for the workers; therefore a close watch must be kept on the operation of the Common Market, so that the trade unions may be in a good position to bring pressure to bear at the appropriate time for Treaty amendments. These could be introduced to rectify faults shown in the light of experience.

The general picture emerging is that all three national trade union centres in Italy are in favour of European integration for economic reasons; that is because of the benefits it will bring for Italy and Italian workers. The CISL and the UIL, more particularly, also support it through a desire for greater European political consolidation, which will buttress the strength of the combined Community countries. The CGIL does not share this viewpoint fully, as there are political implications in it unsavoury to communist tastes. However, it is in agreement with the other two organisations that integration should bring a welcome extension of co-operation and solidarity with other European trade union organisations.

CHAPTER XVIII

BENELUX

Economically speaking, Belgium, the Netherlands and Luxembourg must now be considered as one unit. Belgium and Luxembourg, in fact, have been one economic unit sine 1921, when they were first linked in an economic union. From the beginning of 1948 a customs union was operating between all three countries; that is, all customs duties on goods passing over their borders were abolished, and a common external tariff was applied to the rest of the world. In February, 1958, the Benelux Economic Union Treaty was signed. This sets out to complete the whole economic integration process. Its purposes, as defined in Article I, are to promote the free movement of people, goods, services and capital within the Union, the co-ordination of national economic policies and the pursuance of a common trade policy towards other countries. It is intended that the Benelux Union should function within the framework of the European Economic Community.

Although it is early, yet, to attempt an assessment of the results of the full economic union, there can be little doubt that ten years experience of the customs union, alone, has inspired confidence in the larger project of the Community of Six, insofar as the two schemes are comparable. On the face of it there appeared to be a number of rocks on which Benelux might have foundered, but all have been avoided without much difficulty. There have been some disturbances to the smoothness of transition but, generally speaking, they have been minor ones. Although Belgium adopted a high wages policy after the war, the subsequent difference in the general level, compared with that of the Netherlands, did not cause much trouble when a large measure of free labour movement was first brought about several years ago. The movement of labour over the national borders has not been great, and Belgium's wage levels have not been pulled down, although they have been reasonably stable since about 1955, while the Netherlands' have been rising.

The removal of tariffs did not cause any grave difficulties, and the maintenance of some quantitative restrictions during the earlier years of the Union helped the smooth transition. There were special provisions made for agriculture, and in all other branches of industry there were hardly any setbacks due to the customs union. In fact, a considerable increase in trade has resulted, without markets being flooded. During the first eight years there was an increase of nearly 200% in trade between the three members, and of nearly 100% between Benelux and the rest of the world.

It is not surprising, in the circumstances, that the Benelux countries have been, perhaps, the foremost advocates of the larger Community of the Six, and were favourable to the creation of a wider Free Trade Area (FTA) in addition. Having a large interest in coal and steel, they had earlier joined the European Coal and Steel Community, eagerly, and have found it to their benefit since.

While Benelux may be regarded as one unit for economic purposes, there can be no question of regarding it as such when examining the trade union movements. There is a considerable difference of outlook and structure between the trade unions of Belgium, and those of the Netherlands. Not only that, but in neither country is there a single trade union viewpoint which can be said to represent the nation as a whole. As in France and Italy, the unions are split into separate national centres, with allegiances along differing political and religious lines. The parts the trade unions play in the national life are dissimilar in several ways, the systems of collective bargaining in Belgium and the Netherlands are quite different, and their views on European integration, although united in enthusiasm, are not identical in matters of detail. Even Luxembourg has its own trade union movement, and disunity in it, although on policy matters the main organisations are very closely allied to their counterparts in Belgium.

Although from one point of view it is convenient to consider the Benelux countries together in a single chapter, for the main purpose of examining the trade unions, and their impact upon integration questions, it is necessary, for the reasons outlined, to consider them separately.

Belgium

The history of central organisation in Belgian trade unions dates back to 1898, when a Commission of Trade Unions was set up by the Belgian Workers Party. Trade union membership has risen fairly consistently since then. In 1904 the Commission adopted a constitution of its own, and became independent of the Workers Party. Since that time, trade unions have attempted to maintain a nominal independence of political parties, and, indeed, they have no organic connection with them. However, unofficially, they work in close collaboration, as is done in the other Community countries. Much of the Commission's work, up to the second world war, was concerned with welding local and regional trade unions into national federations, as well as campaigns for reduced hours and a minimum wage.

The name was changed to the General Confederation of Labour of Belgium in 1937, and greater powers over its affiliates were taken. But the war period drove trade union work underground, and towards the end of hostilities there were a number of disunited groups. Four of these merged in 1945 to form the *Fédération Générale du Travail de Belgique* (FGTB), or General Federation of Labour of Belgium. But a large number of specifically christian trade unionists were not included in this new organisation, and the division between them and the FGTB has been perpetuated. The christians are organised in the Roman Catholic *Confédération des Syndicats Chrétiens belges* (CSC), or Belgian Confederation of Christian Trade Unions.

The main split in the Belgian trade union movement is between the FGTB, with its social democratic outlook, and the CSC, with its allegiance to church and christian political party. But there is a further group of trade unionists organised in what are known as the "Liberal" trade unions, having an estimated membership in the region of 100,000. This compares with a membership of 700,000 claimed for itself by the FGTB, and 686,000 claimed by the CSC. The Liberal unions are rather looked down upon by their larger rivals, and particularly by the FGTB, which regards them as having no set purpose or direction, and being under employer influence.

The FGTB takes the usual socialist view of the CSC–that it is too amenable to the Church and to the Christian Party to be an effective workers' organisation–and the CSC thinks the FGTB is too closely tied in with the socialists. However, the nature of the Belgian system of industrial negotiations makes it essential for the trade unions to be represented jointly on many bodies, including the Works Councils; the National Joint Councils, composed of employers and trade unionists on an equal basis, (which determine wages and conditions in each industry separately); the Central Economic Council and the National Council of Labour, which are bodies set up to advise the Ministry of Economic Affairs and the Ministry of Labour, respectively, and are composed, again, half of employers and half of trade unionists.

Generally speaking, trade union seats on these national bodies are distributed in accordance with the strengths of the unions, and appointments are made by the government. It is inevitable that there is a certain amount of manoeuvring by the various national centres to better their own positions, and the outcome of these may depend on whether the government, at the time, is Christian, Socialist or Socialist-Liberal. The split among the trade unions makes matters more difficult than they otherwise would be for successive governments, with differing political complexions.

The rivalry between the FGTB and the CSC is not as intense, perhaps, as the rivalry between christian and social democratic unions in other countries; partly because they are, to some extent, geographically demarcated–the FGTB having almost a monopoly in the Walloon south, where allegiance to the Roman Catholic Church is more nominal than active. The concentration of christian trade union strength is largely in the north, and in Flanders, although the FGTB has a fair strength in some parts, such as Brussels.

There does not appear to be any immediate prospect of the FGTB and the CSC working more closely together, unless, perhaps, relations between the International Confederation of Free Trade Unions and the International Federation of Christian Trade Unions, to which they are respectively affiliated, became closer. It is probably true to say that although there is not a great deal of difference in their strengths, the FGTB has more influence in the country than the CSC because it takes the initiative more often. The Liberal unions have their membership spread thinly over the country, and over many industries, and have only a very small national influence. As far as integration questions are concerned, only the views of the FGTB and the CSC are of real significance.

In Belgium, there has been a general enthusiasm for further steps towards European integration, which has been fully reflected by the trade unions, although certain developments in 1958-9 have caused a certain hesitancy in places.

Belgium is a country, like Britain, which has only one main source of natural wealth–coal. She has, therefore, to carry on a large amount of international trade to earn a living, and nobody realises this better than the trade unions. There could be no better reason for wishing to abolish restrictions on the flow of trade. The trade unions are careful to stress, however, that economic considerations are by no means the root cause of their support for integration, although important. There are, too, strong ideological and political motives for their support, and there have been some criticisms that the Common Market has lost a good deal of internationalism during its evolution from the Spaak Report.

The FGTB summed up the Belgian trade union attitude, well, in a booklet it published, which is probably the most comprehensive survey and criticism of European integration projects published by any European trade union centre. Its conclusion reads, in part:[1]

"On condition that success is achieved in breaking down structures

1. *La Communauté Economique Européenne et Euratom*, published by FGTB, p. 89.

which are far too nationalist, the European Economic Community will create a market of 162 millions, and if we add the overseas territories, of more than 180 million inhabitants. At the present time it is not possible to say exactly what will be the probable repercussions of this on our economy. But in general–Benelux proves it–it will open new and more stable outlets, and consequently greater possibilities of expansion for our industry. But in order to arrive at that position, our industrialists must adapt themselves to the times and must not miss the opportunities offered."

The industrialists, themselves, do not disagree with this viewpoint. In fact, over the general principles of Belgian support, employers and workers have issued a joint statement; or to be more exact, the Belgian Central Economic Council, which is composed half of each group, has issued a statement supporting the plan for the Common Market and Euratom, and making certain recommendations.[2] What it said, basically, was that it supported the Common Market plan because it hoped for a real European Community which would bring about an improvement in living conditions by a more rational use of natural resources and of labour power. It wanted the closest possible association of the overseas territories with the Common Market, and looked forward also to a free trade area which included other Western European countries. It hoped that Euratom would hasten the joint peaceful use of the atom, and would reduce Europe's power deficiencies.

Having given its general enthusiastic support, the statement went on to make two main recommendations. Firstly, that the Economic and Social Committee of the Community should contain members of diverse economic interests, including equal numbers of heads of undertakings and of wage earners, and should be able to give its own opinions on all matters raised by any one of the groups comprising it. The second recommendation is that the Belgian Government should try to obtain a lowering of the proposed common external tariff. As a reason for this, the Council states that too high a level of protection may tend to isolate the six countries, somewhat, from the rest of the world's trade, at a time when the various regions are becoming more interdependent. It may also tend to raise price levels in the Community countries and weaken their competitive capacities in foreign markets.

These points are all valid, but it is likely that the main reason for wanting a lower common tariff is that the Benelux countries start off with lower tariffs than the other Community countries. As the common

2. Issued on 23 May 1956, published in the CSC's journal CSC, 10 May 1957, pp. 141-5.

tariff is to be an average of existing ones in the Community, Benelux stands to lose a little of her previous trade, all other things being equal, because the new tariffs will be higher in many cases that the old ones.

In addition to this statement on behalf of the full Council, some of the trade union members of it issued a separate one, setting out their own viewpoint. It stated that transitional difficulties would not be overcome, and the possibilities of progress would not be fully exploited, unless the Community became an area of common economic and social policy, included in a wider framework of international economic co-operation.

The structure and powers of the Economic Community's institutions were thought to be inadequate, particularly in the case of the Commission. These deficiencies could jeopardise the operation of effective transport and agricultural policies, as well as schemes for policy harmonisation, social harmonisation, readaptation, investments and the overseas territories.

The Council of Ministers, which would have most of the powers of decision, may prove to be too susceptible to national pressures and interests, and be thereby prevented from exercising the continuous and constructive action which the development of the Common Market will require. There was also a risk that the powers of the Assembly were too few.

The statement pointed to a gap between the aims of the Common Market and the means provided for achieving them. The plans seemed to have been made on the assumptions that economic automatisms will operate without control, and that the permanent goodwill of national and private interests will always be forthcoming. Political reforms greater than those envisaged would be required to achieve the Community's objectives; and the new institutions would require to be reinforced within the framework of a general reorganisation, which would bring about a new division of powers between the legislative and executive institutions of Western Europe, and of its member states.

With regard to Euratom, the trade unionists of the Council, while giving a welcome to it, believed that the way to dangerous national competition had been opened by the proposals for the supply of ores and nuclear fuels, which were too loosely drafted. It was regretted that when much required doing in a short time, the common institutions had not been given the necessary powers to stimulate and co-ordinate national efforts, by taking a hand in investments and the creation of common enterprises within the framework of a European power policy. They were in favour of the communal ownership of fissile materials, particularly for the purpose of assuring public safety.

The FGTB booklet on the Communities goes further, in its criticisms of Euratom, although its main emphasis is the same: that the supranational powers of the Community are too few. It admits that the Treaty does bring a promise of faster nuclear development, but says it would have been much better if Euratom institutions had been given powers, even as great as those in the Coal and Steel Community, particularly as regards the co-ordination of investments among member states. Having said this, it is admitted that the ECSC has by no means used its own power to the full extent. The FGTB thinks that the system of providing stocks in Euratom is quite inadequate, and that, in practice, policy will be decided by the national states. Apart from the other general criticisms, as made by the trade union members of the Central Economic Council, the FGTB has also expressed concern at the inadequacy of the Treaty provisions concerning the co-ordination of research projects.

However, as the Treaty is signed, and unalterable for the time being, the FGTB is of the opinion that action must be taken at national level. In Belgium, electrical and nuclear energy and fuel production should be nationalised, and a national co-ordinating body should be created, for policy purposes. This demand was re-emphasised in early 1959, following the Borinage strikes connected with coal production.

On matters connected with the Economic Community Treaty, also, the FGTB booklet makes most of the suggestions and criticisms made by the Central Economic Council, as a whole, and also those made by the trade union members. Again, the emphasis is put upon the insufficiency of supranational powers in the Community, and the congenital weaknesses of its institutions. In the case of the Economic and Social Committee of the Community, in particular, the FGTB would have liked to have seen radical provisions, such as the right of initiative of the Committee for dealing with problems in its own domain, and effective control over such matters. It should be compulsory for the Committee to be consulted on every decision or recommendation of the other institutions, concerning economic and social questions. Its advice and comments ought, furthermore, to be published. Such a formula would help to base the effective control of Community policy more broadly, and thus strengthen democracy.

The Community institutions should have the necessary power to investigate and obtain information on all matters relating to cartels, or other restrictive trading arrangements. It is regretted that the provisions in Part 3 of the Treaty, in respect of rules governing competition and enterprises (Articles 85-90), are not as strong as they might have been, and it is feared that the decision to leave the application procedure of Articles 85 and 86 to the Council may pave the way for manoeuvres by capitalist interests which oppose the principles of the provisions, to attenuate them.

As far as the overseas territories are concerned, the FGTB believes that the Treaty provisions are good. They should help to stabilise the economies of these territories, as well as the markets between them and their associated European countries. New possibilities for Belgians to trade in French overseas territories are anticipated, and the channeling of finance through Development Funds is welcomed as a step forward to the expressed aims of aiding underdeveloped countries, and sending capital where it is most needed.

In order to obtain a greater degree of supranationalism in the Community, the FGTB believes that the Commission and the Assembly should each have greater powers, so that the former becomes a European executive body, and the latter a European legislature, whose financial resources should be independent of national budgets.

It believes that the Investment Bank has a quite inadequate capital for the function it is to perform, and is therefore not likely to play a decisive role in investment matters.

The FGTB believes that the procedure envisaged in the Treaty for a common agricultural policy is too weighty, and is likely to militate against a common policy being brought into operation within a reasonable period. The endowment of the states with the power of fixing minimum prices is proof of this; and the powers given to the Council in this sector are insufficient to prevent abuses. The whole of the Treaty Chapter on agriculture is regarded as being biased in favour of the producers' interests.

As far as social policy is concerned, the FGTB criticises the assumption that appears to lie behind the Common Market Treaty, that social progress will automatically result from the functioning of the Common Market, and will be promoted automatically by collaboration between the member states. The experiences of the ECSC and of Benelux, it is said, belie this faith in automatisms and voluntary co-operation. The Treaty provisions, it concludes, are weak, and an adequate institutional procedure is not provided for. Those concrete measures which have been written into the Treaty concerning equal pay for equal work, paid holidays and the levelling up of overtime payments have been put in to placate France, rather than through any sense of social compulsion or industrial benevolence. The Treaty, therefore, is lacking, in that it is only trying to establish an equilibrium in certain working conditions rather than to improve them, all round, by specific provision.

The FGTB criticises, also, the Treaty provisions concerning the free circulation of capital, services and labour; particularly the last of these.

The trouble is that only objectives are fixed in the Treaty, and the Council is wholly entrusted with attaining them. Consequently, there is a risk of the objectives not being fulfilled. The automatic freeing of workers to move where they will, as foreseen in the Spaak Report, has been abandoned, says the organisation. This would have run counter to the governments' ideas of the necessities, and changing conditions, of economic life. The object of including free labour circulation in the Treaty, it says, was not so much a desire to give the worker his liberty as a provision to ensure that workers can respond to the jobs actually offered.

As far as the possibility of introducing a Free Trade Area was concerned, the FGTB was broadly in favour of the original plan. It was thought that such a scheme would strengthen the Common Market Bloc, and allow a much wider form of economic unison in Europe. It was suggested by FGTB representatives in attendance at the European Industrial Conference in London, in February 1958, that harmonisation in the social field was essential for a Common Market or a FTA to function satisfactorily, and this may even involve certain sacrifices by the countries which are initially better off. In this, their view was somewhat similar to that of the *Force Ouvrière* in France, although the FGTB's support for a FTA, in principle, was much stronger. But it was felt, as in France, that there should have been some method of harmonisation in the social field which would have taken account of wage scales, social charges, and additional benefits coming from the state, or elsewhere. To achieve this, rules should have been laid down at the beginning, and there should have been an adequate transition period.

On financial and monetary questions, it was thought that, in order to prevent the constant use of escape clauses which would impair the effective functioning of an FTA, co-ordination of monetary policy would be essential between the participating countries. The liberalisation of exchange could not function properly, even if backed by strong supranational institutions, without the co-operation which would provide for harmony in monetary policies. Exchange rates could not remain stable in a FTA unless they were first brought into balance. If even one country had its exchange rate seriously out of harmony with the others, that would prevent a free trade system working, because it would be reflected in terms of production in that country.

The Christian Federation, the CSC, has not had very much to say about the Free Trade Area idea, but some pronounced views on the Common Market were expressed by Monsieur A. Cool, the organisation's President, in January 1958, in his annual address.[3] He stressed

3. Printed in *Notes de la CSC*, January 1958.

the difficulties in becoming Europeans, rather than nationals, but regarded the process as inevitable. He complained that, in spite of this process, workers organisations had not been granted recognition, internationally, in the same way as they had at national level. In the Common Market, trade unionists had representation only in a consultative capacity on the Economic and Social Committee. They had no representation, as they should have, on the bodies where the decisions were taken—the Commission, the Court and the Bank.

M. Cool stressed that it was wrong to believe that social integration would necessarily follow from economic integration. But social harmonisation was essential, although this did not mean that social costs or benefits would have to be the same in each country, or even that wages and conditions would. Even now, there were differences between the various regions of Belgium, alone. But there would have to be some equivalence in the totals of all these benefits, as between the different countries. No obligations of uniform methods should be imposed.

It was inevitable, and desirable, in these circumstances, that the trade unions of the separate countries should be brought more closely together, in order to determine common policies. M. Cool concluded:

> "We may ask ourselves if co-ordination between the trade union organisations of the six countries will be sufficient, and if we ought not to carry on towards a supranational trade union movement, with a supranational authority. There is a trade union nationalism, also, and there are trade union frontiers which ought to disappear. We will not be logical if we argue for the economic, social and political integration of Europe, and if we are at the same time too conservative in matters of trade union integration. This language may appear revolutionary. Today I ask you only to consider it and to brave being logical right to the end so as to be able to act at the chosen moment. The day may come when international collaboration between trade union movements will not be sufficient and when the necessity of international integration of the trade union movements will be forced upon us."

M. Cool, in his advocacy of trade union integration, appears to have gone farther than any other trade union figure in Europe has done, in public. And he has put his finger on a problem which, although some have shied away from it, will come increasingly to the forefront, as European integration proceeds.

It appears that although the rivalry between the two main trade union federations in Belgium is fairly intense, their views on European integration questions are similar, with only slightly differing emphasis. Their enthusiasm for all the integration projects is in line with that of practically all sections of Belgian life, and with that of the wider Benelux Community. It indicates that within the Common Market the smaller countries have less apprehension of their larger neighbours than the larger neighbours have of each other.

Luxembourg

Luxembourg, perhaps, of all the six Community countries, is the most dependent on free trade. Although the country has a number of industries, iron and steel production is completely dominant, and comprises something like 80% of all economic activity. Over two-thirds of production of all goods is exported. Luxembourg, having been a member of the Coal and Steel Community since its inception, is the country which has been most affected by it, because of her dependence on the one industry. The larger Economic Community provisions, however, are unlikely to affect her as much as they will affect her partners.

Luxembourg is a strong supporter of the newer forms of integration provided for under the Rome Treaties, although it cannot be pretended that her small size (1,000 square miles and estimated 310,000 population) give her any large influence in the Communities. But the fact that the ECSC Headquarters and Secretariat has been established in Luxembourg gives the country a stake in the European Communities, quite apart from any other considerations. A Secretariat so large, in a small place, cannot have been other than a great economic boon to the country.

Although Luxembourg is entirely independent, her very close ties with Belgium, especially in the customs union since 1921, have given her an interest and outlook which are, in many respects, virtually identical with those of her larger neighbour. This is very much the case at the trade union level. Although, again, the unions are quite independent, they work closely with their Belgian counterparts, and have a very similar outlook. As far as their views on European integration are concerned, it is sufficient to refer to the previous section on Belgium, bearing in mind that the trade unionists' fortunes are largely bound up with the iron and steel industry, and, to a lesser extent, with coal.

The trade union movement, itself, is split, as in Belgium, into two main sections, the most important national centre being the *Confédération Générale de Travail du Luxembourg* (CGT Lux.), with an estimated 23,000 members. The other national centre of significance is the LCGB, with a membership claimed at 12,000. While the CGT Lux. is affiliated to the ICFTU, and was a founder member of it, the LCGB is affiliated to the christian international, the CISC. In view of the fact that the Luxembourg population is, at least nominally, almost all Roman

Catholic, it is significant that the christian trade union federation is so much weaker than its socialist rival.

It may be thought that Luxembourg is more vulnerable to the freeing of labour movement than the other members of the "Six", because of its high wages and social welfare facilities. But it should be remembered that Luxembourg traditionally employs a higher proportion of foreign workers than its partners, so that the effects of the Rome Treaties may not be serious for the workers. They have already managed to survive the free movement of skilled steelworkers, under ECSC provisions, without much upset, and the trade unions are not likely to be caused too many worries when this is extended to other industries.

The Netherlands

As in the other Benelux countries, the trade union movement in the Netherlands is fairly deeply divided. The division, as with the others, is between religious unions and socialist unions. There is also a very small communist national trade union centre, the *Eenheidsvakcentrale* (EVC), which is affiliated to the World Federation of Trade Unions, but it has hardly any influence in the country. The division between the main national centres is not as straightforward, (if that is the correct word) as the division in Belgium, or France, for instance. The reason is that the christian trade unionists are divided into Roman Catholic and Protestant camps.

The *Nederlands Verbond van Vakverenigingen* (NVV), or Netherlands Federation of Trade Unions, is the oldest and largest of the national centres, having been founded in 1906, and having attained a membership of about 500,000 in 1957, which had dropped to 482,000 in early 1959. The NVV has always been better established than its two major rivals, which were both founded in 1909. It has followed a policy of centralisation, in banding together previously independent unions, and has worked on a policy of industrial unionism, that is, one union for one industry. The NVV has socialist leanings, and a good understanding and relationship with the Netherlands Party of Labour.

As in all countries under German domination during the war, the Netherlands trade union movement was rendered inoperative. Towards the end of the war, however, NVV leaders made approaches to members of the Catholic and Protestant trade union centres, the *Katholieke Arbeidersbeweging* (KAB) and the *Christelijk Nationaal Vakverbond* (CNV), respectively, with a view to the formation of one large centre. Agreement on a merger was not reached, but the centres did agree to co-operate with each other, and things went fairly well until 1954, when a pontifical letter was circulated advising Catholics against joining the NVV. As the KAB did not oppose this, the NVV felt it had no alternative but to break off co-operation with it. Relations were officially restored in 1958.

During the immediate postwar period, the most fruitful co-operation between the national centres was achieved in the Foundation of Labour, a body which advises the Government on social matters, mainly, and is composed of representatives of all three trade union centres, and the employers. Even during the break in relations between the national centres, they continued to work together on this body, and they still do; although it is becoming overshadowed by the larger and wider Social and Economic Council.

The three centres also work together on this national Social and Economic Council, which advises the Government on much wider questions of public policy, and is composed of 45 members–fifteen each, representing Government, employers and workers. The trade union representation on this body provides a fair estimate of the relative influence of the three national centres in the country. The NVV has seven representatives, the KAB five and the CNV three. (1959 figures.) The membership figure of the KAB was claimed at about 400,000 and that of the CNV at about 230,000 at the beginning of 1958.

Relationships between the national centres have been improving and the Roman Church may well be modifying its attitude to the NVV. But, as in other European countries, the alignment of the various centres with political parties, unofficially, is bound to keep a constant barrier between them, as are the differing international affiliations. The NVV is an affiliate of the ICFTU, while both the KAB and the CNV are affiliated to the Christian International, the CISC. The CNV, in fact, is the only sizeable Protestant trade union centre affiliated to this predominantly Roman Catholic International.

It may be thought that two national centres affiliated to the same international would have few differences. But the Netherlands has a background of religious differences and factions, in many aspects of life, and the trade unions are no exception. There is little love lost between the KAB and the CNV. KAB co-operation with the Catholic Political Party in the Netherlands is strong–moreso than in France or Belgium. But the CNV co-operation with Protestant politicians is more complicated because there are two Protestant Parties, one of which is rather conservative, and the other more socially progressive. The CNV has stronger inclinations towards the latter, but its whole position is made rather delicate.

There are several other small national centres and independent unions in the Netherlands, totalling, probably, well under 200,000 membership. The communist EVC is the largest of these. However, none of them is represented on the Foundation of Labour, or on the Social and Economic Council, and none of them has any significant influence in the country. The NVV has decisively rejected unity overtures from the EVC, and the other major national centres will have nothing to do with it, either.

The NVV has been a strong supporter of Western European integration for some years, and at a special congress concerned with integration problems in October, 1954, passed a resolution instructing the Executive to press as strongly as possible for a policy of integration, on which Dutch and European freedom and welfare would depend. It was in favour of breaking down national barriers, and regarded the Coal and Steel Community as having been an important first step in this process. Economic integration was necessary to keep up with the tempo of production increase in Russia and America, but care would have to be taken that it did not lead to cartelisation, as had been the tendency in the ECSC.

Economic integration could raise living standards, but it must be combined with social integration, which would raise cultural and welfare standards. All this would depend, ultimately, on political integration. There would have to be European organs to exercise economic control, advised by bodies representative of trade union and other interests.

The NVV viewpoint has not changed, basically, since its 1954 resolution. But one or two additional aspects have been dealt with, officially. The organisation fully supported the ratification of the Rome Treaties by the Dutch Parliament, and has made it clear that although the supranationalism of the Common Market Treaty is not as far-reaching as it would have liked that is no excuse for rejecting something that goes a good deal of the way to fulfilling an ideal. Supranational institutions must be strong in order that full policy co-ordination of the member countries can be achieved. Liberalising trade, and taking all controls and brakes off the European economy was not good enough. There must be a workable international policy.

The NVV approves of the freedom of movement of labour and capital, but is inclined to think that the freedom of capital movement is potentially of greater value. This is because, wherever possible, jobs should be taken to people, and not people to jobs. Freedom to move capital ought to divert investment to places where jobs are needed. If it does not, then it is the job of a European Investment Fund to do so.

It is strongly felt that the trade unions in the Community countries were insufficiently consulted during the drafting of the Rome Treaties, and the need for close consultation, now the Community is in being, is stressed. The number of delegates allocated to the European Assembly is insufficient, and should be increased, and the Benelux countries, it is felt, are particularly badly hit in this respect.

The Netherlands has, naturally, a particular interest in the agricultural provisions of the Common Market Treaty, and the NVV is pleased that a common agricultural policy is envisaged. It readily admits that minimum prices will have to be fixed, initially, because the agricultural producer, as well as the consumer, must have guarantees of reasonable prices. The organisation is of the opinion, however, that there ought to be provision for these minimum prices to be fixed by a supranational body, and not just supervised by them, even during the initial stages of the Economic Community. Allowing the individual countries to fix their own minimum prices during the Community's formative years, is, it believes, a mistake which may divert the Treaty's other purposes, and prevent a proper integration of agricultural policies.

Perhaps the section of the Common Market Treaty dealing with transport has caused as many misgivings among Dutch unions as any other. The NVV stresses that while other Community countries consider transport only as a means to certain economic and political ends, the Netherlands considers it as an independent and equal branch of production, which also provides a substantial amount of foreign currency for balance of payments purposes. Protection of their own transport industries by other Community countries, to keep out the Dutch, particularly by Germany, is deprecated, and it is regretted that the Treaty provisions are not strong enough to overcome this completely. The lack of facility for trade union participation in European transport policy-making is also regretted. Although the NVV wants a common transport market, which the Treaty does not envisage, it does appreciate the fact that the Netherlands will stand more chance of getting its particular views and problems across within the new institutions, than it previously did in its dealings with separate countries.

The NVV welcomes the Euratom Pact, and thinks that a combination of efforts by the "Six" in the peaceful development of nuclear energy is essential to solve their power problems, and to keep up with the progress of other nations. Having said that, the Euratom Treaty has not the full measure of supranational power the NVV would have wished, and the organisation is also uncertain that the provisions for the health and safety of workers, and general population, are sufficient. It is believed that the Netherlands, having large areas of its territory contiguous with river estuaries, is particularly vulnerable to dangers from the outlet of radio-active materials.

Although the NVV prefers, in principle, the closer form of integration offered by the Common Market, it believes that it is politically and economically desirable that there should be some form of close co-operation with the other countries of Western Europe. For this reason it supported the original idea of the wider Free Trade Area. It was felt that the Netherlands had closer affinity, in some respects, with Britain and the Scandinavian countries than it did with, say, France or Germany, because all the former have comparatively low tariffs. Consequently there was apprehension in case the higher common tariff of the "Six" should eventually stifle Dutch trade with other outside countries. Britain was among those nations with whom the country trades, and it was felt that the more countries that could be brought inside some West European tariff-free association, the less amount of external trade stood to be lost through the higher tariff of the "Six". The common tariff would, in any case, raise production costs.

The NVV has some reservations on the "wider zone" idea, though. It anticipates the problem of deflection of trade, and thinks that some attempt at tariff harmonisation, as opposed to unification, would have to be made. It believes that the possibilities of a common social-economic policy in the Community of the Six are already minimal, and would not want the countries in a wider association to be freed of the minimum Community responsibilities of contributing to a Social Fund, an Investment Bank, and helping overseas territories. It is felt, strongly, that although a Common Market in agriculture would not be possible, or necessary, in this wider association, a common policy would be essential. It would be quite unrealistic for Britain to insist that agriculture should be excluded from some form of common treatment, particularly as 45% of Dutch exports to Britain have been agricultural products.

The christian centre, the KAB, has not defined its position on European integration as thoroughly as has the NVV. It bases its attitude on that of its own international movement, the CISC. The General Secretary of the KAB has summarised his organisation's standpoint in three principles. First, it strongly supports the Common Market and Euratom, and considers them necessary for raising European welfare and keeping West European political influence strong in the world. Second, the policies of the Communities must be such as to benefit the workers reasonably, particularly in economic welfare. Third, it is hoped, and believed, that the economic integration of the "Six" will not lead to their isolation, but will, on the contrary, stimulate trade with outside countries.

Its position on a wider association is similar to that of the NVV. The KAB was a potential supporter of the original FTA plan, and thought that sort of scheme a necessary complement to the Economic Community, provided the Community was a composite part of it. The conditions for support of the idea were that a FTA should not in any way harm the effective operation of the Common Market, and that it should not make for unfair competition as between the "Six" and the other FTA members.

The smaller Protestant centre, the CNV, does not differ much in its view from the other two centres. It believes that economic nationalism in the past has been the cause of much suffering in the Netherlands, and elsewhere, and that the integration taking place will make for a healthier employment position and higher living standards, as well as increasing the prospects for wider social and economic co-operation. It expresses the same sentiments about the agricultural and transport industries as the NVV does: that they are of special importance to their own country and that the very real problems in these sectors must not be glossed over. The Treaty provisions are weak, here, the CNV believes, and far too many questions of policy have been left to be decided at a later date, instead of having the lines of approach incorporated in the Treaty.

The Treaty is also considered weak on balance of payments problems, and it is regretted that although the provisions are deferential to the special problems of several countries, the special problems of their own country–the rapid growth of the professional population, poverty in raw materials, and Indonesian interests – have not appeared to qualify for special concessions. It is thought that the provisions to ensure fair competition are not strong enough.

One point of difference with many other European trade union centres is that the CNV believes social harmonisation must come after, and not before, integration. In any case, there should not be harmonisation to an extent which might undermine the right of a member nation to give expression to its individual desires in this field.

The CNV is a great believer in a strong Economic and Social Committee within the Economic Community, and regrets that the one provided for will not be competent to tender unsolicited advice to the European Commission, or the Council of Ministers, but will have to wait until asked for its opinions on any given subject. The organisation also believes that parity of representation between members of the Committee with a trade union background, and members with a background in industrial enterprises, should be decided on. There is nothing prescribing or preventing this. It is pointed out that the Consultative Committee of the Coal and Steel Community, which is supposed to have a third of the members from employers, a third from workers and a third from consumers, has, in fact, a composition which draws all those in the consumer group from enterprises, or from transport. This unbalances the employer-worker representation in favour of the former.

In spite of the possible weak points, the CNV believes the Economic and Social Committee to be a good institution, in principle, because it is thought it will make concrete, on a European level, the christian idea of co-operation between enterprises and employees which is so much a Dutch national feature, at present.

CNV feelings are favourable to some form of wider European association, outside the Community, and the organisation supported the principle of the original Free Trade Area plan. Such an association was thought necessary because of the Netherlands' large overseas trade. The high external tariff of the Common Market could be dangerous, and tend to an unhealthy shutting off of the "Six" from outside trade.

Looking at the Netherlands' position as a whole, it can be said that the unions are among the strongest supporters of integration, ideologically, even though their national position is more vulnerable than that of most other Community members–due to their special agricultural and transport interests, and the initial low tariff structure of Benelux. In spite of this, and in spite of some misgivings about the ECSC's working, all three of the main national centres are keen on integration–in the wider context if it does not harm the Common Market–and want strong supranational powers in the institutional structure, presumably to counterbalance the weight of other national interests, which may often go against their country. There is little difference between the attitudes of the three centres, and their enthusiastic support for integration, although all have some serious misgivings. It seems to be a case of mind over matter.

In Benelux, as a whole, there is enthusiastic support by the trade unions for European integration, although there are a number of differences in the details of their approach, and each national centre emphasises different points. The three countries have in common being the smallest partners in the Economic Community, each without the chance of exercising a strong influence in its councils. But, together, they can form a very substantial power in the Community. The framework of Benelux does not appear to have been used, yet, to the full extent, in achieving this united influence.

If this is true on a governmental level, it is surely valid as far as it concerns the trade unions. If the unions were to co-ordinate their efforts more closely, within Benelux, on questions such as European integration, on which they have a great deal of common ground, then their prestige and influence in the international trade union bodies of the "Six", and in the ICFTU's and the CISC's Regional Organisations, would be greatly enhanced. Such unity would probably help to counterbalance the strength of the unions from larger countries, and win more consideration for the special problems of the Benelux countries. It would probably not be possible to align the unions belonging to different Internationals, or of differing political persuasions, in this way, but there seems no good reason why, in particular, the FGTB and the NVV; and the CSC, the KAB and the CNV should not come to a much closer working arrangement between themselves.

CHAPTER XIX

BRITAIN

The British Trades Union Congress (TUC) holds a unique position among European national trade union centres. It is the largest of the ICFTU's affiliates in Europe, it has a continuous history from 1868, it holds an established place in Britain as an organisation consulted by governments, and, although its viewpoint is often rejected, it is never ignored. It holds a large degree of moral authority over its well organised affiliated unions, it has no rival centres of any significance, and hardly any political or religious divisions to contend with in the movement at large.

Because of the TUC's prestige and traditions it is widely respected by its continental counterparts, even when they differ from its viewpoint, as is the case, for instance, on European integration matters. There was a widespread feeling among continental trade unions that Britain ought to have joined the Coal and Steel Community and the Common Market, and that the TUC could then have joined forces more closely with its contemporaries, and lent them strength. One school of thought was also of the opinion that the TUC's presence would have been useful as a counterweight to the might of the other large national centre, the German DGB, in the trade union councils of the Communities.

However, neither the British Government nor the TUC were to be enticed into a policy of full economic integration of Western Europe which would include Britain. Both Governments and trade unions in Britain are traditionally insular in their attitudes to the European continent and tend to believe that ties with the far-flung countries of the British Commonwealth are closer, and potentially more beneficial than any which would have to span the English Channel. The need for closer co-operation between Britain and the countries of continental Europe is well recognised, and has become manifest in the close ties with OEEC. The decision of the continental countries to integrate themselves is noted and approved. But, according to official viewpoints, integration is too strong a concept for most Britons to stomach, themselves.

Charles Geddes (now Lord Geddes), who was the TUC's representative on the Executive Committee of the ICFTU's European Regional

Organisation, until his retirement in 1957, has made an outspoken comment on the TUC's attitude.[1] He said in 1957:

"Now that Britain is favourably considering a Free Trade Area, pressure on the TUC to go even further into an integrated Europe will be more vigorously applied.

The British TUC's attitude to all this has been sceptical tolerance. Despite the creation of the Council of Europe, the formation of the European Coal and Steel Community, their general idea was that this was alright for those who wanted it; they did not mind watching the wagon go by so long as they were not committed to ride on it. My personal task as the TUC's representative on the ERO economic committee was to ensure that the wording of the reports and recommendations was in such terms that they could be swallowed without too much mental indigestion. The general council was prepared to accept the terms 'adaptation and harmonisation' in place of 'integration and co-operation', an almost classic example of turning the blind eye to an unwelcome development."

In spite of its reluctance to go deeply into Europe, the TUC put out a policy statement supporting the principle of a wide Free Trade Area, as originally proposed by the British Government, if it were carried through on what the TUC considered to be the right lines – that is with adequate guarantees and safeguards for the workers. The TUC published a highly informative pamphlet on the subject[2] which was both a statement of policy and a background report on Europe. It has submitted well-reasoned memoranda to Government Departments and had meetings with Government Ministers on questions appertaining to the Common Market and the proposed Free Trade Area, after consultations with the ICFTU's European Regional Organisation.

In these respects the TUC's research efforts have outshone those of some of its continental counterparts who are committed heart and soul to integration. Its approach, though, has been very cautious and pragmatic by comparison with the approach based more, perhaps, on idealism and the will to create, which is rather characteristic of most continental trade union centres.

The initiative to do anything at all about European integration or co-operation questions has come entirely from the top in the British trade union movement. If it had been left to come from lower levels, it is very likely that nothing at all would have been done; or if it had, it

1. Third Programme BBC broadcast on "Wages and the Common Market", reproduced in the *Listener*, 4 April 1957.

2. *Economic Association with Europe*, November 1956.

may even have been to move in an opposite direction, away from closer ties.

Uninspired by any ideals to press for a closer-knit Europe, the Common Market and Free Trade Area projects fail to fire the imagination of the average British trade unionist. The consequence is that the subject appears prosaic and technical, and this impression is not dispelled by the tentative and empirical manner in which it is treated in official documents, and in the press. The sporadic reports of negotiations appearing in the newspapers over several years have been confusing through apparent lack of continuity, and the upshot is that trade unionists at all levels are mostly without a working knowledge of the subject. A large number of trade unionists are unable to distinguish the various integration and free trading schemes, one from another.

The lack of interest in the original Free Trade Area plan at ground-floor level was shown by the fact that out of 77 resolutions sent in by affiliated organisations on the agenda for the Trades Union Congress in 1957, only one was on the subject of the Free Trade Area. This called for continued protection of the jute industry. The 1958 agenda did not contain a single resolution on the subject, although it was probably the most important economic plan for many years, and trade union agendas are normally packed with resolutions on economic policy.

Knowledge of, and interest in, European integration questions in the British trade union movement is mainly confined to those members of the TUC General Council who sit on the Economic and International Sub-committees, and whose job it is to draft TUC policy on the subject. The policy decided – cautious support for the Government's Free Trade Area proposals – was reported to the 1957 Congress, composed of delegates from all affiliated unions, and, in spite of some opposition, was confirmed. However the TUC is not able to speak on behalf of its affiliated organisations in such a way as to bind them to its own decisions. Unlike some national centres, the TUC is a consultative organ only, and does not have any executive power over its affiliates. Individual trade unions were therefore free to speak out against the European Free Trade Area, and one or two of them did so. But generally, there is a tendency among them to adopt the attitude that the TUC General Council knows more about the subject than they do, and its effective policy, in consequence, will not be seriously challenged.

Once the General Council had decided, after studying the documents prepared by its secretariat, that British industry, generally, stood to make gains in a wide Free Trade Area, it gave the lead by issuing a policy statement favouring it. Had this initiative not come from the top, straight away, it might have been left for the delegate Congress to decide at some later date. If this had been the case it is doubtful whether the project would have been supported.

Most British trade unions regard themselves as socialist organisations, and, indeed, the majority of trade unionists are affiliated to the Labour Party, directly. There is a widespread and traditional aversion, generally speaking, in the British Labour Movement (that is in the Labour Party and trade unions combined) to the words "free trade". Socialists have been brought up to believe that free trade smacks of 19th. century *laissez-faire* policies, and *laissez-faire* was a basic tenet of the capitalist system to which they were, and are, opposed. This mode of thought is dying out a little, owing to changing circumstances and changing standards, and it is often recognised that a Free Trade Area in Europe would not be similar to the universal free trade that was advocated in the last century. But the suspicion of free trading schemes lingers, in Labour eyes, because of their name.

The other traditional argument against close associations with the continent, to be found at all levels in the Labour Movement, is that British Socialism may be swamped in a right wing Europe. Having had majority Socialist Governments in Britain, the Labour Movement feels that if the country is inveigled into any close form of association which implies eventual political unification, then the lack of socialist strength in Europe generally, and the predominance of alien right wing and Roman Catholic political parties will emasculate British Socialism, and prejudice the chance of creating a socialist society in Britain. For similar reasons there is grave suspicion of entering into Treaty commitments which would deprive a British Government of any of its national powers to plan the country's economy as it thought fit. Economic planning, and the need for it, is a constant theme among British Labour figures. Many of them do not realise that a good deal of economic planning, on an international scale, has gone into the European Coal and Steel Community, and is likely to go into the Common Market; more perhaps than has been carried out on a national scale by some British Governments.

The very close partnership of the trade unions and the Labour Party in Britain has probably been a further factor making for a cautious policy by the TUC. It is normal for the TUC and the Labour Party to consult each other before publishing policy statements on important matters, and there was a prior exchange of views on the question of economic association with Europe. But as the National Executive Committee of the Labour Party includes one or two people, for example, Aneurin Bevan, who are not convinced of the merits of a Free Trade Area, what was decided by the TUC had to be conservative enough not to give offence to any section of the Labour Movement. Because of this, the Labour Party, itself, said only the minimum it had to say in support of the original scheme in Parliament, and it refrained, for two years, from publishing any comprehensive document for circulation and discussion among its general membership. As the TUC and the Labour Party consider that public harmony between them is of paramount importance, the Party's lack of enthusiasm, and its policy of inactivity on European integration questions has probably had some effect on the TUC approach, as well.

Having regard to these complications, it is not possible to assess the future of British trade union attitudes to European integration without taking account of the feeling in the political side of the Labour Movement. It is extremely unlikely that the TUC and the Labour Party will fall out of step in public, but the attitudes which are adopted in common are the direct result of diverse pressures working in private between them.

TUC Policy on Economic Association with Europe[3]

As may have been expected, the TUC's main concern in considering proposals for a Free Trade Area has been that full employment must be the chief aim, and that participating countries should be bound to this principle by a specific obligation incorporated in any Treaty or Agreement. Not only that, but member countries should be required to draw up adequate plans for internal action to maintain full employment, and a Treaty should include a general statement on the methods which they will adopt, individually and collectively, in furtherance of the aim.

The TUC General Council submitted a draft clause to the Chancellor of the Exchequer which set out these methods. Member countries would not only be obliged to formulate a full employment objective under this clause, but would be required to prepare, publish and lay before the appropriate international body, annual reports on the measures being undertaken to reach the objective. Members would commit themselves to influence the levels of consumption, demand and investment in such a way as to maintain full employment, and would also ensure a balanced distribution of industry to this end. Maximum use of national employment services would be developed with the aim of providing the

---

3. Most of the information in this section is drawn from the TUC Report 1957, paras. 312-318 inclusive, pp. 267-276 inclusive. This section includes reproduction of the texts of the policy pamphlet *Economic Association with Europe*, and of the memorandum submitted to the British Government giving observations on its FTA policy, as published in the White Paper (Cmnd. 72) *A European Free Trade Area*, February 1957.

maximum information on employment opportunities, etc., assisting in the placing of workers, establishing training and retraining facilities, easing the movement of labour by overcoming financial and other obstacles, and assisting in the formulation of policy on the location and establishment of industry.

Consultation on full employment between the member countries was provided for, and, in addition, members would undertake to interpret the other Treaty provisions in the light of the full employment programmes. The TUC was convinced that if a full employment policy based on these principles was carried out in Western Europe, the foundations for steadily rising living standards would have been laid, and Europe would be able to develop its full economic and political strength, enabling it, among other things, to give more aid for the development of economically backward countries.

The reason that the TUC centres its attitude to free trade on the various facets of the full employment question, to the exclusion of most other labour questions, is because it is less interested in the other questions, or less enthusiastic about the attitudes taken to them by its counterparts in the "Six" countries.

It will be recalled that, apart from full employment, the main concerns of the European Regional Organisation of the ICFTU, and many of its affiliates, were the questions of workers' representation, social harmonisation, adequate supranational authority, the free movement of labour and a strong institution to stimulate international investment, free from private influence.[4]

Rather strangely, the TUC placed no stress in its early documents on the question of workers' representation in a FTA. All it said was that it would expect to be kept informed of the progress made in negotiations, and to be fully consulted on matters which became the subject of negotiations with other Governments. There was no mention of the necessity for consultation with the trade unions if a wider economic association actually came into being. During 1958, however, the TUC came round to the view that an Economic and Social Committee, on which trade unions would have substantial representation, was a proper institution to have in such an association, and should be modelled, presumably, on the Economic and Social Committee operating in the Community of the "Six".

The TUC agreed with the Government that a comprehensive FTA should have been established within the OEEC, the Organisation for European Economic Co-operation. But it made no mention of any new

4. Details of the differences in viewpoint between the TUC and other trade unions in the ERO will be found in Chapter III.

facilities that would have been necessary for trade union consultation within it, commensurate with its new functions. Neither did it make mention of the Trade Union Advisory Committee, operated jointly between the ICFTU and CISC unions, that is already working hard within the OEEC. Subsequently, the TUC has taken a rather stronger line over the desirability of consultation with the unions in the European Free Trade Association.

It has said little about the general institution required to guide a free-trading scheme. Continental unions have continually pressed for greater supranational powers to be given to their Community institutions. They want to sweep away what they regard as outmoded national interests. This, the TUC thinks, may be all very well for those countries which wish to integrate their economies. But it has no desire to see Britain's economy integrated with Europe–it wants nothing more radical than harmonisation. Hence the original TUC preference for working within the OEEC–basically a body for promoting co-operation, and not integration.

Another vital aspect of European unity on which TUC and ERO opinions are divergent is the question of social harmonisation. The TUC is not prepared to endorse compulsory harmonisation, but supports a complaints procedure which enables countries considering their interests to be damaged, through another not having equivalent social provisions, to approach a competent authority for remedial action. A similar provision might operate in respect of complaints against a country which did not ratify ILO Conventions. These are believed to be better objectives than having a legal obligation on harmonisation written into an international treaty. Traditionally, British trade unions are strong advocates of improving pay, conditions and fringe benefits by collective bargaining, and have not much sympathy with continental methods of obtaining improvements statutorily. They believe that what the law can give, it can also take away, and this is the basic reason why they are opposed to upward harmonisation by means of a treaty clause.

Another respect in which British trade union thinking is not in harmony with that on the continent is on the subject of the free movement of labour. The TUC is not in favour of the type of provision such as that in the Common Market Treaty which will ensure free movement of labour between Community countries. It believes that the present system operating in Britain, whereby employers must make efforts to find British workers to fill vacancies, before obtaining permission to employ foreigners, is fair and reasonable. The General Council originally stated that it did not consider that a European policy on movements of labour was necessary, and that the existing consultative

machinery within the OEEC and the ILO would require no modification
for FTA purposes. Its subsequent thoughts on the matter are that the
existing machinery might be further developed. Even so, this is a far cry
from the determined pleas for free migration put forward by some
others in the ERO, and is indicative of a deep-rooted British trade union
fear of permitting anything which may possibly prejudice a strong
trade union bargaining position, or may decrease the scarcity value of
labour.

Thus it can be seen that the TUC's policy towards a closer-knit
Europe has, so far as direct trade union interests are concerned, been
centred almost entirely on the different aspects of full employment,
because some of the other issues considered vitally important by its
continental colleagues—strong supranational authority, social harmonisation and free movement of labour—would appear to commit Britain
to Europe further than the TUC thinks expedient.

Consequently, the remainder of the TUC documents on the European
question are almost entirely concerned with issues which are less
industrial, and are more technical and political. In these fields it exceeded
the efforts of most of its continental colleagues in providing well-
reasoned arguments on aspects and problems of a FTA which were
of less direct importance to trade unionists, but were, nevertheless,
important.

The TUC is in favour of the Government making provision, in conjunction with other Governments concerned, for action to deal with
restrictive business practices within a wider economic association, such as
international cartels. It would like to see some form of complaints-
procedure operate within any scheme, so that any member country
could complain about unfair competition from any other member,
whether it arose from the operation of cartels, low labour standards in
other countries, export subsidies, tax remissions to exporters or
currency retention schemes.

But having said this, the TUC is not prepared to see regulations so
strict on these matters that they would restrict the rights of national
governments to plan their economies, or to give financial assistance in
specific cases. It does not consider that fair competition codes should
preclude governments from providing temporary assistance for the re-
equipment of an industry lacking the necessary capital, or assisting
industries which are essential for strategic purposes, or are vital to
national cultural standards. The European Free Trade Association
Convention appears to have incorporated TUC views on most of these
procedural and political matters.

On a good number of mainly commercial aspects of a wider economic association, the TUC appears to have made such qualifications to its support as to almost qualify it out of existence. This may not have been their intention, but it is a situation which is, perhaps, attributable to the painstaking caution and conservatism of the organisation and to the fact that the members of the General Council have their main loyalties to their individual unions which employ them. Sectional interests can be difficult to reconcile with international free trade; but not many strained loyalties have been apparent.

The TUC has modified its views on the right of establishment, and the free movement of capital. It now supports the former, and is not opposed to the movement of non-speculative capital for genuine purposes. But a free-trading arrangement would be bound to bring some reorganisation of production and this would make it necessary to have some internal control over capital movement. Individual governments should retain full control of their internal fiscal policies, which affect industry, and should be allowed to promote particular economic or social policies, in the TUC's view.

As far as a FTA catering for all Western Europe is concerned, the General Council believes that the established OEEC methods of trade liberalisation should be adequate for the United Kingdom's purposes. A number of industries have been built behind traditional tariffs, and the sudden removal of the tariffs would be too radical a method of freeing trade. A reasonably extended transitional period would be acceptable to them in principle, but it is stressed that there should be some flexibility. This viewpoint is well in line with the operating principles of the Common Market.

The General Council would expect to be consulted on any criteria it was intended to adopt regarding tariff removal. They consider that in a wide FTA the Government should maintain a right to levy duties on imports, for revenue and social purposes, and also for the regulation of consumer purchasing power in relation to available supplies, always provided that this is done in a manner which does not discriminate for or against any particular member country.

There were several more points in its own 1956 and 1957 documents where the TUC expressed reservations which were even more cautious and painstaking than those of the official OEEC Working Party, which published a report on the possibility of creating a Free Trade Area.[5] The TUC agreed with the Working Party that some provision for escape clauses would have to be provided to meet exceptional circumstances in member countries, but also went further than them by stating its belief

5. *Report on the Possibility of Creating A Free Trade Area in Europe*, published by OEEC, Paris, January 1957.

that such provisions might have to be retained even after the end of the transitional period.

The General Council also stated the view that member countries should have the right to determine their own priorities during a gradual reduction of quantitative import restrictions, and flexibility in the method of removal should be allowed. As far as commodity agreements were concerned, the United Kingdom should have the same right to make long term trade agreements with Commonwealth and other countries as at present, in any FTA.

On the question of balance of payments difficulties the TUC took the conventional viewpoint that member countries should have the right to restrict imports if their payments difficulties reached emergency levels, and also that there should be provision for the restoration of equilibrium without forcing deficit countries to resort to internal deflation. Consultation on remedial action between member countries should be provided for. The more original and interesting suggestion on balance of payments problems, however, was that the burden of restoring equilibrium should be shared between the creditor and the debtor countries, through automatic credit. It can be taken that most of these 1956 and 1957 views still largely apply to the Free Trade Association and possible wider developments.

The TUC was a firm believer in the merits of the European Payments Union (EPU), and had hoped that it would be maintained in any Free Trade Area. It considered that the linkage the EPU had established between the sterling area and the European convertible currency countries was valuable, and thought it desirable to maintain the institution's structure as it was. It can be taken that the decision to wind up EPU was unwelcome to the TUC.

The policy points outlined show clearly the pragmatic and prosaic approach of the TUC to questions which arouse emotional as well as practical interest among its continental counterparts. The British preference for assessing the European situation, rather than pushing it, was well shown in a speech by Mr. Alan Birch, the Chairman of the TUC Economic Committee, when he spoke at a European Industrial Conference held in London, in February 1958. Speaking of a proposed Free Trade Area Treaty, he said:[6]

"The first effects of the Treaty will be to increase competition. To the whole question of competition the British Trade Union Movement has avoided a doctrinaire approach. Experience shows that competition

6. *European Industrial Conference*, verbatim Report, published by United Kingdom Council of the European Movement, p. 16.

can sometimes be beneficial and sometimes detrimental–both to workers and to consumers. We should, therefore, be realistic and recognise that some limitations will, in effect be necessary to the free play of competitive forces ... free trade in the context of present day Europe and the world cannot mean a reversion to nineteenth century *laissez-faire*. Therefore each country should not be precluded from taking certain measures which might be necessary, and would be possible without limiting the benefits to be derived from free trade in Europe."

In contrast to Mr. Birch, many trade union and political figures in the Labour Movement are lacking in a clear knowledge of what has happened already in European integration questions, what the provisions of the Rome Treaties and the Free Trade Association Convention are, what the prospects for a wider association are, and what are the real issues involved in negotiating it. The less well-informed ones are downright suspicious of the whole business, and, if they were publicly to voice their scepticism, would possibly have considerable support from the rank and file.

They have not, generally speaking, voiced their suspicions because the majority decision favoured an FTA, and because they are not sufficiently sure, themselves. Most of those in the trade union movement who have a good working knowledge of European integration are much more inclined to look favourably on the process, but even they feel their way forward very gingerly, half afraid of betraying their insular past, though intellectually impressed by the possibilities of a form of internationalism that may really work. They will continue to keep a wary eye, though, on the reactions of members in their own unions. Internationalism, they may think, is all well and good in theory, but where does loyalty lie if the short term interests of their own particular industries appear to be in conflict with the international good?

However hesitant and qualified the TUC's support of a closer-knit Europe has been, at least its ground shifted over a period of two years, or so, from 1956, to a rather more positive attitude. Mr. George Woodcock, the organisation's Assistant General Secretary, summed it up in an article in which he wrote:[7]

". . . while trade union support for the idea of a free trade area was given in the first place for the negative reason that it would avoid discrimination against U.K. goods in Western European markets, there has been a shift in the TUC position since that decision was

7. *Financial Times Annual Review*, 1958, "British Industry in a Free Trade Area", p. 28.

taken. We are now more inclined to recognise the possibilities of greater industrial specialisation and higher living standards in the market of 250 million people which would be created by the establishment of a free trade area; we also realise that the failure of the negotiations would result in the economic division of Western Europe with potentially disastrous effects on European political unity."

In conclusion, it can be said that the TUC will continue to decide its attitude to the problems of a wider association as they arise, in consultation with the Labour Party, and that neither body will take up any radical new position without the assent of the other. For this reason, the Labour Movement, as a whole in Britain, will continue, in all probability, to be edged forward, inch by inch, into the acceptance of closer ties with its European neighbours. But the complete process may well take a good many years.

PART FIVE

CONCLUSION

CONCLUSION

Since the end of the second world war there has been an unprecedented number of organisations for international co-operation set up in a large variety of fields by the governments of the world, or of particular regions of the world. The world-wide ones have frequently been less successful than the regional ones, because they had more differences to reconcile than common interests to promote. The political ones have generally been less successful than the economic and social ones, for similar reasons.

The various Western European integration schemes, other than defence pacts, are of a character mainly economic and partly social, and cater for nations whose interests, in these respects, have a good deal in common. They are therefore working in a comparatively favourable climate for international organisations. Because their potentialities for success are good, the participating governments have been prepared to relinquish a certain amount of their national sovereignties, and, occasionally, to put real power into the hands of supranational institutions. Unless political factors encroach a great deal, the policies of these supranational authorities will not often be openly flouted by national governments.

The international trade union movements are mainly concerned, also, with economic and social matters, and their regional bodies have been able to make a good deal of progress, through affiliates relinquishing a certain amount of national sovereignty, in order to pursue a united purpose in a limited geographical area. While the governments change from national to international commercial and industrial policies, the trade unions, in order to perform their normal functions, are willingly adapting themselves to the international level, also. As the evolution of the European Communities takes the member states further into the fields of international administration, so will the trade unions require to develop their own international organisations to keep pace with the growth of their supranational tasks. Substantial progress has already been made but more will require to be done as the situation develops.

One of the problems that the ICFTU and CISC-affiliated trade unions make particularly their own concern, is to attempt to ensure that the existing Communities of the "Six" have a strongly supranational character. This springs partly from their conviction that authorities with a large measure of independence of national governments tend to follow enlightened social policies, and partly from a belief that the influence of the nation state should no longer dominate, and that true internationalism holds more promise for peace and prosperity. The WFTU, and most of its affiliated unions, representing a minority view in Western Europe, state that the supranationality which the Communities bring is harmful to the workers' interests, it will allow monopolies to control the Communities, and that this erosion of national sovereignties is therefore undesirable.

The fact that the Common Market Treaty gives fewer specific supranational powers to its Commission, *vis à vis* the Council of Ministers, than the ECSC did to its High Authority in similar constitutional circumstances, is presumably welcome to the WFTU, on the grounds that a larger degree of national sovereignty is thus maintained. The ICFTU and the CISC, and most of their European affiliates, have looked upon this trend with some dismay. But while it was the opposite of what they wished to see, it was, to some extent, inevitable.

In the case of the ECSC, the original initiative came from a war-weary France, anxious to put the basic German industries of coal and steel– her main war potential–into some form of straightjacket which would prevent their future use for the wrong purposes. In this respect, a strong supranational institution seemed the best way of lessening any feelings of political constraint that Western Germany may have had about the Plan, concerning other member states. National sovereignty over two basic industries was dispensed with, in return for a form of guarantee of their good behaviour in Germany.

In the case of the Common Market the position was reversed, to some degree. Western Germany, with her economy greatly strengthened in the intervening years, was in a position to gain substantial benefits, competitively, through extending the common market in coal and steel to other industries. It was France which was wary, unsure that the Coal and Steel Community had had the desired authority over German basic industry, and demanding concessions, often at German expense, as the price of agreement for her to enter the new scheme. German interests stood to gain, not only economically, but through the country's full re-establishment as a respected member of the Western World, and of European Communities.

Because the Common Market, economically speaking, is a very much larger scheme than the ECSC, and because its size, and other factors, give it greater political implications, it was to be expected that member states would approach it circumspectly, and refrain from committing themselves too far at an early stage. The somewhat uncertain political and economic situation between France and Germany is reflected in the tentative nature of many Common Market Treaty provisions. Anything affecting the relations of these two countries is bound to resound within the Community; and this was another factor that counselled caution for all six governments negotiating the Treaty, and caused them to agree on an institutional framework which, although supranational in character, could quickly be made responsive to the views of nations which felt their interests were being jeopardised.

The trade unions have reacted against what they feel is a significant loss of supranationality and independence for the Economic Community, as compared with the ECSC. This loss is partly because trade union representatives are all but excluded from membership of its executive institutions. It is felt that not only has the EEC less independence of national governments, because of this, but the trade unions also have less possibility of influencing the course of events.

Even if they can work as effectively in the purely advisory Economic and Social Committee, as they did in the ECSC's Consultative Committee (which is considered doubtful), it is felt that they now have the Council of Ministers to convince on many occasions, in addition to the Commission. In the ECSC, it was often necessary to persuade only the High Authority of a viewpoint for it to be effective. But these considerations apart, as they had, in 1958-9, one-third of the membership of the High Authority of the ECSC, they feel entitled to some representation on the Common Market Commission.

It is strange that most member governments appear to have set their face against seating trade unionists on the executive bodies. Apart from one alternate member on the Board of Directors of the European Investment Bank, there is no trade unionist seated in an executive institution of the Common Market. Neither is there one in the new Court of Justice, although there was one in the Court it replaced. In view of the fact that the trade unions, in most cases, have been among the keenest and most consistent supporters of integration projects in Western Europe, and are in large part responsible for the broadly-based and positive support the Communities have in the six countries, the governments appear to have made a substantial error of judgment in this respect.

There could hardly be a better way of providing raw material for the WFTU-affiliated unions in France, Italy and the Netherlands, in their campaigns against the Common Market, in principle or in detail, than to deprive the trade unions of representation in the executive and judicial institutions, against ECSC precedents. This might have the effect not only of confirming the suspicions of these unions, but also of arousing serious doubts in the minds of the ICFTU and CISC affiliates, as to whether their faith that the Common Market was intended to benefit all sections of society was fully justified. Doubtless, the unions will continue to press hard for representation; perhaps by asking for trade unionists to be co-opted, in the short term, but probably also by following a long term policy of persuading governments to consider appointing trade unionists when the terms of some of the present office-holders expire. There have been signs that the unions have found a sympathetic hearing in the Assembly, concerning representation, and this factor could influence the future policy of governments.

As far as their concern with increasing the Economic Community's supranational authority is concerned, the trade unions will regard their campaign for representation as one method of helping to assure it. But it will not necessarily be the quickest way, or the only way. There may be a long-term campaign to amend the Articles of the Treaty to give greater supranational powers to the Commission, or to give it more specific supranational functions to perform. But this does not seem the most profitable channel for trade union energies. They may well decide that it will be more effective if they use their influence to have the Community institutions interpret the existing Treaty Articles in a liberal manner as they offer plenty of scope for supranational action, provided the Council of Ministers is prepared to sanction their wide interpretation.

To achieve this result, the unions are likely to develop the techniques which have been used with effect in the Coal and Steel Community. There, they had the advantage of direct representation on the High Authority, but even in the absence of representation on the European Commission, the systems of personal contact and discreet lobbying, can be developed most effectively. The Economic and Social Committee will naturally be important, but the unions believe that it has limitations because of the likelihood that the employers represented on it will be able to outvote union advice on matters about which the unions feel strongly, such as decisions concerning the degree of industrial concentration, or price fixing, to be allowed.

They are therefore likely to put a good deal of effort into developing relations with the European Commission and their staff in the Brussels headquarters, through the separate Liaison Bureaux which the ICFTU unions and the CISC unions maintain there. These Bureaux are otherwise the Secretariats of the Executive Committee of the "Six", in the case of the ICFTU unions, and of the European Organisation in the case of the CISC unions. Viewpoints put in an informal atmosphere between individuals who respect each other's positions, are often more influential than stands taken officially, with, perhaps, a show of strength, in formal meetings. Experience in Brussels is likely to confirm this.

Lack of formality may also prove to be the keynote of good trade union policy co-ordination, as the overlap of trade union personalities in the Economic and Social Committee with those sitting on the trade union Executive Committee, and the European Organisation, mentioned above, is fairly extensive, and should result in a good deal of unofficial co-operation.

Many of the trade unionists on these bodies will also have close contact, although acting, perhaps, in other capacities, with members of the new Assembly for the three European Communities; and this may provide a valuable lobby for trade union interests. Although the Assembly has very few direct powers over the other Community institutions, its *raison d'être* is to provide broadly-based and democratic guidance for those institutions. The trade unions will work hard to ensure that such guidance has been well primed by their own viewpoint.

Whether the main trade union influence will operate at Community level or at national level will depend partly on the amount of supra-national authority wielded by Community institutions. In others words, trade union pressure will be brought to bear at the real seats of power, whether national or international. But there is not likely to be any sudden or drastic change from the normal division of functions between international organs, national centres and individual unions. The inter-national organs have already begun to take over some of the tasks previously performed at national level, but only to a limited degree. The continuation of this process is likely to be slow, but perceptible. In the short term, many of the problems which integration poses to the unions will demand that action be taken partly, if not wholly, at the national level, if significant results are to be achieved.

Although international trade union organisations may be effective in their representations to international institutions, they normally carry comparatively little weight with national governments. These govern-ments are more used to working with national trade union centres, and will usually be more susceptible to pressure from those sources. It follows that if national governments are to reserve most of the fundamental powers of the new Communities to themselves for some years, the trade unions will work most effectively by concentrating a good deal of their efforts at national level, also, during that period.

This particularly applies to the traditional function of trade unions, which is to obtain for their members an equitable share of the wealth which they help to produce. The Community institutions will not be employers in the general sense, and will not be parties to collective bargaining concerning rates of pay. The level of remuneration will still be determined in the Communities' industries, by agreement at national or at workshop level, or by a combination of both, usually through established collective bargaining machinery. It follows that efforts to ensure that the extra wealth created, through the increased specialisation and productivity expected from the Community, must be directed mainly through these traditional national channels if they are to raise living standards all round, in accordance with international trade union policy.

There will certainly be an increasing necessity for the policies of individual unions and national centres to be harmonised at the international level, so that there can be a levelling-up process between the member countries. But the main results must be expected from action taken within the member countries, during the early years of the Common Market, at least.

This does not preclude the possibility of international collective bargaining to determine levels of pay, at some time in the future. It is hardly possible to predict when this may occur but it is not likely to be for a number of years—perhaps after the transitional periods of the Communities are completed. There is more than one reason why international collective bargaining, over pay, is not an immediate proposition.

There are, in many cases, no international organisations of employers who would be competent to take on the task of bargaining for a group of countries, and the trade unions might not be keen to stimulate their opposite numbers in strengthening their international co-ordination at the present time. They will usually consider it a better proposition to try and use differing national circumstances as bargaining points, during the first years of the new Communities. Future action would depend on how circumstances developed; and most trade union leaders with international experience recognise that international collective bargaining is something to be provided for at a future date.

But these leaders often tend to regard the date as one which they, themselves, will not see. The established negotiating machinery, they feel, has taken many years and much hard work to build. They do not like relinquishing power any more than politicians or governments do, and many of them will therefore be opposed, through quite natural conservatism and caution, to turning over functions which they traditionally perform, to international organisations. That is, until they are absolutely certain that doing so will not decrease the effectiveness of the bargaining, from the standpoint of their particular membership, or deprive them, personally, of the influence they hold at present. They do not believe that such guarantees can be quickly forthcoming and neither, therefore, will be international collective bargaining over rates of pay.

The trade unions, for the most part, will not oppose the extension of the principle of international determination of certain conditions of employment, whatever they may feel about rates of pay being a national prerogative. Indeed, they have, by pursuing their policy for upward social harmonisation and minimum standards, implicitly asked that some conditions now determined nationally, should become the concern of international organisations. This is not a new departure; only a development of a policy which has been supported in the International Labour Organisation for many years. The policy, for most countries, is not an unprecedented encroachment on the collective bargaining principle, for it has been the practice for some years to have certain conditions of employment regulated statutorily, rather than established through collective bargaining between unions and employers. One prominent example is the 40 hour normal working week in France.

Some countries are ahead of others in some social provisions, or conditions of work, but have less favourable conditions than those same countries in other specific respects. There is no Western European country with a clear lead in every field. This means that if upward social harmonisation takes place, a process provided for in the Common Market Treaty, all countries will need to level up in some respects. The stress is likely to fall, increasingly, on doing this by statutory means, even in those countries where it is usually done by collective bargaining, as no other method is likely to be as effective for pursuing a positive harmonisation policy.

One method of achieving harmonisation might be an agreement among the member nations of the Common Market, or of a wider association, to work towards a given level in each category of social or industrial provision which it is intended to harmonise. This could be done all at once, or in stages, to suit the convenience of each country. Inasfar as the minimum provisions would be laid down internationally, this would be a continuation and development of present procedures, whereby Conventions are agreed at the ILO, and some Social Conventions at the Council of Europe, and are afterwards ratified by national parliaments.

In this respect, an important development within the framework of the Council of Europe, since 1953, gives promise of future beneficial possibilities for an integrated Europe. Since that year, a European Social Charter, fixing minimum social standards for member countries, has been under discussion and in draft. In December 1958, a Tripartite Conference (that is representing governments, employers and workers) was convened by the ILO, at the request of the Council of Europe, to consider the draft Charter. The Conference made a number of amendments and suggestions, before sending it back to the Council, and a good deal of progress was made towards establishing the precise terms on which all the parties could come to agreement. The Charter deals with many of the social provisions with which ILO Conventions concern themselves, and also covers a good deal of the same ground as the ERO has suggested for its minimum social provisions under a social harmonisation programme. It also deals with questions which the Community of the "Six" countries will have to take up in its moves towards harmonisation.

The European Social Charter is ambitious in that it attempts to reconcile a large number of countries' differing interests. That is one of the main reasons why the drafting and agreement of it are taking a long time. It is bound to run the risk, in these circumstances, either of being whittled down until it has little substance, or of not being implemented through trying to achieve too much. The important thing is that whether the Charter is ever adopted, fully, in Western Europe, or not, the progress up to 1958 indicated that the Council of Europe may well be the most suitable medium for achieving social harmonisation, either in the "Six" countries, or, better still, in all the countries of any wider European Economic Association which is negotiated.

An agreement to use the Council of Europe for this purpose would have a number of advantages. It would tend to enhance the status of the Council, which sometimes seems to be in danger, from indifference and financial stringency in member states. It could follow the formula, already adopted, of asking the ILO to convene tripartite meetings for member countries in Western Europe, or, perhaps, even for the "Six", if necessary. This would surmount the difficulty of the Council, itself, not being a tripartite body, and also the constitutional problem the ILO might otherwise have, of convening regional meetings at which the Soviet Union and Eastern European countries were not present. This formula could also ensure the continued close co-operation of the ILO with the Council, on matters on which the former has a vast fund of experience and information at its disposal. Council pressure on member countries to ratify ILO Conventions has increased the rate of such ratification in recent years, and has already shown the fruits of close working between the two organisations.

There could be further valuable benefit from an agreement which would encourage social harmonisation by means of Western European Conventions originating in the Council of Europe. If such Conventions could be linked up, for example, with the specific provisions in the Common Market Treaty for equal pay for men and women doing equal work, the levelling up of overtime payments and the equivalence of paid holidays; it would ensure that any legislation necessary to bring about these conditions would take the form of national ratifications of international Conventions, rather than statutory acts or orders originating in the legislatures of member states.

The distinction may seem, at first, unimportant. But it could prove to be an opening for bringing the opinions of the trade union movements of the Community countries, and the other OEEC members nearer together, on social harmonisation. If that were achieved, the gap between the Free Trade Association and the Economic Community, in the settlement of a wider European association, might also be narrowed.

The position is that while the trade unions in a number of continental countries do not object, on principle, to certain social provisions connected with employment being regulated by statute, the British TUC, and the Scandinavian trade unions are traditionally wedded to determining these through collective bargaining. Even though statutory regulations in countries with fairly weak trade union movements have frequently yielded better results, in respect of the length of the working week, paid holidays, equal pay, and other provisions; the TUC, particularly, has never been convinced of the merits of statutory improvements. It does, however, approve of industrial provisions which are ratified by Parliament, if they originate as Conventions passed by the ILO, or, presumably, by a similar tripartite body having connections with the Council of Europe.

It would probably be to the advantage of the international trade union movements to press for the social harmonisation of Western Europe through machinery jointly operated by the Council of Europe and the ILO. This could, on the one hand, serve their intentions for the Community countries, and, on the other hand, stand a good chance of overcoming TUC and Scandinavian trade union objections to the social harmonisation of Europe by legislative provisions. If the TUC could be convinced of the merits of accepting planned social harmonisation as an integral part of an agreement for a wider European association, then there is a chance that the British Government could also be persuaded of this. As this question was one of those over which the original Free Trade Area negotiations stumbled, a solution along these lines may help considerably in the larger problem of concluding some other form of wider European association embracing the "Six" and the "Seven".

There would be a need for more powerful machinery to operate than that dealing with the European Social Charter, if social harmonisation were to be achieved by means of such European Conventions. And it would certainly have to be capable of operating at a much faster pace, if it were to serve the ends of the Rome Treaty provisions on social harmonisation, or to open up new fields for settlement in a wider association. These are matters which it would pay the trade union organisations to examine earnestly, and immediately, in view of the importance of concluding an agreement for some kind of comprehensive West European association as early as possible.

Their desire for effective supranationalism may even cause them to consider whether they should campaign for this sort of machinery as a beginning of a long-term plan for a supranational parliamentary institution in Western Europe, which could legislate on social questions, for example, without recourse to national parliaments.

But first it will be necessary for the continental trade unionists to convince their British and Scandinavian colleagues that attempts to regulate certain conditions of employment by legislation can sometimes show better results than attempts to regulate them by agreement reached through collective bargaining. In Britain, for instance, the main efforts of the whole trade union movement, nearly every year, go into making claims for higher pay. Although claims are frequently presented for higher overtime premiums, equal pay for equal work, more paid holidays in line with continental countries, and other "fringe" benefits, the progress on these is slow or negligible. The reason is that the unions are not prepared to dissipate their energies or resources on forcing these issues to a successful conclusion, at the risk of prejudicing their priority claims for more pay. The employers are not usually prepared to make concessions in both fields, simultaneously.

On the other hand, many continental countries, including Community countries, have gained clear leads over Britain in some conditions of employment, and "fringe" benefits, because they have not shared British trade union fears about the encroachment of legislation. Although their weaker union organisation, in many cases, has not enabled them to obtain wages, through collective bargaining, comparable to those in Britain; trade union pressure and influence in political circles has provided them, often, with more advanced benefits in industrial conditions. They have found that even governments of a political complexion they do not favour have been responsive to pressure, and to public opinion on these matters. Politicians, after all, depend on votes and public support. Employers do not, and will frequently decline to make concessions to the trade unions that governments would find inexpedient to refuse. And there does not seem much danger, today, of governments taking their actions to improve industrial conditions as a precedent for withdrawing privileges at a later date, as the TUC seems to fear may happen. That would be a certain way to lose popular support, at any time.

It is difficult to see the logic of the British trade union attitude on this question. The TUC is quite happy to press hard for Conventions to be passed at the ILO Conferences, and, afterwards, to urge the British Government to ratify them. Such was the case, for example, with Convention No. 100, passed in 1951, providing for equal remuneration. If Britain had ratified it, the trade union movement would have welcomed it, but as she has not, it is prepared to attempt, year after year, to obtain equal pay on an industry by industry basis, through collective bargaining. This has had little effect, generally.

The question that arises in respect of equal pay, or any number of other conditions of employment, is what difference in principle there is between the trade union movement in Britain supporting legislation for improvements originating as ILO Conventions, and suppoting legislation for improvements originating in national parliaments. The British Government has, after all, been legislating in the industrial field for many years, on questions of health, safety and other factory conditions. The results are incorporated in the various Factories Acts.

An extension of industrial legislation to conditions connected with social harmonisation in Western Europe would not seem, in the circumstances, to be a radical or dangerous departure from accepted practice. If the unions of the Community countries wish to draw Britain and Scandinavia, and their trade union movements, into closer association with themselves, they will take effective steps to convince the TUC that an agreement for international social harmonisation, achieved through statutory means, would not be harmful to their interests. If this were accepted by the TUC, which may well carry the British Government with it, it could prove a boon both to the future of trade union co-ordination in Europe, and to the future of governmental negotiations for a wider, comprehensive, association.

However, there is one factor that will cause trade unions to be wary about the conditions under which governments may agree to harmonise social conditions. There is the possibility that a government committed to harmonisation may say that any wage increases given would tend to increase the disparities between the different countries; and it may use its influence, therefore, to prevent them taking place. Unions are used to dealing with this argument from employers, and are not likely to be deterred by it. But if governments did press this view with any determination, it is likely that it would result in a much more rapid co-ordination of trade union action in Europe than would otherwise be the case. The unions would almost certainly counter by presenting simultaneous claims in the countries affected; which could mean an early beginning to Community-wide bargaining.

Whether this happens or not, it seems probable that in the Economic

Community, and possibly in a wider association, also, those countries which are, at the outset, less favourably placed regarding rates of pay, will tend to use this factor as a bargaining agent, as has been done in the ECSC, to raise their levels towards those of the higher paid countries. This process has occurred in the ECSC, without wage rates being levelled out, though percentage differentials have been narrowed. It has not caused the higher-paid countries to forego wage and salary increases. Real living standards for coal and steel workers have tended to rise in all ECSC countries, although in Italy they have not risen as fast as in the others, which is probably the result of a high unemployment level and comparatively weak trade unions. Provided the Western European economy continues to expand, and the extra wealth accruing is equitably distributed, then it seems likely that the same basic pattern for wages will develop in the Common Market, but possibly with Italy more favourably placed; owing to increased emigration opportunities, and the influx of capital from the Investment Bank, and other sources, probably giving increased productivity as an extra bargaining factor for the unions.

The certainty of greater co-ordination of trade union policy in Western Europe poses the question of the channels through which it is likely to be achieved. As far as the Community countries are concerned, in the matter of general policies, the Executive Committee of the "Six" together with its Sub-Committees and Industrial Committees, will probably be adequate for the ICFTU organisations; and the European Organisation working with the Trade Internationals, will probably fulfil the purposes of the CISC unions. But it does not seem likely that there will be adequate facilities for the detailed examination of the comparative conditions prevailing in the specific industrial sectors of the various countries. These facilities will be required more and more as the tendency grows to harmonise trade union claims.

The International Trade Secretariats of the ICFTU unions have been providing these facilities for their affiliates for many years; not only in Europe, but the world over. As was concluded in Chapter IV, the most logical and efficient course might be for the ITSs to expand their activities in Europe, and to set up their own European Sections, possibly sharing a regional headquarters in Brussels. Co-ordinated claims for each industry might eventually originate in the appropriate ITS, or alternatively, model agreements in respect of pay or conditions might be agreed, to serve as a basis for individual national claims. Not only could this machinery be valuable for Community countries, but it could encourage the harmonisation of trade union policies throughout the OEEC countries, which should ease the advent of a wider European association. The advantage would be that the individual unions of the "Six", and the others, would have a constant liaison which is not provided for in the Executive Committee of the "Six" or its Industrial Sub-Committees.

Although it was, no doubt, wise for the Community country trade unions to decide to set up their own co-ordinating structure, in view of their common interests and closely shared viewpoints on integration questions, there is a danger that they may concern themselves so much with their internal Community problems that they risk neglecting the problems confronting Western Europe as a whole. If certain difficulties outlined in preceding chapters can be overcome, this wider liaison could be established through the close working of the Executive Committee of the "Six" with the ERO. But that would only be at the general policy level, and could not deal comprehensively with the problems relating to specific industrial sectors. European Sections of the ITS's could fill this gap in co-ordination. Such liaison would be valuable for ensuring that the unions were conversant with any negotiations being conducted between governments for a wider association embracing the "Six" and the "Seven", especially if the negotiations were based on a sector by sector study, as has been suggested on several occasions. And it should prove of even greater value as a medium for policy co-ordination in the different industries, if such an association came into being.

However much attention the unions pay to their international co-ordinating machinery, they will not succeed in creating a fully European outlook among trade unionists at humbler levels unless they can make them feel directly implicated. Meetings of national union leaders in Brussels or Luxembourg do not catch the imagination of workers in Milan, Marseilles or Cologne, unless they, too, are stimulated by new experience, and caught up in the European spirit. There is a necessity for the international trade union organisations in Western Europe to attract this broadly-based support by a series of practical measures.

What the detailed measures should be, the unions will work out themselves, but there are one or two fairly obvious approaches. It would be perfectly legitimate for the trade unions to promote their own interests by sponsoring a campaign for European solidarity through the "Union Label". This system, which operates widely in the United States, and is being introduced in Britain, consists of reaching an agreement with employers to attach a Union Label to goods made by union labour, and then urging trade unionists to ask for goods, so labelled, when doing their shopping. The system is best known in the clothing industry but it has an almost unlimited application, in theory. The psychological impact of a European Union Label campaign upon the rank-and-file trade unionist could serve the interests of trade unionism, and of a wider European unity.

The unions might consider an extension of the system operating in some countries, of paying union contributions by the purchase of stamps, which are attached to contribution cards. If agreement could be reached in the case of ICFTU-affiliates, through the ITSs and the ERO, a European stamp could be issued, over-printed with the appropriate union name and purchase price. Any trade unionist migrating could be accepted as a fully paid-up member of an appropriate union in his new country, providing he produced his contribution card containing the requisite European Stamps. This, again, would be of mainly psychological value for all other trade unionists, but it could serve a very practical purpose, also, if agreement were reached that a small percentage of the stamp purchase price were to go to appropriate international trade union organisations. For them, a strengthened financial basis would be a solid foundation for the assumption of greater responsibilities.

Other methods of arousing interest in European unity would be for the international trade union organisations to extend their educational and publications services considerably, especially by running more international schools, publishing popular trade union journals or newssheets for mass consumption, inaugurating a broadcasting service and increasing the number of languages in which all these facilities were provided.

These are fields in which national organisations, could, as a basis for effective trade union supranationalism, relinquish some of their functions in favour of the international organisations, without feeling the loss too badly. The extra finance needed by the international organisations might be found through increased contributions from national affiliates, and from the proposed percentage payment from the sale of European contribution stamps. Although most European trade unions are keen on having stronger supranational powers for intergovernmental institutions, they tend to be conservative about relinquishing any of their own sovereignty for the purpose of strengthening their own international organisations. But that strengthening will be needed if trade unionism is to maintain its influence. The methods outlined could provide a fairly painless start to the process.

One major test of the international intentions of the trade unions will arise out of the provisions for workers' mobility in the Community. The matter may not be urgent for some years, but it will be necessary for the national centres to agree on the principles of a European policy at an early stage, if serious disagreement is to be averted when the issues become more pressing. The free movement of workers is to be assured in the Community by the end of the transitional period of the Common Market. The mobility provision in the ECSC Treaty did not cause the unions many problems because it applied to skilled workers. As unemployment existed, and still does, mostly among unskilled workers, there has been little movement of coal and steel workers over national borders. The Common Market provisions will free all workers, skilled and unskilled, and the problems raised are therefore liable to be more severe, unless tackled well in advance.

There are two main reasons why workers should want to migrate. First, the existence of employment opportunities in other countries which do not exist in their own. Second, a higher level of wages in other countries. As may have been expected, the unions in the countries with high unemployment, low wages, or both, are much more enthusiastic about the free movement of workers than are the unions in countries with higher employment levels, high wage levels, or both. In order that a serious clash of interests does not occur several years, hence, the unions will probably consider that a co-ordinated programme of action is needed now.

They might well reach the conclusion that there are two main policies to pursue, vigorously, to forestall difficult problems ahead. The first would be an insistence that the Community should ensure a high rate of investment in countries or areas where there is heavy unemployment, or a low wage level. This would normally provide extra employment and a tendency for wages to rise. But there might be some instances where increased investment would bring redundancy to workers previously underemployed, at least in the short-term. The unions might insist that such investment plans be closely linked with readaptation provisions, or with planned migration schemes involving efficient co-ordination of the national employment services in the various countries.

Second, the unions are likely to find it in their interests to pay more attention than is customary to vocational training programmes for workers in countries with high unemployment levels. If they can persuade the Community authorities to sponsor large scale training schemes for workers, it should result in the easing of mobility problems. It would enable more workers to be trained for the skilled jobs which provide the vacancies in the high employment countries, and help to overcome the present situation in which jobs offered are for skilled personnel, while most of those unemployed are unskilled, or skilled in other trades. Large scale training programmes would also ensure that there was a smooth flow of trained workers into the new industrial occupations created by Community investments in underdeveloped countries and areas.

In order to ensure that such an international trade union policy has the best chance of success, it may be necessary for some national unions to reconsider their policies in relation to the regulation of entrants into skilled trades, with a view to greater flexibility. Not only the number of apprenticeships approved, but the age at which it is acceptable for workers to train for a new trade, might be critically reviewed in order to liberalise the position.

There will undoubtedly be a variety of other issues, large and small, whose exact natures are difficult to prophesy, but will provide a conflict of loyalties for national trade union organisations called on to take joint decisions in their international bodies. The main conflicts are likely to be between supporting planned supranational solutions which may cause some temporary economic difficulties to particular countries, and supporting what appears to be a policy of self-protection, in line with immediate national interests. Alternatively, loyalties may be strained between supporting action which a unified international policy would seem to necessitate, and opposing it for internal national reasons, connected with relations between rival trade union organisations or between unions and political parties or church.

It would be unrealistic to expect that national trade union organisations will be able to put internationalism first and last in the many decisions they will be called upon to make. National interests, party interests, and sectarian interests are too deeply ingrained in their histories and traditions. The rivalries between the Eastern and Western Blocs of the world, between left and right wing politics in European countries, between clericals and anti-clericals, is bound to be reflected in the national and international trade union organisations for some considerable time ahead. There may be a tendency towards increasing co-operation between the ICFTU and the CISC, owing to the joint representation of their affiliates on the Economic and Social Committee of the Common Market and Euratom, but it is not likely to reach substantial proportions while national rivalries remain keen; or, indeed, while there are disagreements over whether CISC support for setting up new christian national centres can be regarded as splitting the trade union movement, as the ICFTU alleges. There is no prospect, at all, as far as can be seen, of the ICFTU or the CISC co-operating with the WFTU over European questions. Their philosophical divergences are much too fundamental. And the same applies to the national affiliates of these organisations in Europe.

The foregoing relates mainly to the position in the six Community countries, because the rivalry between the three trade union Internationals is not strongly reflected in most of the other OEEC countries. In particular, there is no serious opposition for ICFTU affiliates to contend with in Britain or the Scandinavian countries, either from CISC or WFTU affiliates. Because these latter Internationals have little or no organisational interests in these countries, and have not much potentiality for increasing them, the CISC was not as interested in the original Free Trade Area plan, or in the Free Trade Association, as it was, and is, in the Communities of the "Six". And the WFTU has not expressed such persistent opposition to the later developments as it did to the Communities. It will be the international machinery of the ICFTU unions which will continue to play the important role of formulating European trade union policy towards any wider association. The ICFTU has made it clear that it supports all the moves towards regional economic integration already made, in Europe and elsewhere, and that it regards them as a step towards wider integration and the liberalisation of international trade generally. It hopes for a close, outward-looking association between the Common Market grouping and the Free Trade grouping in Western Europe; and it is likely to support any such development to the full, including, possibly, a wider, Atlantic, basis for economic co-operation; provided that governments do not ignore the requests for reasonable guarantees which the unions have already made in connection with each of the schemes.

The ICFTU and CISC-affiliated organisations, representing the vast majority of trade unionists in Western Europe, have already staked their claims in their respective European groupings, and have provided a broad base of popular support, without which governments would be hard put to it to bring about successful economic integration. Provided the unions are allowed to play their full part in the future, and provided their members share in the fruits of the wealthier economy which is planned, it can be expected that they will support the greater unity of Europe in the political field also.

BIBLIOGRAPHY

This is a selected bibliography of some of the more important books, articles and statements – mootly in the English language.

PART ONE

Bras, Marcel, "TheWorkers and the European Common Market", Article in *World Trade Union Movement*, WFTU, London, February 1959.

CGT and CGIL, Joint article on "Danger of Common Market", *World Trade Union Movement*, WFTU, London, March 1959.

Dange, S. A., *Trade Union Tasks in the Fight Against Colonialism*, WFTU, London, 1957.

European Regional Organisation of ICFTU; Statement on the Revival of the European Idea in *Free Labour World*, Brussels, September 1955.

Ford, Charles, "The Trade Unions and European Free Trade", Article in *Trade Union Information*, European Productivity Agency, Paris, July–August 1958.

ICFTU, *Constitution of the ICFTU*, Brussels 1957.

ICFTU, *Report to the Fifth World Congress*, Brussels, July 1957.

ICFTU, *Statutes and Standing Orders of the European Regional Organisation*, Brussels, May 1956.

ICFTU-ERO, Commentary on Draft Treaty of Common Market submitted to Council of Ministers, *ICFTU Information Bulletin*, Brussels, 15 February 1957.

ICFTU-ERO, Statements of Policy, in *Free Labour World*, Brussels, September 1955, June 1956, July 1956, February 1957, June 1957 and June 1958.

International Federation of Christian Trade Unions; *Constitution*, Brussels, 1952.

International Federation of Christian Trade Unions; Various Articles in *Labor*, 1956 onwards, Brussels.

International Federation of Christian Trade Unions; *Program*, Brussels, No date.

International Metalworkers Federation, *Report to 18th, International Congress*, IMF, Geneva 1957.

Lorwin, Lewis L., *The International Labor Movement*, New York 1953.

Metal and Engineering Workers Trade Union International; *Report of Activity 1949-54*, WFTU, London, 1954.

Metal and Engineering Workers Trade Union International; *Second International Conference, Vienna.* WFTU, London, 1954.

Price, John, *The International Labour Movement*, Oxford 1945.

Saillant, Louis, *Report to Fourth World Trade Union Congress*, WFTU, London 1957.

Schevenels, Walter, *Forty-Five Years* (History of the IFTU) IFTU, Brussels.

Trade Union Co-ordination and Action Committee of the Common Market Countries (WFTU); Official statement of policy etc. in *World Trade Union Movement*, November 1958, and in *World Trade Union News*, 16-31 January 1959, WFTU, London.

Transport, Port and Fishery Workers Trade Union International; *The Transport 'Pool' Its Meaning, Its Aims and Its Social Consequences*, WFTU, 1954.

Vignaux, Paul, Christian Trade Unionism Since World War II, in book *Church and Society* editor J. N. Moody.

World Federation of Trade Unions, *Miners Unite Against the Schuman Plan*, London 1953.

World Federation of Trade Unions; *Texts and Decisions of the 4th World Congress*, London 1957.

Yearbook; *Yearbook of the International Free Trade Union Movement* (ICFTU auspices), London 1957.

PART TWO

Committee of 21 of the ICFTU Unions; *Position vis-à-vis de la Revision du Traité instituant la CECA*, Luxembourg, July 1957.

ECSC, *Agreement concerning relations between the ECSC and the U.K.*, Luxembourg 1954.

ECSC, *A Problem for Europe: The Supply of Energy*, Luxembourg, February 1958.

ECSC, *Bulletin Mensuel d'Information*, all issues, Luxembourg.

ECSC, *Bulletin* (English Language), all issues, Luxembourg.

ECSC, *Europe's First Common Market*, Luxembourg 1957.

ECSC, *General Reports on the Activities of the Community*, Annual Reports from. 1952 onwards, Luxembourg.

ECSC, *Real Incomes of Workers in the Community*, Luxembourg, January 1957.

ECSC, *Towards European Integration*, Luxembourg, June 1956.

ECSC, *Treaty Establishing the European Coal and Steel Community*, Luxembourg 1952.

ECSC, *What is the Community?* Luxembourg, November 1956.

Federation of Christian Trade Unions in the ECSC, *Position de la Fédération des Syndicats Chrétiens dans la CECA relative à la Revision du Traité Instituant La Communauté Européenne du Charbon et de l'Acier*, Luxembourg, January 1958.

Federation of Christian Trade Unions in the ECSC; *Statuts de la Fédération des Syndicats Chrétiens dans la Communauté Européenne du Charbon et de l'Acier*, Luxembourg, September 1955.

Haas, Ernst B., *The Uniting of Europe*, London 1958.

Weir, Sir Cecil, *The First Step in European Integration*, London 1957.

PART THREE

Banker, The, *Europe—the parting of the Ways?*, London, December 1958.

Britain in Europe, *Britain, the Commonwealth and European Free Trade*, London, August 1958.

Driscoll, James. *Britain and the European Market*, London, December 1956.

Economist, The, Supplement to 12 October 1957 issue, London.

Economist Intelligence Unit; *Britain and Europe*, A Study of the Effects on British Manufacturing Industry of a Free Trade Area and The Common Market, London 1957.

Euratom, *A Target for Euratom*, May 1957.

Euratom, *First General Report on the Activities of the Community*, Brussels, September 1958.

Euratom, *Treaty Establishing the European Atomic Energy Community*, Brussels 1957.

European Economic Commission, *L'Evolution Récente de la Situation Economique*, Brussels, September 1958.

European Economic Commission, *Exposé sur la Situation Sociale dans la Communauté*, Brussels, September 1958.

European Economic Commission, *First General Report on the Activities of the Community*, Brussels, September 1958.

European Economic Community, *Treaty establishing the European Economic Community*, Brussels 1957.

Federal Union, *A Survey of Commonwealth Parliamentary Opinion on British Participation in a Free Trade Area*, London, September 1958.

Federation of British Industries, *European Free Trade Area, A Survey for Industrialists*, London, April 1957.

Hansard, *House of Commons Debates*, 26 November 1956, Cols. 34 to 164.; 28 March 1958, Cols. 715 to 807; 12 February 1959, Cols. 1368 to 1494, London.

Information Service of the European Communities; *Bulletin from the European Community*, all issues, London.

Lewis, Russell, *Challenge from Europe: Britain, the Commonwealth and the FTA*, The Bow Group, London, No date.

OEEC, *Report on the Possibility of Creating a Free Trade Area in Europe*, Paris, January 1957.

Ouin, Marc, *The OEEC and the Common Market*, Paris 1958.

P.E.P., *Designs for Europe*, London, September 1957.

P.E.P., *Free Trade and Social Security*, London, July 1957.

P.E.P., *The Spaak Report*, London, September 1957.

Times, The, Articles on "The Free Trade Area", in editions of 8, 9, 10, 11, 14, and 15 October 1957, London.

White Paper, *A European Free Trade Area*, United Kingdom Memorandum to the OEEC, Cmnd. 72, London, February 1957.

White Paper, *Negotiations for a European Free Trade Area*, Documents Relating to the Negotiations from July 1956 to December 1958, Cmnd. 641, London, January 1959.

White Paper, *Negotiations for a European Free Trade Area:* Report on the Course of Negotiations up to December 1958, Cmnd. 648, London, January 1959.

Williams, Shirley, *Britain and the Free Trade Area*, Fabian Society, London, November 1958.

Williams, Shirley, *The Common Market and its Forerunners*, Fabian Society, London, October 1958.

PART FOUR

ICFTU, *The Norwegian Trade Union Movement*, Brussels, July 1956.

Odhe, Thorsten, "The Nordic Customs Union on the Way?", Article in *Cartel*, London, April 1958.

Bacher, Maria, "Die Integration–eine schicksalsfrage Europas", Article in *Gewerkschaftliche Rundschau*, Vienna, March 1957.

Der Offentlich Bedienstete, Editorial Article *Europa schliesst sich enger zusammen*, Vienna, March 1957.

ICFTU, *The Austrian Trade Union Movement*, Brussels, January 1956.

Kienzl, Heinz, "Gewerkschaftsinternationale und Freihandelszone", Article in *Arbeit und Wirtschaft*, Vienna, July 1957.

ÖGB, *Aktions Programm*, Vienna, October 1955.

USS, *Commission Syndicale*, Procès-Verbal, Berne, 26 April 1957.

USS, *Rapport de Gestion*, 1953-1956, Berne.

Swiss Federation of Trade Unions, *The Trade Unions in Switzerland*, Berne, September 1947.

Becker, Richard, Article on DGB Congress proceedings, *Free Labour World*, Brussels, November 1956.

Friedrichs, K-H, "Wirtschaftspolitik im Gemeinsamen Markt", Article in *Gewerkschaftliche Monatshefte*, Köln-Deutz, October 1957.

Goettlicher, Erich, Der Wirtschafts–und Sozialausschuss im Gemeinsamen Markt", Article in *Gewerkschaftliche Monatshefte*, Köln-Deutz, October 1957.

Henkel, W., and Zweig, G., Article in *Gewerkschaftliche Monatshefte*, Köln-Deutz, September 1957.

Le Creuset, Articles in issues of 19 July 1956 and 7 February 1957, CGC, Paris.

ICFTU, *The French Trade Union Movement Past and Present*, Brussels, February 1953.

Force Ouvrière, Article in Journal of this name, 16 May 1957, Paris.

Rassengna Sindacale, Articles on pp. 420-1, of issue 31 July 1957, and on pp. 470-2 of issue 15 August-15 September 1957, CGIL, Rome.

CISL News (English Language Edition), Article in issue of 30 July 1957, CISL, Rome.

La Palombara, J., *The Italian Labor Movement, Problems and Prospects*, New York, 1957.

Au Travail, Article in issue of 4 January 1958, CSC, Brussels.

CSC, Article in Journal of this name, 10 May 1957, CSC, Brussels.

Notes de la CSC Pour les Militants, Brussels, January 1958.

FGTB, *La Communauté Economique Européenne et Euratom*, Brussels, No Date.

de Gids, Articles in issues of this journal for 23 February, 4 May and 5 October 1957, published by CNV, Utrecht.

NVV, *De Integratie Van Europa*, Amsterdam, 1954.

De Vakbeweging, Articles in issues of this journal for 5 February, 19 March, 16 April, 14 May, 28 May, 15 October and 10 December. 1957, NVV, Amsterdam.

Oosterhuis, H, "Fifty Years of Trade Unionism in the Netherlands", Article in *Free Labour World*, ICFTU, Brussels, May 1956.

Geddes, Charles, "Wages and the Common Market", Radio talk reprinted in *The Listener*, 4 April 1957, BBC, London.

ICFTU, *The British Trade Union Movement*, Brussels, 1954.

TUC, *Economic Association with Europe*, London, November 1956.

TUC, *Trades Union Congress Reports*, annually, especially 1957, London.

Woodcock, G., Article in *Financial Times Annual Review*, "British Industry in a Free Trade Area", London, 1958.

European Industrial Conference; Verbatim report of Conference held in London, 19-21 February 1958, published by United Kingdom Council of the European Movement, London, 1958.

Galenson, Walter (Editor), *Comparative Labor Movements*, New York, 1952.

Turner, H. A., *Wage Policy Abroad*, Fabian Society, London, 1957.

GENERAL

Council of Europe, *European Conventions*, Strasbourg, 1956.

Council of Europe, *Concise Handbook of the Council of Europe*, Strasbourg, 1954.

Economic Commission for Europe, *Economic Survey of Europe, 1956 and 1957*, Geneva, 1957 and 1958.

European Productivity, Various articles in this Journal, February 1958, European Productivity Agency, Paris.

European Regional Organisation of ICFTU, *The Problems of European Unification*, Brussels, 1954.

Heilperin, M. A., "Freer Trade and Social Welfare", *International Labour Review*, March 1957, ILO, Geneva.

ILO, *Constitution of the International Labour Organisation*, 1955 edn., Geneva.

ILO, *Social Aspects of European Economic Co-operation*, Report by a Group of Experts, Studies and Reports New Series, No. 46, Geneva.

Industry and Labour, Article in issue of 1st. April, 1959, on the Tripartite Conference on the Draft European Social Charter, ILO, Geneva.

Kienzl, Heinz, Article in *Free Labour World*, June 1957, ICFTU, Brussels.

Monnet, Jean, Interview with, Reported in September 1955 issue of *Free Labour World*, ICFTU, Brussels.

Morse, David, *Report of ILO Director General to 1st European Regional Conference Jan.-Feb. 1955*, ILO, Geneva, 1955.

OEEC, *At Work for Europe*, an account of the activities of the OEEC, Paris, 1956.

Philip, André, "Social Aspects of European Economic Co-operation", article in *International Labour Review*, September 1957, ILO, Geneva.

Schevenels, W., "A Social Charter for Europe", article in *Free Labour World*, April 1959, ICFTU, Brussels.

Schevenels, W., Article in *Free Labour World*, July 1956, ICFTU, Brussels.

Sturmthal, Adolph, Article on Comparative Collective Bargaining in *Free Labour World*, September 1956, ICFTU, Brussels.

Sturmthal, Adolph, *Unity and Diversity in European Labor*, Glencoe, Illinois, 1953.

Zoeteweij, H., "Social Harmonisation and European Free Trade", article in *Trade Union Information*, European Productivity Agency, Paris, July-August issue, 1958.

SUPPLEMENTARY LIST

Bulletin of the European Economic Community (occasional); EEC. Brussels.

Camps, Miriam, *Problems of free trade in Europe*, P.E.P, London., June 1958.

Camps, Miriam, *The European Free Trade Association*, P.E.P., London, September 1959.

Camps, Miriam, *The Free Trade Area Negotiations*, P.E.P., London, April 1959.

Camps, Miriam, Stockholm: Bridge or Barrier? Reproduction of BBC Third Programme broadcast. *The Listener*, December 31st, 1959, London.

Central Office of Information, *European Co-operation in Brief*, a Reference Handbook, HMSO, London.

European Free Trade Association – The Stockholm Convention and Free World Trade, published by the seven EFTA governments, 1959.

European Labour Bulletin, all issues, Britain in Europe, London.

Hansard, *House of Commons Debates*, 14 December 1959, Cols. 1057 to 1180, London.

Information Division of the Treasury, *The European Free Trade Association* HMSO, London, December 1959.

Layton, Christopher, *Britain's European Dilemma*, European Youth Campaign, London, 1959.

Monthly News Letter, all issues, Britain in Europe, London.

P.E.P., *European Organisations*, London, 1959.

Robertson, A. H., *European Institutions–Co-operation: Integration: Unification*, London, 1959.

Schevenels, Walter, Article in *Free Labour World*, November 1959, ICFTU, Brussels.

Strauss, E., *Commonsense about the Common Market*, London, 1958.

White Paper, *European Free Trade Association*, Text of Convention and other Documents Approved at Stockholm on 20 November 1959, Cmnd. 906, London, November 1959.

White Paper, *Stockholm Draft Plan for a European Free Trade Association*, Cmnd. 823, London, July 1959.